/973

This book may be kept

FOURTEEN DAYS

F

AN ANTHOLOGY OF SPANISH LITERATURE

IN ENGLISH TRANSLATION

AN ANTHOLOGY OF
SPANISH LITERATURE
IN ENGLISH TRANSLATION

EDITED BY
SEYMOUR RESNICK, Ph.D.
AND
JEANNE PASMANTIER, M.A.

VOLUME II
EIGHTEENTH CENTURY
NINETEENTH CENTURY
TWENTIETH CENTURY

FREDERICK UNGAR PUBLISHING CO.
NEW YORK

Third Printing, 1971

ISBN 0-8044-2722-4 Vol. I
ISBN 0-8044-2723-2 Vol. II
ISBN 0-8044-2721-6 Set

CONTENTS

VOLUME II

xxxi

EIGHTEENTH CENTURY

BENITO JERÓNIMO FEIJÓO Y MONTENEGRO
[1676–1764]

The erudite Benedictine monk, Benito Jerónimo Feijóo y Montenegro, published two voluminous collections of his essays entitled Teatro crítico universal and Cartas eruditas y curiosas. While his writing is sometimes undistinguished, Feijóo, fighting against injustice, ignorance and superstition, was for Spain far in advance of his time.

TEATRO CRÍTICO UNIVERSAL
A DEFENCE OF WOMEN

Father Malebranche argues in another manner, and denies women to be equal in understanding to men by reason of the fibres of their brain being more soft and impressible. I, for my part, know not whether there be any thing in this supposed softness or not. I have read two anatomical treatises which say not a word about it. The female brain having been supposed moister, it has been inferred to be likewise softer; yet, this is no absolute consequence. Ice is moist, and far from being soft; metal in fusion is soft, but cannot be said to be moist. Woman, as of the more soft and pliant temper, has likewise been conjectured to be more soft in the material part of her composition : for some men of superficial knowledge form their ideas, by such analogies; and afterwards, not being duly digested, such reveries spread even among persons of sense.

But be it so, what analogy is there between the softness of the brain, and the dubility of reason? Or rather, the brain being thus more impressible by the spirits, one would conceive it better adapted to mental operations, and this argument receives an additional force from our author's doctrine, for in another part, he says that the vestiges, left in the brain by the motion of the animal spirits, being the lines with which the imaginative faculty delineates in it the effigies of objects; the more strongly marked and more distinct those vestiges and impressions are, the more clearly and sensibly will the understanding perceive the very objects themselves.

Now it is clear, that the brain being softer and its fibres more flexible, the spirits will more easily impress it, and the vestiges be more strongly marked and distinct. The resistance of the substance being less and the more distinct, as the fibres in males,

333

being something rigid, make, by their power of elasticity, some effort to recover their former position; and thus, in some measure, efface the path made by the motion of the spirits, whereas the fibres of female brains, being more flexible, will form those images larger and distinct, and women of course, will have better perceptions of the objects.

Let it not be thought, that on this account, I am for giving more understanding to women than to men. I only take the liberty of animadverting on Father Malebranche and indicating that such an advantage may be inferred from his doctrine, contrary to what he himself asserts in another part of his work; but what I affirm is, that by these philosophical ratiocinations, any thing may be proved, and nothing is really proved. Every one philosophises according to his fancy; and did I write from adulation, humour, or to display my wit, I could easily, by deducting a chain of consequences from received principles, shew that man's understanding, weighed in the balance with female capacity, would be found so light as to kick the beam. But I am far from any such thoughts, all I intend, is to declare my mind, and I therefore aver, that neither Father Malebranche, nor any other writer hitherto, knew the precise mode or specific mechanism, by which the organs of the head assist the faculties of the soul. We know not yet, how fire burns, or water freezes though objects of sense and within the verge of the sight and touch; yet would Father Malebranche, with the other Carthesians persuade us, that they have clearly seen into all that passes in the most secret recesses of the rational soul. . . .

But this greater softness of the brain, in reality, neither implys the one nor the other, neither a superiority nor an inferiority in the female intellects, as the impressions of the spirits, cannot from it be inferred to be larger; and from this largeness, it is that both the contrarieties are deduced. The reason is, the movement or impulse of the spirits may be proportioned to the impressibility of the substance, and thus make no greater impression than that of more rapid spirits on a brain of a stronger texture, as by moderating the action of the hand as superficial a line may be traced on wax, as those which a greater force of the hand would make in lead. After all, what I think of this whole system of female brains is that bodily motions may be less vigorous and forcible in them than men, as the nerves which have their origin in the fibres of the brain, and the spinal marrow must of course be less strong or moved by fainter impulses; but not that the mental operations of women are more or less perfect. . . .

I shall conclude this discourse with an exception, which may be raised against the whole tenor of it; which is, to promote a persuasion, that both sexes are equal in intellectual qualities, is so far from being of any public advantage, that it may rather occasion many mischiefs, as fomenting the pride and presumption of women.

This difficulty may be removed only by saying, that in every thing, which comes under the cognizance of reason, it is of use to display truth, and explode error. A true knowledge of things is valuable in itself, without regard to any other end. Truth has an intrinsical worth, and of such coin the whole treasure of understanding consists. Some pieces indeed are more valuable than others, but not one is useless. Neither can the truth which we have proved, of itself elevate women to vanity and presumption. If they be really our equals in mental faculties and in virtue, there is not the least harm in their knowing it and thinking so. St. Thomas, speaking of vain glory says: *Quod autem aliquis bonum suum cognoscat, et approbet, non est peccatum,* 'that for any one to know and feel a complacency in any good or perfection of which he is possessed, is no sin'. And in another part, speaking of presumption, he says, that this fault always arises from some error in the understanding; therefore, as women's knowing what they are does not lead them to entertain any overweaning conceits of their accomplishments, it cannot puff them up with vain glory or presumption; or rather, the rectitude of mind, which it is the scope of this discourse to establish by removing a vulgar error, adds no presumption to women, and abates it in men.

But I claim a still greater merit; the maxim which we have corroborated, so far from tending to any moral evil, may bring about much good. Let it be considered how many men this imaginary superiority of talents has prompted to undertake criminal conquests on the other sex. In all disputes, a confidence or diffidence in one's own strength, greatly contributes to the gain or loss of the battle. Man relying on his superiority in reasoning, speaks boldly; and woman, thinking herself inferior in argument, hears with deference and timidity. Who can deny but that here is a great presage that he will compass his ends, and she fall the victim?

Let women therefore be intimately convinced, cherish a strong persuasion that they are not inferior in sagacity to men, then will they confidently encounter their sophisms, and confound their seducers, however artful in disguising their injurious fallacies with the pigments of argumentation. If woman be brought to a persuasion that man, in respect to her, is an oracle, she will listen to the basest proposal, and acquiesce in the most notorious falsity, as a truth which she is not to question. It is well known to what shocking infamies those heretics called Molinists have inveigled many women, who, before, were not only irreproachable in their lives, but of shining characters; and whence arose this sad seduction, but from entertaining strange notions of man's superior intellects, and an extreme mistrust of their own understanding, when those poisonous doctrines were urged to them?

Another very interesting consideration is, that any woman yields the more easily to the man whom she fancies to be greatly her superior. A man finds little reluctancy to serve another of higher birth, but where that circumstance is equal, servitude goes sorely against the grain. It is the very same in our case. If a woman is so far mistaken as to think man of a much more noble sex, and that as for herself, she is but an imperfect animal, a kind of inferior being, she will think it no shame to submit to him, and the flattery of compliments and promise of obsequiousness working on her own debasing notion, she may be led to account that honour which is the very worst of infamies. Therefore, according to the energetic St. Leo, *Woman, entertain a due sense of thy dignity. Know that our sex is not in any respect preferable to thine; and therefore to allow man the dominion over thy body, except when authorised by the sacredness of marriage, is servile, infamous and sinful.*

I have not yet displayed all the moral benefit, which would accrue from men and women being cured of their mistake, with regard to the disparity of the sexes. It is my real belief, that this mistake is of infinite prejudice to the marriage bed. Here some may imagine, I am running into a strange paradox, yet, it is an evident truth, as a little attention will shew.

When some months are elapsed after two hearts were united in the bands of marriage, the woman loses that high value, which was before placed on her as a new piece of furniture. The husband passes from fondness to coldness, and coldness often degenerates into a settled and declared contempt. The husband once come to this culpable extremity, begins to play the master, and insult his spouse, building on the imagined superiority of his sex. Having imbibed those common sayings; *that the most knowing woman, knows as much as a raw school boy; that their scull is as empty as a bladder full of soap suds,* and the like elegant apothegms, every thing his poor wife says or does, he sneers at. If she argues, she raves, every word is an absurdity, and every action a blunder. The allurement of beauty, if she has any beauty, is now overlooked.

Fruition has thrown a shade over its brilliancy, and being at the husband's command, it is undervalued. All the husband thinks on, now is, that woman is a defectuous creature; and, when out of humour, the best word he can afford his wife, though ever so neat and cleanly, is, *that she is a foul vessel.*

Whilst the unhappy wife labours under this tyranny, a gallant begins to ogle her; a smiling countenance must naturally please one wearied out of her life with frowns, contemptuous looks, and imperious gestures. This suffices to bring about a conversation, in which, to be sure, every thing is calculated to please her. Before, it was nothing but taunts, threats, and insults; whereas, every word of the gallant is fraught with complaisance, praise, and adoration. Before, she was not treated even like a woman; now, she sees herself exalted to a deity; before, she was bluntly told that she was a fool; now, she hears herself extolled for incomparable wit and sense; to the husband, she was an object of vain ridicule and disgust; the gallant approaches her with the awe of a submissive slave. And though the enamorato, if a husband, may act the same part as the other within his own walls, the wretched wife, unacquainted with this dissimulation, thinks there is as much difference between them, as between an angel and a brute. In the husband, she sees a heart bristled with thorns, and in the gallant, a heart crowned with flowers. On one side, she sees a chain of iron, on the other, a bracelet of gold; here slavery, there despotism; with one a dungeon, the other a throne.

In such a situation, how shall the most discrete, the most resolute woman act? How resist two impulses, directed to one and the same end, one impelling her, the other gently drawing her? Without the powerful support of heaven, fall she must; and if she falls, who can deny, but that it was by the hand of her own husband. Had he not treated her with contempt, all the blandishments of the gallant, would not have prevailed against her. The rigour of the one, enforced the complaisance of the other. Such are the evils which frequently spring from that mean opinion of the other sex, which married men so often harbour and delight in exemplifying. Would these but throw aside such false maxims, their wives would spurn at every temptation to infidelity. God has enjoined affection to them, and that contempt and affection towards the same object can ever dwell in one heart, is utterly irreconcilable, a contradiction; and thus to treat a wife with contempt, is a breach of the divine command, than which, words cannot express any thing more horrible.

ANONYMOUS

JOSÉ FRANCISCO DE ISLA
[1703–1781]

El Padre Isla, a member of the Jesuit order, wrote the best Spanish novel of the eighteenth century, Historia del famoso predicador Fray Gerundio de Campazas. *It is a satire ridiculing the pompous, affected preachers of the time. Isla also made an excellent translation of* Le Sage's Gil Blas de Santillana, *with the assertion that he was restoring this picaresque novel to its original tongue.*

FRAY GERUNDIO DE CAMPAZAS

A POMPOUS PREACHER

He was in the full perfection of his strength, just about thirty-and-three years old; tall, robust, and stout; his limbs well set and well proportioned; manly in gait, inclining to corpulence, with an erect carriage of his head, and the circle of hair round his tonsure studiously and exactly combed and shaven. His clerical dress was always neat, and fell round his person in ample and regular folds. His shoes fitted him with the greatest nicety, and, above all, his silken cap was adorned with much curious embroidery and a fanciful tassel,—the work of certain female devotees who were dying with admiration of their favourite preacher. In short, he had a very youthful, gallant look; and, adding to this a clear, rich voice, a slight fashionable lisp, a peculiar grace in telling a story, a talent at mimicry, an easy action, a taking manner, a high-sounding style, and not a little effrontery, —never forgetting to sprinkle jests, proverbs, and homely phrases along his discourses with a most agreeable aptness,—he won golden opinions in his public discourses, and carried every thing before him in the drawing-rooms he frequented. . . .

It was well known, that he always began his sermons with some proverb, some jest, some pot-house witticism, or some strange fragment, which, taken from its proper connections and relations, would seem, at first blush, to be an inconsequence, a blasphemy, or an impiety; until, at last, having kept his audience waiting a moment in wonder, he finished the clause, or came out with an explanation which reduced the whole to a sort of miserable trifling. Thus, preaching one day on the mystery of the Trinity, he began his sermon by saying, 'I deny that God exists a Unity in essence and a Trinity in person', and then stopped short for an instant. The hearers, of course, looked round on one another, scandalized, or, at least, wondering what would be the end of this heretical blasphemy. At length, when the preacher thought he had fairly caught them, he went on,—'Thus says the Ebionite, the Marcionite, the Arian, the Manichean, the Socinian; but I prove it against them all from the Scriptures, the Councils, and the Fathers.'

In another sermon, which was on the Incarnation, he began by crying out, 'Your health, cavaliers!' and, as the audience burst into a broad laugh at the free manner in which he had said it, he went on :—'This is no joking matter, however; for it was for your health and for mine, and for that of all men, that Christ descended from heaven and became incarnate in the Virgin Mary. It is an article of faith, and I prove it thus : *"Propter nos homines, et propter nostram salutem descendit de cœlis et incarnatus est."*' —whereat they all remained in delighted astonishment, and such a murmur of applause ran round the church, that it wanted little of breaking out into open acclamation.

GEORGE TICKNOR

JOSÉ CADALSO
[1741–1782]

José Cadalso, a colonel in the Spanish Army, died at forty-one fighting the British in the siege of Gibraltar. He had already achieved fame as a writer and as a literary mentor who exercised great formative influence particularly upon the poet Juan Meléndez Valdés.

His prose works include Noches lúgubres, *an elegy in imitation of Edward Young's* Night Thoughts*; Los eruditos a la violeta, a literary satire on pseudo-knowledge; and* Cartas marruecas. *The latter, inspired by Montesquieu's* Lettres Persanes, *is a criticism of Spanish society, as seen—supposedly—in the letters of two Moors, one of whom is travelling through the country. Cadalso also published a volume of verse called* Ocios de mi juventud.

MOROCCAN LETTERS

LETTER 26—DIVERSITY OF THE PROVINCES OF SPAIN

By your last letter, I see how strange has seemed to you the dissimilarity of the provinces which compose this monarchy. After having visited them, I consider the information which Nuño had given me, regarding this diversity, to be very accurate.

In point of fact, the Cantabrians, understanding by this name all those who speak the Biscayan language, are a simple people, famed for their truthfulness. They were the first mariners of Europe, and they have always maintained their reputation as excellent seamen. Their land, although extremely rugged, has a most numerous population, which does not seem to diminish even with the colonies which it continually sends to America. Even when a Biscayan is away from his fatherland he always feels at home as soon as he meets a fellow-countryman. They have such unity among themselves that the highest qualification which one can have for another is the very fact of being a Biscayan; with no greater difference among several of them, when they seek to attain the favour of a potentate, than the greater or lesser proximity of their respective villages. The seigniory of Biscay, Guipuzcoa, Alava, and the kingdom of Navarre enjoy such solidarity that some call these territories the *United Provinces* of Spain.

The people of Asturias and Montaña place high esteem on their lineage, and on the memory of it having been their country which engendered the Reconquest of Spain with the expulsion of our forefathers. Their population, too great for the poverty and physical limitations of the land, causes a considerable number of them to employ themselves continually in Madrid in liveried positions, which is the inferior class of servants; so that, if I were a native of this territory and were to find myself in the Court, I should examine with much prudence the papers of my coachmen and lackeys, so as not to experience one day the mortification of seeing a cousin of mine throwing barley to my mules, or one of my uncles cleaning my shoes. Regardless of all this, various respectable families of this province maintain themselves with rightful splendour, are meritorious of the highest regard, and continually produce officers of the greatest merit in the army and navy.

The Galicians, notwithstanding the poverty of their land, are vigorous. They scatter themselves throughout all of Spain to undertake the hardest physical occupations, in order to bring a bit of money into their homes at the cost of such laborious industry. Their soldiers, although they lack that outward glitter of other nations, are excellent for the infantry because of their subordination, firmness of body, and their ability to suffer discomforts of hunger, thirst, and fatigue.

The Castilians are, of all the peoples of the world, those who merit first place in the ranks of loyalty. When the army of the first Spanish king from the royal house of France was destroyed in the battle of Zaragoza, the province of Soria alone gave to its sovereign a new and large army with which to take the field, and it was that army which won the victories that resulted in the destruction of the Austrian army and faction. An illustrious historian who relates the revolutions of the beginning of this century—with all the precision and truth which History demands in order to distinguish itself from fiction—extols the faithfulness of these peoples so greatly, that he says it will live eternal in the memory of kings. This province still preserves a certain pride born of its ancient glory, lost today but for the ruins of its cities and the integrity of its inhabitants.

Extremadura produced the conquerors of the New World, and it has continued to be the mother of outstanding warriors. Its people are little inclined to learning, but those among them who have cultivated letters have achieved no less success than their compatriots in the military.

The Andalusians, born and reared in an abundant, delightful, and passionate land, possess the reputation of being somewhat arrogant. But if this defect is real, it should be attributed to their climate, since the influence of the physical over the moral is so well-known. The good things with which nature endowed those provinces make them regard with scorn the poverty of Galicia, the ruggedness of Biscay, and the austerity of Castile. But, be this as it may, among them there have been outstanding men who have bestowed much honour on all Spain, and, in ancient times, the Trajans, Senecas, and others like them, who may well fill with pride the country in which they were born. The gaiety, cunning, and charm of the Andalusian women makes them incomparable : I assure you that just one of them would be enough to throw the Moroccan empire into a tumult, so that we should all kill one another over her.

The Murcians share the character of the Andalusians and Valencians. The latter are considered to be men of excessive slightness, this defect being attributed to the climate and soil : some claiming that even in their very foods there is lacking that pith which is found in those of other countries. My impartiality does not permit me to acquiesce to this prejudice, universal though it may be; rather I should observe that the Valencians of this century are the Spaniards who make the greatest advances in the natural sciences and in the dead languages.

The Catalonians are the most industrious people of Spain; manufacturing, fishing, navigation, commerce, contracts, are matters scarcely known in the other provinces of the Peninsula in comparison with the Catalonians. Not only are they useful in peacetime, but also they are of the greatest service in war: the casting of cannon, manufacture of arms, equipment for armies, conveyance of artillery, munitions, provisions, the formation of light troops of excellent quality, all this comes from Catalonia. The fields are cultivated, the population grows, wealth increases, and in sum, that nation seems to be a thousand leagues away from the Galician, Andalusian, and Castilian. But they are by temperament rather unsociable, and are dedicated solely to their own profit and interest, and therefore some call them the Hollanders of Spain. My friend Nuño tells me that this province will flourish so long as there are not introduced into it personal luxury and the mania of ennobling artisans: two vices which until now are opposed to the talent which enriched the country.

The Aragonese are men of valour and spirit, honourable, tenacious in judgment, lovers of their province and notably prejudiced in favour of their fellow-countrymen. In other days they cultivated the sciences with success, and they bore arms with much glory against the French in Naples and against our forefathers in Spain. Their land, as all the rest of the Peninsula, was thickly populated in ancient times, and so much so that there is a familiar tradition among them that for the wedding of one of their kings there entered into Zaragoza ten thousand noblemen, each one with a servant, and the twenty thousand mounted on an equal number of native horses.

Because of the many centuries that these peoples were divided, warred with each other, spoke different languages, governed themselves under different laws, wore different costumes, and in sum, were separate nations, there was nourished among them a certain hatred, which without doubt has lessened and even come to disappear. But there still continues a certain coolness among those of distant provinces. And if this can do harm in time of peace, because it is a considerable obstacle to perfect union, it can be most advantageous in time of war, through mutual rivalry: a regiment made up entirely of Aragonese will not view with dispassion the glory acquired by an all-Castilian troop; and a ship manned by Biscayans will not surrender to the enemy so long as another, manned by Catalonians, resists.

JEANNE PASMANTIER

SATIRICAL LETRILLA

That much a widowed wife will moan,
When her old husband's dead and gone,
    I may conceive it :
But that she won't be brisk and gay,
If another offer the next day,
    I won't believe it.

That Chloris will repeat to me,
'Of all men, I adore but thee,'
    I may conceive it :
But that she has not often sent
To fifty more the compliment,
    I won't believe it.

That Celia will accept the choice
Elected by her parents' voice,
    I may conceive it :
But that, as soon as all is over,
She won't elect a younger lover,
    I won't believe it.

That, when she sees her marriage gown,
Inez will modestly look down,
    I may conceive it :
But that she does not, from that hour,
Resolve to amplify her power,
    I won't believe it.

That a kind husband to his wife,
Permits each pleasure of this life,
    I may conceive it :
But that the man so blind should be
As not to see what all else see,
    I won't believe it.

That in a mirror young coquettes
Should study all their traps and nets,
    I may conceive it :
But that the mirror, above all,
Should be the object principal,
    I won't believe it.

ANONYMOUS

JOSÉ IGLESIAS
[1748–1791]

José Iglesias de la Casa, a Salamanca-born cleric, wrote some charming lyric and bucolic poetry. But he is best known for the scintillating wit of his satirical letrillas *and epigrammatic verse.*

ALEXIS CALLS ME CRUEL

Alexis calls me cruel;
    The rifted crags that hold
The gathered ice of winter,
    He says are not more cold.

Where even the very blossoms
    Around the fountain's brim,
And forest-walks can witness
    The love I bear to him.

I would that I could utter
    My feelings without shame,
And tell him how I love him
    Nor wrong my virgin fame.

Alas! to seize the moment
    When heart inclines to heart,
And press a suit with passion,
    Is not a woman's part.

If man come not to gather
    The roses where they stand,
They fade among their foliage;
    They cannot seek his hand.

WILLIAM CULLEN BRYANT

TOMÁS DE IRIARTE
[1750–1791]

For all the dedicated scholarship of this Canary Island-born author, Iriarte's dramatic works and serious poetry are now forgotten. His fame rests on the seventy-six Fábulas literarias, in which he ridicules, among other things, the literary vices of his contemporaries. Iriarte skilfully employs a great variety of metrical forms in these fables, many of which have become extremely popular.

THE BEAR, THE MONKEY AND THE HOG

A Bear, with whom a Piedmontese
A wandering living made,
A dance he had not learn'd with ease,
On his two feet essay'd :

And, as he highly of it thought,
He to the Monkey cried,
'How's that?' who, being better taught,
' 'Tis very bad,' replied.

'I do believe,' rejoin'd the Bear,
'You little favour show :
For have I not a graceful air,
And step with ease to go?'

A Hog, that was beside them set,
Cried, 'Bravo! good !' said he;
'A better dancer never yet
I saw, and ne'er shall see.'

On this the Bear, as if he turn'd
His thoughts within his mind,
With modest gesture seeming learn'd
A lesson thence to find.

'When blamed the Monkey, it was cause
Enough for doubting sad;
But when I have the hog's applause,
It must be very bad !'

As treasured gift, let authors raise
This moral from my verse :
'Tis bad, when wise ones do not praise;
But when fools do, 'tis worse.

JAMES KENNEDY

THE ASS AND THE FLUTE

This little fable heard,
    It good or ill may be;
But it has just occurr'd
    Thus accidentally.

Passing my abode,
    Some fields adjoining me
A big ass on his road
    Came accidentally.

And laid upon the spot,
    A Flute he chanced to see,
Some shepherd had forgot
    There accidentally.

The animal in front
    To scan it nigh came he,
And snuffing loud as wont,
    Blew accidentally.

The air it chanced around
    The pipe went passing free
And thus the Flute a sound
    Gave accidentally.

'O then,' exclaimed the Ass,
    'I know to play it fine;
And who for bad shall class
    This music asinine?'

Without the rules of art,
    Even asses, we agree,
May once succeed in part,
    Thus accidentally.

                                        JAMES KENNEDY

THE SWORD AND THE SKEWER

(Against two kinds of poor translators)

On many a gallant battle-field
A sword had served, its fine, well steeled,
Sharp and pridefully polished blade
The best a Toledan smith had made.
Many a day it had saved with grace
Till passing through hands, from place to place
It went by untold circumstance
To more than one auction and by chance
Reached at length (ah, sad to say)
A roadside inn and there it lay,
Unknown, unused, a thickening crust
Obscuring it with shameful rust.

The innkeeper ordered his kitchen maid
(Though he was crack-brained, she obeyed)
To take the sword to the hostel kitchen
And use its blade to cut up a chicken.
The sword once held in honour secure
Became, alas, a common skewer.

While this was taking place, toward
The court there came, to buy a sword,
A late arrived and foreign knight,
Transformed from bumpkin overnight.
The bladesmith, seeing this new lord
For an ornament only wished a sword
And that a fine blade would not count,
The style of the hilt being paramount,
Told the knight to return; he'd fix
A worthy sword; he was up to tricks.
He took a skewer, filed and burnished it,
Then as Tomás de Ayala's furnished it
To the poor and gullible foreign lord.
This bladesmith with his tricked-out sword
Was a knavish villain, a rogue as great
As the innkeeper was a silly pate.

But is it not true we are no better off
And, as a nation, that we cannot scoff?
Are we not afflicted with two evil phases
Of translating gentry with ill-spoken phrases?
Some take our classics and turn them quite badly
From swords into skewers, and others as sadly
Take our worst works and their finished translations
From skewers to swords have wrought transformations.

ALICE JANE M^CVAN

FÉLIX MARÍA DE SAMANIEGO
[1745-1801]

*Iriarte's rival as Spain's leading fabulist is Félix María de Samaniego,
author of* Fábulas morales. *While he is less original than Iriarte—
Samaniego often imitated La Fontaine and Phèdre—he is considered by
many critics the better poet of the two.*

THE WOLF AND THE DOG

A prowling wolf, whose shaggy skin
(So strict the watch of dogs had been)
Hid little but his bones,
Once met a mastiff dog astray;
A prouder, fatter, sleeker Tray
No human mortal owns.
Sir Wolf in famished plight,
Would fain have made a ration
Upon his fat relation;
But then he first must fight;
And well the dog seemed able
To save from wolfish table
His carcass snug and tight.
So, then in civil conversation,
The wolf expressed his admiration
Of Tray's fine case. Said Tray, politely,
'Yourself, good Sir, may be as sightly :
Quit but the woods, advised by me;
For all your fellows here, I see,

Are shabby wretches, lean, and gaunt,
Belike to die of haggard want;
With such a pack, of course, it follows
One fights for every bit he swallows.
Come, then, with me, and share
On equal terms our princely fare.'
'But what, with you,
Has one to do?'
Inquires the wolf. 'Light work indeed,'
Replies the dog; 'you only need
To bark a little, now and then,
To chase off duns and beggar-men,—
To fawn on friends that come or go forth,
Your master please, and so forth;
For which you have to eat
All sorts of well cooked meat,—
Cold pullets, pigeons, savoury messes,—
Besides unnumbered fond caresses.'—
The wolf, by force of appetite,
Accepts the terms outright,
Tears glistening in his eyes.
But, faring on, he spies
A galled spot on the mastiff's neck.
'What's that?' he cries. 'O, nothing but a speck.'
'A speck?' 'Ay, ay, 'tis not enough to pain me;
Perhaps the collar's mark by which they chain me.'
'Chain,—chain you? What, run you not, then,
Just where you please, and when?'
'Not always, Sir; but what of that?'
'Enough for me, to spoil your fat!
It ought to be a precious price
Which could to servile chains entice;
For me, I'll shun them, while I've wit.'
So ran Sir Wolf, and runneth yet.

ANONYMOUS

THE YOUNG PHILOSOPHER AND HIS FRIENDS

A gentleman young and carefully reared
By a venerable scholar of learning,
Abandoned the books which he long revered—
For the taste of the world he was yearning.

He found himself soon with light company
In whose manner and charm he delighted.
He joined in their quests for gay revelry
And to dine with them soon was invited.

But when he arrived with his comraderie
To sup at the table's sweet savours,
—Unspeakable horrors! Brute savagery!—
The table was full of cadavers!

'You eat unashamed these spoils of death?'
Declaimed the young man with a sigh.
The guests, looking up without catching breath,
Whilst devouring a bird, did reply :

'If you want to live with us happily,
Our manners and customs you'll follow.'
So saying, they passed to him graciously
A bird they implored him to swallow.

'That may be so, what you have just said;
Remorse your reflections instill.
But after all, it's already dead,
And if you don't eat it, we will.'

Looking on those who partook with delight
Of the food in this sumptuous feast,
And breathing the scent of the bird did excite
In the young man a lust for the beast.

'Who could have said that me too they would find
Eating an innocent creature !'
But still he ate on, not seeming to mind
His own philosophic forfeiture.

Once having fallen, he fell once again;
From his early maxims he did stray.
From quail to woodcock he went without strain,
Like a wild beast devouring his prey.

In this way we may see how bad habits creep in,
And our hearts from good ways they sever.
Enslaved we become and continue to sin,
Their whims we must follow forever.

So rash never be in deed or in word—
Take heed and beware : resist the first bird!

LILLIAN RESNICK

JUAN MELÉNDEZ VALDÉS
[1754–1817]

Juan Meléndez Valdés was the outstanding lyric poet of the eighteenth century. A teacher, magistrate and high government official under Joseph Bonaparte, Meléndez Valdés died in exile after the defeat of the French invaders.

The early compositions of this elegant and graceful poet include traditional eclogues, odes, love poetry and ballads, all distinguished for their technical perfection. He later cultivated the neo-classic school of poetry, and his works of this second period bear a strong philosophic tendency.

SACRED ODE

Lord! in whose sight a thousand years but seem
A fleeting moment,—O Eternal Being!
Turn towards me thy clemency,
Lest like a shadow vain my brief existence flee!

Thou who dost swell with thine ineffable
Spirit the world,—O Being Infinite!
Regard me graciously,
Since than an atom more invisible am I!

Thou in whose mighty, all-protecting hand
The firmament of heavens abides,—O Power!
   Since of my soul thou know'st
The fallen and abject state, unveil the virtuous boast!

Thou who dost feed the world's immensity,
O Fount of Life, still inexhaustible!
   Hear my despised breath,
Since before thee my life will seem but wretched death!

Thou who dost see within thy boundless mind
Whatever was or will be!—knowledge vast!—
   Thy light I now implore,
That I in error's shades may wander lost no more!

Thou, who upon the sacred throne of heaven
In glorious light dost sit, Immutable!
   For thine eternal rest,
Exchange, my Lord, the thoughts of this unstable breast!

Thou, whose right hand, if from the abyss withdrawn,
Doth cause the stars to fall,—Omnipotent!
   Since I am nothing, take
Sweet mercy upon me, for thy dear Jesus' sake!

Thou, by whose hand the sparrow is sustained,
Father of all, God of the universe!
   Thy gifts with gracious speed
Scatter upon my head, since I am poor indeed!

Being Eternal, Infinite! Soul! Life!
Father all-knowing! wise, omniscient Power!
   From thine exalted throne,
Since I thy creature am, look down upon thine own!

ANONYMOUS

JUVENILITIES

When I was yet a child,
   A child Dorila too,
To gather there the flowerets wild,
   We roved the forest through.

And gaily garlands then,
  With passing skill display'd
To crown us both, in childish vein,
  Her little fingers made.

And thus our joys to share,
  In such our thoughts and play,
We pass'd along, a happy pair,
  The hours and days away.

But ev'n in sports like these,
  Soon age came hurrying by!
And of our innocence the ease
  Malicious seem'd to fly.

I knew not how it was,
  To see me she would smile;
And but to speak to her would cause
  Me pleasure strange the while.

Then beat my heart the more,
  When flowers to her I brought;
And she, to wreathe them as before,
  Seem'd silent, lost in thought.

One evening after this
  We saw two turtle-doves,
With trembling throat, who, wrapt in bliss,
  Were wooing in their loves.

In manifest delight,
  With wings and feathers bow'd,
Their eyes fix'd on each other bright,
  They languish'd, moaning loud.

The example made us bold,
  And with a pure caress,
The troubles we had felt we told,
  Our pains and happiness.

And at once from our view
  Then, like a shadow, fled
Our childhood and its joys, but new,
  Love gave us his instead.

JAMES KENNEDY

NISÉ

When first a gentle kiss
Upon Nisé I pressed,
Paradise-grain and cassia
Her lovely breath confessed.
And on her smiling lips
Such luscious sweets I found
As never knew the hills
Or bees of Hybla's ground.
To purify its balm
With love's essential dews,
A thousand and a thousand times
Each day her lips I choose;
Until the sum and total
Of all our score amount
To kisses more than Venus
Did from Adonis count.

THOMAS WALSH

RAMÓN DE LA CRUZ
[1731–1794]

The first dramatic efforts of Ramón de la Cruz were translations and adaptations of French, Italian and Spanish classics. But on the basis of his own numerous sainetes—*comic one-act plays developed as a genre from the* pasos *of Lope de Rueda and the Golden Age* entremeses—*he became the most popular playwright of the eighteenth century.*

The sainetes, *all in verse, paint in their totality a realistic and historically priceless picture of life in Madrid, with subjects ranging from fiestas and fairs to dandies and dancers. De la Cruz often ridicules a human or social foible, but always with the good humour of a detached, tolerant observer. One of the best* sainetes, La presumida burlada, *is given here in a slightly abridged version.*

PRIDE'S FALL

Characters

Don Carlos
Don Gil Pascual
María Martín, his wife
Old María, her mother
Tonilla, her sister
Colas Morado, a peasant
Perico, Pascual's valet
Lady and Gentlemen visitors

SCENE I

A street in Madrid
From one side Gil *enters, from the other, his friend* Carlos,
military costume.

CARLOS. I saw you the minute I turned on to this street. Did you see how I most ran my head off to say hello to you? How's good old Gil? But what does this mean? Why aren't you still in mourning? Here, I've been away from Madrid barely a month and I come back to find you dressed in your gayest clothes, you who are supposed to be still in mourning for your wife!

GIL. Well, I may not look so, but I'm more in mourning than ever.

CARLOS. I'd never think it to look at you.

GIL. The veil of my fine clothes is hiding the mourning of my heart.

CARLOS. What do you have to mourn for now?

GIL. Because I'm married again. I had to pretend tears when my wife died, but they're real tears now.

CARLOS. What's so sad now?

GIL. Alas, that's a long story, Carlos.

CARLOS. Oh, well, if you won't tell your troubles to an old friend like me, I won't insist. But at least tell me whom you married.

GIL. The devil.

CARLOS. I take it she's not much to look at, so no doubt, you fell in love with her cleverness, since that's where the devil is subtle.

GIL. If she were as discreet as she is good-looking, that would be another story.

CARLOS. But who is she? Do I know her?

GIL. As well as you do me or my first wife, may she rest in peace!

CARLOS. Then tell me who she is.

GIL. Do you remember that servant girl from Cuacos that we hired five or six years ago?

CARLOS. Do you mean the girl called María the Drudge?

GIL. She's the girl, but go easy. Fortune has made her my wife and I insist that she be treated with respect.

CARLOS. I mean no disrespect. That's the only name I knew.

GIL. Well, that's the girl I lost my head over, and thanks to her I've got the brain of a donkey now.

CARLOS. What did she do to you?

GIL. People talk about the fatal hour. She gave me my fatal quarter of an hour. She was such a good servant and knew where everything belonged around the house, so she won the esteem of her mistress and also of her master. A man is so crazy about marrying, you know. Well, after I became a widower, one day while I was walking in the Prado, I had an unfortunate idea, and I returned home thinking it was better to marry and settle down rather than gad about all the time. Just as I was threshing over the problem the girl came into my room to set the table. I don't remember what we talked about at first but I know we got into an argument. Somehow or other I found I'd got engaged to her and a couple of days later we were secretly married.

CARLOS. But everybody knows about it, don't they?

GIL. Of course they do! No sooner had she married me than she put on more airs than a peacock and began to boss not only the servants, but me as well. And the way she treats me! Thinking about it is enough to make me stand on my head, and I swear to you on the word of an honourable man, that I spend more money on her than if I had married the daughter of a marquis.

CARLOS. She makes you hustle, then?

GIL. And you should see her vanity.

CARLOS. Lowborn people are always that way when they get the opportunity.

GIL. It isn't because she's low born, for she tells me that her father came from one of the noblest families in that part of Spain, though he became poor and had to work, afterward; and in Madrid she says she has a lot of relatives in high society.

CARLOS. That's what she says; but I suppose you haven't tried to verify it and don't know them.

GIL. It's too late for that. I believe her and keep quiet; besides, she's proving it by the ambitions she has. As soon as we were married, she made me go and hire the best teachers of music and dancing. And the way she sits at ease in the drawing room and makes people wait on her! She's got a bad disposition, but I must confess, she is a surprising woman.

SCENE II

An elaborate room in the house of Don Gil Pascual
(Enter don Carlos.)

CARLOS. Your husband, my best friend, just told me about his marriage. I'm sorry I was so slow in coming with my congratulations.

SENORA. Don Carlos, you are very welcome; but tell me, where did you leave my husband?

CARLOS. With some relatives who have just come from the country and will soon be here.

SENORA. Coming to my house? That's a pretty note! I'm not fond of guests, and if that man doesn't listen to reason, they'll all be kicked out of the house, he and his relatives both.

FIRST MAN. There's nothing like everybody staying in his own house. You are absolutely right, señora.

SECOND MAN. And especially relatives.

CARLOS (*aside*). How you'll be fooled!

SENORA. I've refused even to write to any of mine about my marriage so as to save the expense of sending the letter, and my relatives are a very different sort of people. Why, my mother owns a palace, and after a while she'll be heir to an estate as big as Madrid; and I have an uncle, a curate, with six or seven houses even larger.

CARLOS. Must be a regular kingdom!

SENORA. You'd better believe it! Why, my least important relative is a grandee, and the poorest of them has two hundred lackeys.

65132

VALET. The other day I saw a thief with as many as that. (*Exit the valet.*)

CARLOS. I suppose that your esteemed mother is a widow.

SENORA. Yes, I'm sorry to say. Not because she doesn't have an income of twenty thousand ducats, but if I'd had a father, I wouldn't have married anyone under a Count. But now, it can't be helped. The mistake is made, and one just has to put up with it.

FIRST LADY (*aside to second lady*). They tell me she comes from very lowborn people!

SECOND LADY. There's always someone to say bad and good about everyone.

(*Enter the valet.*)

VALET. Señora, there's a woman outside who'd have walked right in and made herself at home if I hadn't stopped her.

SENORA. Who is she?

VALET. She says her name is María Martín.

SENORA (*aside*). Merciful Heavens, my mother! (*To valet.*) Tell her to come back tomorrow when the master isn't here.

VALET (*aside*). What'll you bet she isn't the barber's wife trying to act as go-between in some love affair? (*He goes out.*)

SENORA. It's a poor old woman to whom I sometimes give alms.

(*Re-enter the valet.*)

VALET. She says there's some mistake, because she's your mother and wants to give you a hug, and with her is your sister and Colas Morado.

SENORA. How amusing! Now I know who they are. They are some poor peasants, and I called her mama because she used to look after me when I was a year old.

VALET. Well, I've looked after you, too, but you never called me 'mama'.

SENORA. Have her come back tomorrow, as I tell you; and if she gets obstinate, order her never to come back, for I don't want anything to do with people who put on airs.

(*Enter don Gil and the three country people.*)

GIL. Neither do I. And nothing has made me so angry with you as when you, out of vanity, refused to recognize the woman who gave you life.

TONILLA. Marica, darling, how I've wept because I couldn't see you!

COLAS (*seriously*). Well, I'd never have thought it of one who received all that your mother gave you, as I'm a Christian!

VALET. I wonder how much she has left of that twenty thousand ducats a year the mistress said she gets to feed the family and repair the palace.

MARIA. So you don't know me?

SENORA. Yes, mother, with arms and lips I beg your pardon at your feet.

MARIA. I'm not surprised that you're ashamed of us, because everybody looks upon poverty as something dishonourable.

SENORA. I'm sorry only for those who are looking at us, and on account of my husband who thought I was noble.

GIL. I'm glad to learn the truth, and provided you make amends, you'll see how you'll be forgiven.

FIRST LADY. And don't be sorry on our account, because if the relatives of all these here should suddenly appear, there'd be a lot of apologizing to do.

CARLOS. There's no shame in being born humble if one has virtue to make up for it.

GIL. Enough of this conversation; let's go on enjoying ourselves, for I want to be different from the common run of son-in-law.

MARIA. Blessings on my son-in-law. He's gay and very different.

GIL. And blessings on my mother-in-law if she helps make my marriage a success.

MARIA. Because of your kindness we three are slaves rather than relatives.

SENORA. And I'll be, too, of so kind a husband, if I have his permission to give away some of the abundance of this house.

GIL. Of course. From now on the appearance of your family and the care of your mother are in my hands.

ALL. Hurray for don Gil!

VALET. I hope we are going to see miracles in this house.

GIL. Come on, then, have a good time; and what's past is past.

SENORA. Then let's have some music, and let the dance we planned begin.

ALL. And let those who witnessed this play grant us at least your pardon, if you didn't like it well enough to applaud.

WILLIS KNAPP JONES

LEANDRO FERNÁNDEZ DE MORATÍN
[1760–1828]

Leandro Fernández de Moratín, son of the poet and dramatist Nicolás Fernández de Moratín (1737-1780), was the foremost eighteenth-century playwright of the neo-classic school. Of his five plays the best is El sí de las niñas. This skilfully executed comedy criticizes parental choice of a young girl's husband—and the type of education which taught the daughter to obey her elders' edict wordlessly, her own emotions notwithstanding.

WHEN A GIRL SAYS 'YES'

Characters

Don Diego
Don Carlos, his nephew
Doña Francisca, a young lady
Doña Irene, her mother
Rita, a servant

The scene is an inn in Alcalá de Henares.

ACT III

SCENE VIII

Don Diego, Doña Francisca

DON DIEGO. So you didn't sleep last night?
DONA FRANCISCA. No, sir. And you?
DON DIEGO. I didn't either.
DONA FRANCISCA. It has been very hot, hasn't it?
DON DIEGO. What is bothering you? (*Sits down beside her.*)
DONA FRANCISCA. It's nothing. Just a little . . . oh, it really is nothing at all, sir.
DON DIEGO. It must be something for you look so downcast and tearful and distressed. What is the matter, Fanny? You know I love you so much.
DONA FRANCISCA. Yes, sir.
DON DIEGO. Then why not have a little more confidence in me? Will you believe me when I say nothing gives me greater joy than to do something to make you happy.
DONA FRANCISCA. I know that is true.

DON DIEGO. Why then, knowing that you have a friend, will you not open your heart to him?

DONA FRANCISCA. Because that very thing compels me to keep silent.

DON DIEGO. By that you mean that I am the cause of your trouble.

DONA FRANCISCA. No, sir, you have in no way offended me. It is not of you that I complain.

DON DIEGO. Of whom then, my dear girl? Look here, Fanny. For once at least, let's talk without evasions or dissimulations. Tell me, isn't it true that you look upon this proposed marriage with something akin to repugnance? If you were left entirely free to choose would you marry me?

DONA FRANCISCA. I would marry no one else.

DON DIEGO. Isn't it barely possible that you know someone else more attractive than I, one whom you love and who reciprocates your love as you deserve?

DONA FRANCISCA. No, sir; there is none such.

DON DIEGO. Are you very sure of that?

DONA FRANCISCA. I tell you there isn't anyone else who loves me.

DON DIEGO. Then must I believe perchance that you have a longing for the convent in which you were brought up, that you prefer its pious atmosphere to a life more . . .

DONA FRANCISCA. Not that either, sir. I have never thought of that.

DON DIEGO. I shall not press you further. But there is a serious contradiction in what I have heard. You do not, it seems, feel inclined to the life of a nun. You assure me that you have no complaint to make of me, that you are persuaded how much I love you, have no thought of marrying anyone else, that I ought not to suspect that anyone disputes with me the possession of your hand. If all this is true, why all this weeping? What is the reason for this profound sadness which in a little while has changed your appearance so that I hardly know you? Are these to be taken as signs that you love me exclusively, that you will be glad to marry me in a few days? Is it in such ways that love and happiness announce themselves?

(*The theatre becomes light gradually, as if dawning.*)

DONA FRANCISCA. And what has given you reasons for this lack of trust?

DON DIEGO. What indeed! If I ignore these considerations, if I hasten the preparations for our wedding, if your mother continues her approval and the affair reaches a point . . .

DONA FRANCISCA. I will do what my mother commands me, and marry you.

DON DIEGO. And afterward, Fanny?

DONA FRANCISCA. Afterward—while my life lasts I will be a faithful wife.

DON DIEGO. I do not doubt that in the least. But if you consider me the one who must be till death your companion and friend, then tell me, do not these titles merit some confidence on your part? Can't you reveal to me the cause of your grief? I'm not asking this, Fanny, to satisfy an impertinent curiosity, but to give myself wholly to the task of consoling you, of bettering your lot in life, of making you happy—if my efforts and zeal can accomplish as much.

DONA FRANCISCA. Happiness, for me! That is all ended.

DON DIEGO. And why, may I ask?

DONA FRANCISCA. I can never tell you why.

DON DIEGO. But what an obstinate and unwise silence when you might at least have a surmise that I am not ignorant of how matters stand.

DONA FRANCISCA. If you are ignorant, Don Diego, then for God's sake don't pretend that you know. And if you really know, then don't ask any more questions.

DON DIEGO. So be it. If there is no more to be said, if this affliction and these tears signify nothing, then today we reach Madrid and within eight days you shall be my wife.

DONA FRANCISCA. And make my mother happy.

DON DIEGO. And you will be happy, don't you think so?

DONA FRANCISCA. Oh, yes, I too : yes, surely.

DON DIEGO. Here are the fruits of our system of education. This is what we call bringing up a girl right. We teach them to belie and hide their most innocent feelings with a perfidious dissimulation. They are called honourable when they are expert in the arts of silence and lying. We are determined that neither temperament nor age nor disposition shall affect their inclinations in the least; their wills must bend to the caprice of those who govern. Everything is permitted except frankness and sincerity. So long as they do not say what they feel, so long as they are willing to utter when they are commanded to do so a perjured, sacrilegious *yes*; source of so many scandals, we call them well brought up. It is an excellent education which inspires in them the fear and cunning and silence of the slave!

DONA FRANCISCA. That is true. Oh, it is all too true! That is what they demand of us, that is what they teach us in the schools. But the reason for my grief is much greater than that.

DON DIEGO. Let it be what it may, my poor child, you must cheer up. If your mother should see you in this plight what will she say? I think she is already up.

DONA FRANCISCA. Oh, my heavens! What will she say!

DON DIEGO. Yes, Fanny, you must try to control yourself. Don't give way entirely. Have faith in God. Our afflictions are never so great as the imagination paints them. You have wept so long that you tremble all over; but give me your word that you will try to brace up a bit, to face her with as much composure as possible. Can you do that, little lady?

DONA FRANCISCA. And you, sir? You know what a temper my mother has. If you don't defend me to whom shall I turn? Who will have pity on me in my unhappiness?

DON DIEGO. Your staunch friend, Fanny. I, myself. I'm not going to abandon you, depend on that. (*He takes her hands.*)

DONA FRANCISCA. Really? Can I believe that?

DON DIEGO. How little you know my heart!

DONA FRANCISCA. I know it well. (*Tries to kneel to him.*)

DON DIEGO. Girl, what are you trying to do?

DONA FRANCISCA. I hardly know. How little I deserve this kindness after being so ungrateful toward you. . . . No, not ungrateful, just unhappy. Ah, Don Diego, if you only knew how unhappy I am.

DON DIEGO. I do know that you are grateful so far as you are able, for the love I give you. The rest has been—oh, what shall I call it —a blunder on my part, yes, a stupid blunder, nothing else. But it is no fault of yours, and you shall not bear the blame.

DONA FRANCISCA. Let us go. Aren't you coming?

DON DIEGO. Not just now, Fanny. In a little while.

DONA FRANCISCA. Yes, but come soon. (*Goes toward* doña Irene's *room, turns quickly and runs to* Don Diego, *kissing his hands.*)

DON DIEGO. Yes, yes, I'll come soon.

SCENE X

Don Diego, Don Carlos

DON DIEGO. Come here, young man, come here, I say. Where have you been since we met last?

DON CARLOS. In the tavern outside the walls.

DON DIEGO. Never left it all night long, eh?

DON CARLOS. Yes, sir, I entered the city and . . .

DON DIEGO. And what . . . Sit down.

DON CARLOS. It was very necessary that I speak with someone. . . . (*Sits.*)

13—SA

DON DIEGO. Necessary?

DON CARLOS. Yes, sir. I am indebted to this person for many favours and it was not possible to return to Zaragoza without explaining . . .

DON DIEGO. I see. And with so many obligations . . . But to come to see this—this person—at three o'clock in the morning seems to me a bit—blundering, indiscreet as it were. Why didn't you write a note? A little note like this for instance. If you'd sent one like this at an opportune time, you wouldn't have needed to keep the person up all night, nor to bother anybody. (*Giving him the paper that had been thrown at the window. Don Carlos, as soon as he recognizes it, returns it, and rises as if to go.*)

DON CARLOS. Very well, since you know all, why did you send for me? Why didn't you let me go my way and escape a dispute which will not add to the happiness of either of us?

DON DIEGO. Your uncle wants to know what is the meaning of all this, and wants you to tell him.

DON CARLOS. Why do you want to know more?

DON DIEGO. Because I wish it, and command it. Hear me!

DON CARLOS. Very well.

DON DIEGO. Sit down here. . . . (Don Carlos *sits down.*) Where did you meet this girl? What love affair is this? Tell me the details. What understanding is there between you? When and where have you seen her?

DON CARLOS. Returning to Zaragoza last year I arrived at Guadalajara without any intention of stopping. But the governor at whose house we alighted, insisted that I stay there all day, it being the birthday of a relative of his. The next day he said he would let me proceed on my way. Among the invited guests there was a Doña Francisca, whom the lady of the house had brought that day out of the convent to amuse herself a bit, and get a little recreation. I don't know what there was in her that aroused in me a constant irresistible desire to look at her, to make myself entertaining and agreeable. The governor said among other things—joking of course —that I was very much in love, and he suggested that I call myself Don Felix of Toledo. I entered into the scheme and conceived the idea of remaining some time in that town and keeping the news from you. I observed that Doña Fanny treated me with a particular courtesy and when we separated that evening I was full of vanity and hope seeing myself the preferred one among many rivals. As a matter of fact . . . but I don't wish to offend you by talking about it.

DON DIEGO. Go on.

DON CARLOS. I found out she was the daughter of a lady in Madrid, a widow and poor, but of a very good family. It was necessary to confide in my friend the love intrigues which obliged me to remain in her company. And he, without approving or disapproving, invented the most ingenious excuses to keep me with him at his country home. As the place was near the city it was easy to go and come by night. There were two or three letters exchanged between Doña Francisca and myself, little brief notes on her part to be sure, but they sufficed to involve me in an ecstasy of passion which will make me unhappy as long as I live.

DON DIEGO. Well, well—go on with your story.

DON CARLOS. My groom, who is as you know a man with an active imagination and knows the world pretty well, contrived in a thousand ways to overcome all obstacles. There was the signal three hand claps responded to by three others from a certain little window looking out on the convent yard. Every night we talked together until a rather unseasonable hour—with a good deal of caution, you may imagine. To her I was always Don Felix of Toledo, an army officer, esteemed by my superiors and a man of honour. I never told her more; I never spoke to her of my relatives nor of my purpose in life; I never mentioned that by marrying me she might gain money and social position. I did not speak to her of you, for I did not want self interest or ambition, but only love, to influence her. Each time I saw her she seemed to me fonder, more beautiful, more worthy to be adored. For almost three months I lingered there; but at last it was necessary that we separate and one sad night I took leave of her, left her forlorn and almost fainting, while I fled whither duty called me. Her letters consoled for some time my exile. Then one day . . . a few days ago there came one which said that her mother had decided she must marry. She assured me that she would rather die than give her hand to any other but me. She reminded me of my promises and begged me to fulfil them. I mounted my horse, I rode in hot haste to Guadalajara. Not finding her there, I came here. You know the rest.

DON DIEGO. And what intention might you have in coming here at this time?

DON CARLOS. To comfort her, to swear to her anew an eternal love; to stop at Madrid to see you, tell you the whole thing and beg of you—not money, not my inheritance, not your protection and patronage—I can get along without all these—only your consent and your benediction upon a longed-for union in which she and I had founded all our hope and joy in life.

DON DIEGO. But Carlos, you surely understand that such a thing is now out of the question.

DON CARLOS. Yes, my lord.

DON DIEGO. If you love her, I love her too. Her mother and all her family approve this marriage. She—whatever may be the promises she has made to you—she herself, not half an hour ago told me she was ready to obey her mother and give me her hand.

DON CARLOS. Her hand—but not her heart! (*Gets up.*)

DON DIEGO. What are you saying?

DON CARLOS. I tell you no. To think that would be an insult to her. You may celebrate your wedding when you please. She will conduct herself always as befits her honour and her virtue. But I was the first and only object of her affection—I was and shall be. You may call yourself her husband; but sometimes or many times, if you come upon her unexpectedly, you will find her beautiful eyes flooded with tears; and they will be shed for me. Never ask her the reason for her sadness. I shall be the cause. Her sighs, which she will try in vain to suppress, will be sighs of love breathed for one absent.

DON DIEGO. What foolhardiness is this? (*Goes angrily toward* Don Carlos.)

DON CARLOS. I have said it and I say it again; though I should have known that it was impossible to speak of her without offending you. So let us end this painful conversation. May you live happy; and do not hate me who never intentionally did anything to displease you. The highest proof I can give you of my obedience and respect is to go away from here at once. But do not deny me the consolation of knowing that you pardon me.

DON DIEGO. So then, you really intend to go?

DON CARLOS. At once, sir. And it will be a long absence this time.

DON DIEGO. Why so?

DON CARLOS. Because in my lifetime it is not fitting that I see her. If the rumours of a coming war are verified then . . .

DON DIEGO. What do you mean by that? (*He seizes* Don Carlos *by the arm and drags him forward.*)

DON CARLOS. Nothing . . . except that I am a soldier, and I love war.

DON DIEGO. Carlos! . . . How horrible! How can you say that to me?

DON CARLOS. Some one is coming. . . . (*Looks uneasily toward Doña Irene's room, breaks from* Don Diego *and makes as if to go through door up stage. Don Diego tries to stop him.*) It may be she. Farewell.

DON DIEGO. Where are you going? No, my boy, you must not go away.

DON CARLOS. There is no other way. I cannot see her. If we should meet face to face even for a moment, it might cause you much unhappiness.

DON DIEGO. I have told you it must not be. Go into that room.

DON CARLOS. But if . . .

DON DIEGO. Do as I command you. (Don Carlos *enters Don Diego's room.*)

SCENE XI

Doña Irene, Don Diego

DONA IRENE. So we are ready to start, Don Diego? Good morning. (*Extinguishes light on table.*) Are you saying your prayers?

DON DIEGO. Yes, I'm in the mood for praying!

DONA IRENE. If you wish it the servants will bring up the chocolate and tell the stage driver to have the horses harnessed. . . . But what ails you, sir? . . . Has anything happened?

DON DIEGO. Yes, there's no end of strange happenings, it seems.

DONA IRENE. But what . . . For God's sake, tell me. You don't know how frightened I am; and any little things upset me so. Since my last miscarriage, you know, my nerves are so delicate. It was nineteen years ago, or maybe twenty; but ever since every trifle positively shocks me to death. And neither hot baths nor snake broth, nor tamarind preserves seem to do me any good.

DON DIEGO. Well, let's not talk about miscarriages or preserves now. . . . There is a more important matter to consider. What are the girls doing?

DONA IRENE. Picking up the clothes and packing trunks so that everything may be in ship shape and no delays.

DON DIEGO. Very well. Will you be seated? And don't get frightened nor cry out (*both sit*) at anything I say; please bear that in mind. Don't lose your judgment when we all need it most. Your daughter, Doña Irene, is in love.

DONA IRENE. Well, haven't I already said so a thousand times? Yes, sir, indeed she is; all I had to do was say . . .

DON DIEGO. That confounded habit of interrupting! Let me speak.

DONA IRENE. Well, go on then.

DON DIEGO. She is in love; but not with me.

DONA IRENE. What's that you say?

DON DIEGO. Just what you hear.

DONA IRENE. Who in the world has been telling you these absurdities?

DON DIEGO. No one. I know it. I have seen it. No one has told me. And when I tell it to you, be sure that I know whereof I'm speaking. Well, well, what is this weeping?

DONA IRENE. Oh, poor unhappy me! (*Cries.*)

DON DIEGO. I can see no reason . . .

DONA IRENE. Because I am a widow and alone, and without means, it seems that everybody despises me and conspires against me.

DON DIEGO. But Doña Irene, please . . .

DONA IRENE. Nearing the end of my days and my chronic ailments, to be treated in this manner, cast aside like a rag, like a smutty cinderella, as I might say. . . . Who would have thought it of you! May the Lord help me! If only my three husbands were alive! . . . The last one alone would be enough, with his devil of a temper. . . .

DON DIEGO. Look, madam, I am coming to the end of my patience.

DONA IRENE. If any one answered back he'd get into a perfect fury. One Corpus Christi day, I don't remember what trifling thing occurred, he struck an army officer in the face, and if it hadn't been for the intervention of two priests he would have choked him to death against the portals of Santa Cruz.

DON DIEGO. Is it possible that you won't listen to what I am going to say?

DONA IRENE. Alas, I understand very well, sir. I'm no fool, I want you to know. You don't want the girl and you're trying to find some pretext for throwing her over. My little girl, the darling of my heart!

DON DIEGO. Doña Irene, I ask you again to listen to me, not to interrupt, not to talk nonsense. Then when you know what it is, you may weep and groan and cry out, and say whatever you please. But in the meantime, for heaven's sake don't drive me to distraction.

DONA IRENE. Well, sir, say anything yc please.

DON DIEGO. And you'll not rage or cry or . . .

DONA IRENE. No sir, I'm not crying any more. (*Wipes her eyes.*)

DON DIEGO. Listen then : for about a year Doña Fanny has had another lover. They have spoken together often, they have written to each other, they have sworn each other love, faith, constancy. And finally there exists in each of them a passion so intense that obstacles and absence, instead of diminishing its ardour, has increased it. This being granted . . .

DONA IRENE. But don't you know, my dear sir, that all this is merely gossip, the invention of some evil tongue that is trying to injure us?

Don Diego. The same thing again! It is not gossip, madam. I repeat anew that I know whereof I am speaking.
Dona Irene. And I repeat that there is not a trace of truth in it. My daughter, the child of my heart, inclosed in a convent, fasting seven Fridays in succession, watched over all the time by those saintly nuns. She who doesn't know what the world is, who is scarcely out of the shell, as the saying goes. Oh, you don't know what an eagle eye Sister Dolores has, and what a temper! She'd be just the easy going woman to pass over the slightest slip on the part of her niece! Yes, indeed!
Don Diego. There is no question here of slips, madam. It is a question of an honourable feeling of love, of which up to now we had had no inkling. Your daughter is a girl of stainless character, no one questions that. What I say is that Sister Dolores and all the rest of the nuns, and you and I, I especially, have committed a colossal blunder. The girl wishes to marry someone else, not me. We've come to our senses rather late. You had forgotten to reckon with the will of your daughter. Just read this letter and you will understand. (*Hands her Don Carlos' letter.* Doña Irene, *without reading it, rises, very agitated, goes to door of her room and calls.* Don Diego *rises and tries to calm her.*)
Dona Irene. Oh, I know I shall go mad! Francisca, my child! Holy Virgin of the Quagmire! Rita! Francisca!
Don Diego. But what is the idea of bringing them here?
Dona Irene. Yes, sir. I want them to come, so that the poor child can have her eyes opened. I want her to know what sort of a person you are.
Don Diego (*aside*). She's upset everything. That's what comes of confiding in a woman.

SCENE XII

Rita, Doña Francisca, Doña Irene, Don Diego

Rita. What is it, my lady?
Dona Francisca. You called me, mother?
Dona Irene. Yes, my daughter, I did, because this fine gentleman, Don Diego, treats us in a way that is not to be endured. What love affairs have you had, my child? Whom have you promised to marry? What entanglements are these, I ask. . . . (*To Rita.*) What do you know about this, hussy? For you must know something. Who has written this letter? What does it say? (*Showing the open letter to* Doña Francisca.)
Rita (*aside to* Doña Francisca.) It's his handwriting.

DONA FRANCISCA. What wickedness! Don Diego, is that the way you keep faith with me?

DON DIEGO. God knows I am not to blame. Come here. (*Takes her by the hand and brings her to his side.*) Don't be afraid. . . . And you, madam, listen and be silent and don't drive to do what I may wish undone. Give me the letter. (*Takes the letter from* Doña Irene.) Fanny, do you remember the three hand claps of last night?

DONA FRANCISCA. I shall hear them as long as I live.

DON DIEGO. At that time this note was thrown in through the window. Don't be frightened, I beg of you. (*He reads.*) 'My darling: If I am not able to speak with you personally I will do my best that this letter shall reach you. I had scarcely left you when I met at the inn the man I called my enemy. On seeing him I was struck dumb with sorrow and amazement. He commanded me to leave the city at once and I could do no other than obey him. My name is Carlos, not Felix. Don Diego is my uncle. May you be happy and forget the unfortunate   Carlos de Urbina.'

DONA IRENE. So that's how the wind blows!

DONA FRANCISCA. Poor miserable me!

DONA IRENE. It's true then what the gentleman said, you great big liar and cheat. I'll give you reason to remember this. (*She goes toward* Doña Francisca *very angrily, as if to strike her.* Rita *and* Don Diego *try to stop her.*)

DONA FRANCISCA. Oh, mother, mother! . . . Forgive me!

DONA IRENE. I'll kill her!

DON DIEGO. What madness is this?

DONA IRENE. I'll kill her, I tell you.

SCENE XIII

Don Carlos, Don Diego, Doña Francisca, Doña Irene, Rita

(Don Carlos *rushes out of the room, takes* Doña Francisca *by the arm to the back of the stage; he places himself in front of her to defend her.* Doña Irene *is startled and draws back.*)

DON CARLOS. No, you won't, while I'm here. Nobody shall touch her.

DONA FRANCISCA. Carlos!

DON CARLOS. (*Approaches* Don Diego.) Forgive my boldness. I saw she was being insulted and I couldn't contain myself.

DONA IRENE. What is happening here anyhow? My God! Who are you? What unseemly conduct! What a scandal!

DON DIEGO. Nothing scandalous about this, madam. This is the man with whom your daughter is in love. To separate them and to kill them amounts to the same thing. Carlos, my boy . . . well, never mind that. . . . Kiss your sweetheart. (*They kiss and kneel before* Don Diego.)

DONA IRENE. So that is your nephew?

DON DIEGO. Yes, madam, my nephew, the fellow who with his hand clapping and his serenading and his love notes has given me the most terrible night I ever spent in my life. . . . What is this, my children, what are you doing?

DONA FRANCISCA. You forgive us then, and make us happy?

DON DIEGO. Yes, treasures of my soul, yes. (*Makes them get up.*)

DONA IRENE. Is it possible that you're going to make this sacrifice?

DON DIEGO. I could separate them forever and claim this lovely girl for myself; but my conscience will not permit it. . . . Carlos! Fanny! It is not without a struggle and much aching of the heart that I do this; for after all I am human. . . .

DON CARLOS. (*Kissing his hands.*) If our love, if our gratitude can console you in your loss . . .

DONA IRENE. So Don Carlos is the fine fellow . . .

DON DIEGO. He and your daughter were madly in love with each other, while you and the aunts built castles in the air and filled my old head with illusions, which have disappeared like a dream. . . . This is the result of the abuse of authority and our young people pay the penalty. These are the assurances which parents and tutors give, and this shows how much you can trust a young girl's *yes*. . . . We learned in time the error of our ways. Woe unto those who learn it too late!

DONA IRENE. Well, may they have a long and happy life. Come here, young man, and let me embrace you. (Doña Irene *and* Don Carlos *embrace;* Doña Francisca *kneels and kisses her hand.*) You've made a good choice, my darling Francisca. . . . My, he's good looking, too. . . . A little dark, but his eyes are captivating.

RITA. Yes, tell her that, for she may not have noticed it. Señorita, a thousand kisses. (Rita *and* Fanny *kiss each other with signs of joy.*)

DONA FRANCISCA. Oh, what great joy! . . . And you, Rita, who love me so much, you will always, always be my friend.

DON DIEGO. Beautiful Francisca (*Embraces* Doña Francisca), receive the first kiss of your new father. I am not afraid now of the terrible loneliness that was threatening my old age. . . . You (*taking* Doña Francisca *and* Don Carlos *by the hand*) will be the delight of my heart; and the first fruit of your love . . . yes, my children . . . he will be for me. And when I caress him in my arms, I shall be able

to say : 'This innocent child owes his existence to me; if his parents
live, if they are happy, I have been the cause.'
DON CARLOS. May you be blessed for all your kindness.
DON DIEGO. Blessed be God for His kindness.

ANNA EMILIA BAGSTAD
(Revised by the editors)

MANUEL JOSÉ QUINTANA
[1772–1857]

*Although he lived well into the nineteenth century, Quintana is classified
as an eighteenth-century author because of his neo-classic style and the fact
that his best poems were written at the turn of the century.*

*A fiery patriot—he is most celebrated for his noble odes in praise of liberty,
progress and love of country—Quintana was secretary of the Junta Central,
which governed unoccupied Spain following the Napoleonic invasion of
1808. He also fought home-grown tyranny, suffering six years of imprisonment for his support of the Constitution during the reign of Fernando VII.
In his final years, Quintana became poet laureate of Spain under Isabel II.*

His passionate ode A España *ranks with Juan Nicasio Gallego's* El dos
de mayo *as the most famous poetic commemoration of the Spanish resistance
to the French occupation. Quintana's principal prose work is an interesting
collection of biographies,* Vidas de españoles célebres.

ODE TO SPAIN—AFTER THE REVOLUTION OF MARCH

What nation, tell me, in the older day
Proclaimed its destiny across the world,
Through all the climes extending its broad sway
From east to west with golden pomp unfurled?
Where from the sunset the Atlantic swept
Its glorious fortunes—there was mighty Spain !—
America and Asia's confines kept
And Africa's upon its boundary main.
The hardy sail upon its fickle course
In vain would 'scape the reaches of its power;
All earth for mineral riches was its source,
All ocean was its pearls' and corals' bower.

Nor where the tempests raged the most
Met they on any but a Spanish coast.
Now to the depths of shame reduced,
Abandoned to the alien eye of scorn,
Like some poor slave unto the market used
To the vile whip and shackle basely borne!—
What desolation, God!—The plague respires
Its deadly breath of poison on the air
And Hunger scarce with feeble arms aspires
For a poor morsel there!
Thrice did the temple gates of Janus ope
And on Mars' trumpet was a mighty blast!
Thrice, but oh see, where even without a glance of hope
The tutelary gods have passed,
And on the sea and land have left us cast!
Throughout thy spreading realms what hast thou seen,
O Spain?—but bitter mourning spread,
Sorrow and misery between
Thy fruits of slavery full harvested?
Thus the sail rends, the hulk is smashed,
And broken goes the bark upon its way;
With every wave a torment it is lashed;
Its prows no more their garlands old display.
Nor sign of hope nor of content appears;
Its standard floats no more upon the air.
The voyager's song is broken by his tears;
The mariner's voice is hushed by weight of care,
And dread of death comes ever on his heart,
A dread of death in silence; there apart
He drifts where the destroying shoals prepare.
Then the fell moment! Reaching forth his hand
The Tyrant threatening the west, exclaims :
'Behold, thou now art mine, O Western Land!'
His brow with barbarous lightning flames,
As from the cloud the summer tempest brings
The horror spreading bolt's appalling wings.
His warriors afar
Fill the great winds with pæans of their war;
The anvils groan, the hammers fall,
The forges blaze. O shame, and dost thou dream
To make their swords their toil, and that is all?
See'st thou not where within their fiery gleams
'Tis chains and bars and shackles they prepare

To bind the arms that lie so limp and bare?
Yea, let Spain tremble at the sound,
And let her outraged ire
From the volcano of her bosom bound,
High justice for its fire,
And 'gainst her despots turn,
Where in their dread they hide,
And let the echoes learn
And all the banks of Tagus wide
Hear the great sound of rage outcried,—
'Vengeance!'—Where, sacred river, where
The titans who with pride and wrong
Opposed our weal so long?
Their glories are no more, while ours prepare;
And thou so fierce and proud
Seeing Castile and thy Castilians there
Urgest thy ruddy waves in seaward pour,
Crying aloud :—'The tyrants are no more!'
Triumph! and glory! O celestial time!
Would that my tongue might speak our country's name
Unto the very winds sublime!
Gladly would I—but not on harp of gold—
My song acclaim; not in the prison hold
Where the inspired breast
Grows weak and cold,
With breathless lips opprest.
Old Tyrteus' lyre untomb,
In the bright sun and the uplifting wind
Of pineclad, rocky Fuenfría's bloom!
High be my flight consigned
To noble singing that shall rouse the plain
And wake Castilians to the sound again
Of glory and of war combined!
War, awful name and now sublime!
The refuge and the sacred shield in time
To stay the savage Attila's advance
With fiery steed and lance!—
War! War! O Spaniards, on the shore
Of Guadalquivir, see arise once more
Thy Ferdinand the Third's imposing brows!
See great Gonzalo o'er Granada rear!
Behold the Cid with sword in mad carouse!
And o'er the Pyrenees the form appear

Of brave Bernardo, old Jimena's son !
See how their stormy wraiths are interspun !
How valour breathes from out their hollow tombs
Where 'War' upon the mighty echoes booms !
And then ! Canst thou with face serene
Behold the fertile plains
Where endless greed would glean
Our heritage and gains,
And to destruction cast? Awake,
O hero-race, the moment is at hand
When victory thou must take—
Our glory owning thine more grand,—
Thy name a higher place than ours to take !—
It was no little day they raised
Nor vain—the altar of our fathers grand;
Swear then to keep its praise;
Swear,—'Rather death than tyrants in the land !'—
Yea, I do swear it, Venerable Shades,
And with the vow mine arm is stronger grown.
Give me the lance, tie on my helm and blades,
And to my vengeance bid me swift be gone !
Let him despairing bow his coward head
To dust and shame ! Perchance the mighty flood
Of devastation on its course shall spread
And bear me on? What matter? One can shed
But once his mortal blood !
Shall I not go to meet
Our mighty ones upon the field of old?
'Hail, warrior forefathers !' there to greet
Their mighty 'Hail.' Where hero-Spain
Amid the horror and the carnage cold
Lifts up her bleeding head again,
And turns anew from her unhappy reign,
A Victress, her reconquered lands to sign
With golden sceptre and device divine !

THOMAS WALSH

GASPAR MELCHOR DE JOVELLANOS
[1744–1811]

One of the noblest figures of eighteenth-century Spain, Gaspar Melchor de Jovellanos was a statesman of high integrity and devotion to his country who held many important government posts. After the Napoleonic invasion he helped organize the Junta *of Spanish patriots, and died while being hounded by the French in 1811. A year before his death he wrote the famous* Memoria en defensa de la Junta Central. *An excerpt is presented here.*

In addition to his prose works—including brilliant treatises on economics, education, government, agriculture and other topics—Jovellanos wrote poetry and several dramas.

IN DEFENCE OF THE CENTRAL JUNTA

. . . And now that I am about to lay down my pen, I feel a secret trouble at my heart, which will disturb the rest of my life. It has been impossible for me to defend myself without offending others; and I fear, that, for the first time, I shall begin to feel I have enemies whom I have myself made such. But, wounded in that honour which is my life, and asking in vain for an authority that would protect and rescue me, I have been compelled to attempt my own defence by my own pen; the only weapon left in my hands. To use it with absolute moderation, when I was driven on by an anguish so sharp, was a hard task. One more dexterous in such contests might, by the cunning of his art, have oftener inflicted wounds, and received them more rarely; but, feeling myself to be fiercely attacked, and coming to the contest unskilled and alone, I threw my unprotected person into it, and, in order to free myself from the more imminent danger before me, took no thought of any that might follow. Indeed, such was the impulse by which I was driven on, that I lost sight, at once, of considerations which, at another time, might well have prevailed with me. Veneration for public authority, respect for official station, the private affections of friendship and personal attachment,—every thing within me yielded to the love of justice, and to the earnest desire that truth and innocence should triumph over calumny and falsehood. And can I, after this, be pardoned, either by those who have assailed me, or by those who have refused me their protection? Surely it matters little. The time has come in which all disapprobation, except that of honourable men and the friends of justice must be indifferent to me. For now that I find myself fast approaching the final limits of human life, now that I am alone and in poverty, without a home or a shelter, what remains for me to ask, beyond the glory and liberty of my country, but leave to die with the good name I have laboured to earn in its service?

GEORGE TICKNOR

NINETEENTH CENTURY

MARIANO JOSÉ DE LARRA
[1809–1837]

The precocious Mariano José de Larra, journalist, novelist, poet, dramatist, critic and costumbrista, *committed suicide at the age of twenty-eight over an unhappy love affair. Had he lived, there is little doubt that he would have become one of the greatest of all Spanish writers. For sharp critical insight and descriptive skill, Larra had no competitors in his own time and few in the entire history of Spanish literature.*

His romantic drama Macías *and his fine historical novel* El doncel de Don Enrique el Doliente *(both 1834) deal with the ill-starred loves of the fourteenth-century troubadour Macías. But it is as a writer of articles satirizing the customs of his day that Larra is most famous. His style is characterized by choice vocabulary, purity of expression, subtle irony and humour. Larra often used the pseudonym* Fígaro, *as he does in* El castellano viejo, *given here.*

THE OLD CASTILIAN

Since I have grown older I very seldom care to change the order of my way of living, which has now been settled a long time, and I base this repugnance upon the fact that I have never for a single day abandoned my Lares to break my system without being overtaken by a most sincere repentance as the aftermath of my deluded hopes. Nevertheless a remnant of the old-fashioned courtesy adopted by our forefathers in their intercourse obliges me at times to accept certain invitations, which to refuse would be rudeness, or at least a ridiculous affectation of delicacy.

Some days ago I was walking through the streets in search of material for my articles. Buried in my thoughts, I surprised myself several times, laughing like a poor wretch at my own fancies, and mechanically moving my lips. A stumble or so reminded me now and again that to walk on the pavements of Madrid it is not the best of circumstances to be either poet or philosopher; more than one malicious smile, more than one look of wonder from the passers-by, made me reflect that soliloquies should not be made in public; and when turning corners not a few collisions with those who turned them as heedlessly as I made me recognize that the absent-minded are not among the number of elastic bodies, much

less among glorious and insensible beings. Such being my frame of
mind, imagine my sensations upon receiving a horrible smack which
a huge hand attached (it seemed to me) to a brawny arm adminis-
tered to one of my shoulders, which unfortunately bear not the
slightest resemblance to those of Atlas!

Not wishing to make it understood that I would not recognize
this energetic way of announcing oneself, nor to rebuff the good-
will, which doubtless wished to show itself to be more than
mediocre by leaving me crooked for the rest of the day, I was
merely about to turn round to see who was so much my friend as
to treat me so badly. But my Old Castilian is a man who, when he
is joking, does not stop half-way. What?—my reader will ask—he
gave further proofs of his intimacy and affection? He clasped his
hands tightly over my eyes from behind, crying out, 'Who am I?'
bubbling with delight at the success of his pretty trick. 'Who you
are? A brute,' I was about to reply; but I suddenly remembered
who it might be, and substituted the words, 'It's Braulio.' Upon
hearing me he loosened his hands, held his sides for laughter,
disturbing the whole street, and making us both very conspicuous.

'Good, good! How did you recognize me?'

'Who could it be but you? . . .'

'Well, so you've come from your dear Biscay?'

'No, Braulio, I have not come.'

'Always the same merry humour. What does it matter? It's a
way we have of talking in Spain. . . . Do you know it's my
birthday tomorrow?'

'I wish you many happy returns of the day.'

'Oh, no formalities between us; you know I'm a plain fellow
and an Old Castilian, and call a spade a spade; consequently I
require no compliments from you, but consider yourself invited——'

'To what?'

'To dine with me.'

'Impossible.'

'You must.'

'I cannot,' I insist, trembling.

'You can't?'

'Very many thanks——'

'Thanks? Very well, my dear friend; as I'm not the Duke of
F., or Count P., of course——'

Who can resist an attack of this kind? Who cares to appear
proud? 'It is not that, but——'

'Well, if it's not that,' he breaks in, 'I shall expect you at two.
We dine early at my house—Spanish style. I expect a lot of people;

there will be the famous improvisor X.; T. will sing after dinner in his usual first-rate style; and in the evening J. will play and sing some trifles.'

This consoled me somewhat, and I had to give way. 'Everybody,' said I to myself, 'has an evil day sometimes. In this world, if one wishes to preserve friends, one must endure their civilities.'

'You won't fail, unless you want to quarrel with me?'

'I shall not fail,' I said in a lifeless voice and low spirits, like a fox vainly revolving in the trap in which it has allowed itself to be caught.

'Then good-bye till tomorrow,' and he gave me a parting slap.

I watched him as the farmer watches the cloud go away from his newly sown field, and remained wondering how one could explain such adverse and fatal friendships.

·   ·   ·

Two o'clock arrived. As I knew my friend Braulio, I did not think it advisable to make myself too fine for his party; that, I am sure, would have annoyed him; nevertheless I could not dispense with a light frock-coat and a white pocket-handkerchief as essential for such birthday festivities. Above all, I dressed myself as slowly as possible, like the wretched criminal confessing at the foot of the gallows, who would like to have committed a hundred more sins the which to confess in order to gain more time. I was invited for two, and I entered the parlour at half-past two.

I shall not dwell on the ceremonious calls made before dinner-time by an infinite number of visitors, among which were not least all the officials of his department with their spouses and children, their cloaks, umbrellas, galoshes, and house-dogs; I shall be silent as to the foolish compliments paid to the head of the family on his birthday, nor describe the monstrous circle which was formed in the parlour by the assembly of so many hetero-geneous people, discoursing upon how the weather was about to change, and how the winter is generally colder than the summer. Let us come to the point: four o'clock struck, and we, the invited guests, found ourselves alone. Unluckily for me, Senor X., who was to have entertained us, being a connoisseur of this class of invita-tion, had had the good idea to fall sick that morning; the celebrated T. found himself opportunely compromised by another invitation, and the young lady who was to sing and play so well was hoarse to such a degree that she was surprised that a single word she said could be understood, and further she had an infection in one of her fingers. Alas, for my beguiled expectations!

'Since all who are to dine are here,' exclaimed Don Braulio, 'let us go to the table, my dear.'

'Wait a bit,' replied his wife in a loud whisper. 'Such a lot of callers prevented my being in the kitchen, and . . .'

'But, look, it's four o'clock . . .'

'Dinner will be ready in a moment . . .'

It was five o'clock when we sat down.

'Ladies and gentlemen,' said our amphitryon, as we staggered into our respective chairs, 'I insist upon your making yourselves quite at home; we don't stand upon ceremony in my house. Oh, Figaro! I want you to be quite comfortable; you are a poet, and besides, these gentlemen who know how intimate we are will not be offended if I make an exception of you; take off your coat; it won't do to stain it.'

'Why should I stain it?' I replied, biting my lips.

'Oh, that's all right; I'll lend you a loose jacket; I'm sorry I haven't one for everybody.'

'I'd sooner not, thank you.'

'Nonsense! My jacket! Here it is; it will be a little large for you!'

'But, Braulio . . .'

'You must have it—bother etiquette!' and he thereupon pulled off my coat himself, *velis nolis*, and buried me in a great striped jacket, through which only my feet and head protruded, and the sleeves of which would probably not permit me to eat. I thanked him; he thought he was doing me a favour.

The days upon which my friend has no visitors he contents himself with a low table, little more than a cobbler's bench, because he and his wife, as he says, what should they want more? From this little table he carries his food, like water drawn up a well, to his mouth, where it arrives dripping after its long journey; for to imagine that these people keep a proper table and eat comfortably every day in the year is to expect too much. It is easy, therefore, to conceive that the installation of a large table for a dinner-party was an event in that house, so much so that a table at which scarcely eight people could have eaten comfortably had been considered capable of sitting the whole fourteen of us. We had to sit sideways with one shoulder towards the dinner, and the elbows of the guests entered on intimate relationship with each other in the most confiding fashion possible. They put me as in a place of honour between a child five years old, raised on some cushions, which I had to arrange every minute, as the natural restlessness of my youthful neighbour caused them to slip, and one of those men that occupy in this world the room of three, whose corpulency overflowed on all sides the chair upon which he was seated like, so to speak, upon the point of a needle. The table-napkins which we silently unfolded were new, for they were commodities of little daily use, and were pulled by these good gentlemen through a button-hole of their frock-coats to serve as intermediary bodies between the sauces and their broadcloth.

'You will have to take pot luck, gentlemen,' exclaimed our amphitryon as soon as he had sat down.

'What ridiculous affectation if untrue,' said I to myself; 'and if it is true, what folly to invite one's friends to take pot luck.' Unfortunately it was not long before I knew that there was in that expression more truth than my good Braulio imagined. Interminable and of poor taste were the compliments with which, upon passing and receiving each dish, we wearied one another. 'Pray help yourself.' 'Do me the favour.' 'I couldn't think of it.' 'Pass it on to the lady.' 'Ah, that's right.' 'Pardon me.' 'Thank you.'

'No ceremony, gentlemen,' exclaimed Braulio, and was the first to dip his spoon into his plate.

The soup was followed by an *olla*, an assortment of the most savoury impertinences of that most annoying but excellent dish; here was some meat, there some green stuff; here the dried beans, there the ham; the chicken to the right, the bacon in the middle, and the Estremaduran sausage to the left. Then came some larded veal, upon which may the curse of Heaven alight, and after this another dish, and another and another and another, half of which were brought over from a hotel, which will suffice to excuse our praising them, the other half made at home by their own maid and a Biscayan wench, a help hired for this festivity, and the mistress of the house, who on such occasions is supposed to have a hand in everything, and can consequently superintend nothing properly.

'You must be indulgent with this dish,' said the latter of some pigeons, 'they are a little burnt.'

'But, my dear . . .'

'I only left them for a moment, and you know what servants are.'

'What a pity this turkey was not half an hour longer before the fire! It was put in too late. And don't you think that stew is a little smoked?'

'What can you expect? A woman can't be everywhere at once.'
'Oh, they're excellent!' we all exclaimed, leaving the pieces on
our plates—'delicious!'
'This fish is bad.'
'Well, they said in the fish market that it had only just arrived;
the servant is so stupid!'
'Where does this wine come from?'
'Now there you're wrong, for it's . . .'
'Detestable.'
These short dialogues were accompanied by a number of furtive
glances from the husband to acquaint his wife of some negligence,
and both tried to give us to understand that they were quite at
home in all those formulae which in similar cases are reputed
correct, and that all the blunders were the fault of the servants,
who can never learn to serve. But these omissions were so
numerous, and looks were of such little avail, that the husband
had recourse to pinches and kicks, and his wife, who, until the
present, had barely succeeded in rising superior to her spouse's
persecutions, now became inflamed in the face, and had tears in
her eyes.
'Dear madam, do not distress yourself about such trifles,' said
her neighbour.
'Ah! I assure you I shall not do this kind of thing in the house
again; you don't know what it means; another time, Braulio,
we'll dine at the hotel, and then you'll not have . . .'
'You, madam, shall do what I . . .'
'Braulio! Braulio!'
A terrible storm was about to burst; however, all the guests
vied with each other in settling these disputes born of the desire
to demonstrate the greatest refinement, and of which not the
smallest components were Braulio's mania, and the concluding
remark which he again directed to the assembly with regard to
the inutility of ceremony, by which he understood being properly
served and knowing how to eat. Is there anything more ridiculous
than those people who wish to pass for refined in the depths of
the crassest ignorance of social usage, and who, to favour you,
forcibly oblige you to eat and drink, and will not allow you to do
what you like? And why are there people who only care to eat
with a little more comfort on birthdays?
To add to all this, the child to my left was making olives jump
into a dish of ham and tomatoes, and one of them hit one of my
eyes, and prevented me from seeing clearly for the rest of the day;
the stout gentleman to my right had taken the precaution to heap

up on the tablecloth, by the side of my bread, the crumbs of his own and the bones of the birds which he had gnawed; and the guest opposite me, who piqued himself on his carving, had taken upon himself to make the autopsy of a capon, or cock, for nobody knew which, and whether by reason of the advanced age of the victim, or the lack of anatomical science of the executioner, the joints never appeared.

'This bird has no joints!' exclaimed the poor wretch, the drops of perspiration running down his face from his struggles, looking more like a person digging than carving. And then a wonderful occurrence took place! Upon one of the attacks, the fork slipped upon the animal as if it had scales, and the bird, thus violently dispatched, took flight as in its happier days, and then quietly alighted on the tablecloth, as on a roost in the poultry yard.

The fright was general, and the alarm reached its climax when a sauce-boat, impelled by the bird's wild career, upset, splashing my snow-white shirt. At this point the carver rose hastily, with a mind to chase the fugitive fowl, and as he precipitated himself upon it, a bottle to the right, which he knocked with his arm, abandoning its perpendicular position, poured out an abundant stream of Valdepeñas wine over the capon and the cloth. The wine ran; the uproar increased; salt was abundantly sprinkled over the wine to save the cloth; to save the table a napkin was inserted below the cloth, and an eminence arose on the site of so many ruins. A terrified maid, bearing away the capon now reposing in a dish of gravy, tilted it slightly as she lifted it over me, and an accursed shower of grease descended like the dew upon the meadows to leave lasting traces on my pearl-grey trousers. The anguish and confusion of the girl were beyond bounds; she withdrew, unsuccessful in her excuses, and, turning round, collided with the waiter, who was carrying a dozen clean plates and a salver for the dessert wines, and the whole business came to the ground with the most horrible clatter and commotion.

'By St. Peter!' roared Braulio, and a mortal pallor diffused itself over his features, while a fire broke out on his wife's face. 'But no matter; let us continue, friends,' said he calming down.

Oh, honest homes where a modest stew and one more course constitute the daily happiness of a family; flee from the tumult of a birthday dinner-party! The custom of eating well and being well served every day can alone avert similar discomfiture.

Are there any more disasters? Alas, there are for my miserable self! Doña Juana, the lady with the black and yellow teeth, holds out to me from her plate and with her own fork a dainty bit, which I am bound to accept and swallow; the child amuses himself by shooting cherry-stones at the eyes of the assembly; Don Leandro makes me taste the delicious orange liqueur, which I had refused, in his own glass, which preserves the indelible traces of his greasy lips; my fat friend is smoking, and makes me the flue of his chimney; finally, oh last of miseries! the clamour and uproar increase, voices already hoarse demand couplets and stanzas, and Figaro is the only poet present.

'You must. It's for you to say something,' they all shout.

'Start him with the first line; let him compose a couplet for each of us.'

'I'll start him : *To Don Braulio on this day* . . .'

'Gentlemen, for Heaven's sake !'

'There's no getting out of it.'

'I've never improvised in my life.'

'Don't play the bashful.'

'I shall leave.'

'Lock the door. He shan't leave here until he recites something.'

And so I repeat some verses at last, and vomit absurdities, which they praise, and the smoke, the hubbub, and the purgatory increase.

Thank Heavens, I succeed in escaping from that new pandemonium. At last I again breathe the pure air of the street; there are now no more lunatics, no more Old Castilians around me.

'Ye gods, I thank you !' I exclaimed, breathing freely like a stag who has just escaped a dozen dogs and can barely hear their distant barks. 'Henceforward I do not pray for riches, office, or honours. But deliver me from invitations to dinner and birthday parties; deliver me from those houses in which a dinner-party is an event, in which a decent table is only laid for visitors, in which they think they are doing you a good turn while they are doing you a bad one, in which they are over-polite, in which they recite verses, in which there are children, in which there are fat men, in which, finally, there reigns the brutal frankness of the Old Castilians ! If I fall by similar temptations, may I ever lack roast beef, may beefsteaks vanish from this world, may timbales of macaroni be annihilated, may there be no turkeys in Perigueux, nor pies in Perigord, may the wines of Bordeaux dry up, and finally may everybody but myself drink the delicious foam of champagne !'

SUSETTE M. TAYLOR
(Revised by the editors)

RAMÓN DE MESONERO ROMANOS
[1803–1882]

Mesonero Romanos' delightful sketches of life in Madrid are gathered in Escenas matritenses *and other volumes. A businessman turned writer, he often chose a foible of Madrid society—or its members—as the object of his good-natured satire. He published some of his works under the pseudonym* El curioso parlante.

THE NEARSIGHTED LOVER

'What!' (some critic will exclaim with surprise upon reading the title of this discourse). 'Even physical shortcomings are not beyond the range of the *Curioso's* potshots? Doesn't this fellow know that it is not proper for him to particularize circumstances which may rob his scenes of general application? And who has told him that it is fair to ridicule a physical shortcoming, unless—at the very least—it is accompanied by some moral.'

——Patience, my friend, and let's understand each other, which is not perhaps difficult. Come, now; when certain physical defects are so common among a people that they help to describe its particular physiognomy, is it wise for a chronicler of customs and habits to ignore them, without profiting from the various vignettes which they ought to provide him? If, for example, there were an entire nation composed of the lame, would it not be interesting to know the manner of march of their armies, their games, their dances, their gymnastic exercises? Well, why can't one describe nearsighted love when there is hardly a lover alive who isn't?

And furthermore, who has told you that this stylish infirmity does not present its own moral aspect? Would it be so difficult to prove its origin in the depravity of customs, the shortcomings of education, or the excesses of youth? Therefore you see, Mr. Critic, that this subject falls naturally under the jurisdiction of my benign lash; therefore you perceive that there is nothing wrong in speaking of it—No?—well, to work.

Examples come to me instantly, and I have but to choose one. Today the lot falls to Maurice R——, and pardon if I use him to unwrinkle the foreheads of my kind readers. And who is this Maurice? This Maurice, my dear ladies, is a young man of twenty-three years, whose expressive countenance and sentimental air reveal at first glance a heart which is tender and inclined to love; it is not, therefore, strange that he should find favour among you. Well, that is what has happened, and a few little flirtations in the streets and the boulevards made young Maurice aware of his advantageous circumstances; but, unhappily, the budding young man has a major defect, and it is—he is nearsighted, *very* nearsighted, a fact which upsets all his plans.

Just a minute, ladies; don't laugh, because my hero does not regard it as a joke, nor does he know how to take advantage of this defect, as many others do, in order to be more daring and demanding, in order to display above his nose shiny gold-rimmed spectacles, or in order to surprise with his inevitable pince-nez the furtive glances of the ladies. Far from that, Maurice is sensitive but very obliging; he would rather deprive himself of comfort than cause another person displeasure. He might well have wanted to wear glasses all the time, as some do unnecessarily and just as a whim; but a pair of eyeglasses bouncing to the quick rhythm of the mazurka harmonize so poorly! And Maurice, at twenty-three, could not bring himself to stop dancing the mazurka. A good remedy, of course, would be a dangling monocle; but aside from the reluctance with which these were used, how was one to foresee the scenes which might occur in order to be prepared with it in hand? If a beautiful damsel quickly turned her lovely eyes to him, or let her handkerchief fall in order to give him a chance to speak with her; how was he to foresee it a moment before? If, thinking he was asking the prettiest girl in the room to dance, he found that he had offered his arm to an Egyptian mummy, what good would his monocle be a moment later? Come, it is clear that the monocle is useless, and Maurice, who realized this, truly despaired.

Love, which for a long time had been satisfied merely to prick him lightly, came at last to slash his heart in two, and one night at the ball of the Marquesa of ——, Maurice, who was dancing with the beautiful Matilda de Lainez, could not refrain from blurting out a straightforward declaration of love. The young lady, on whom the charms of Maurice undoubtedly had their effect, did not reprehend him,

'*Faute d'avoir le temps de se mettre en courroux.*'

And here we have my fine young man in the happiest moment of love, that of seeing his feelings shared by the adored person.

By now our sweethearts had conversed extensively; three rigadoons and one galop had done no more than fan the flame of their passion; but the ball was ending and the conquered Maurice renewed his protestations and vows; he jotted down exactly the hour and minute in which Matilda would appear upon her balcony; the church where she went to hear mass; the boulevards and gatherings which she frequented; her mother's favourite operas; in short, all those preliminaries which you, skilled youths, do not overlook in these matters. But the inexpert Maurice at the same time forgot to take a good look at the mother and an older sister of Matilda who were at the ball; he did not observe her father, a colonel of the cavalry, and, lastly, he did not dare to apprise his beloved of the fatal circumstance of his nearsightedness. What happened later led him to realize his mistake.

When, the next day, the appointed hour had barely arrived, he ran to the street where his lady lived, checking carefully the address of the house. Matilda had told him it was Number 12 and that it was on the corner of a certain street, but inasmuch as the house on the other corner, which was Number 72, looked like 12 to the unfortunate lover, *that* was the one which he chose as the object of his siege.

Matilda, who saw him come (feminine eyes, what don't you see when you are in love!), tossed away her embroidery, and rushing out to the balcony, she displayed to her lover all the charms of her pulchritude in a simple gown; but all in vain, for Maurice, six yards away on the other corner, his eyes fixed on the balconies of the opposite house, scarcely noticed the beauty which had appeared on the other verandah.

This unexpected disdain stung Matilda's ego beyond measure; she coughed twice, she pulled out her white handkerchief, all was useless; her heartsick lover glanced at her quickly, and turned his back to her in order to concentrate upon the other object. This scene lasted for an hour or more until, despairing and believing himself abandoned by his lady, the fine young man felt strong temptations to employ the time profitably with the other neighbour who remained so motionless. Finally, not being able to resist the enticement, and seeing that otherwise he was completely wasting the afternoon, he decided at last (although with anguish in his heart) to digress from his love and talk with the graceful neighbour.

No sooner said than done; he crosses the street, he goes determinedly under Matilda's balcony; he raises his head to speak to her; but at the very same moment she tosses in his face the handkerchief that she held in her hand (in which, during her rage, she had made a few knots), and without saying a single word to him, she goes inside and slams the balcony door. Maurice unfolded the handkerchief and recognized embroidered on it the same initials which he had seen on the one Matilda carried the night of the ball. Then he looked at the house and managed to make out *Number 12*. How can one describe his desperation?

Three days and three nights he walked her street in vain; the implacable balcony remained shut, and the entire neighbourhood, except the object of his love, bore faithful witness to his sighs. The third night one of the mother's favourite operas was being presented in the theatre; located in his orchestra seat, with the help of opera glasses Maurice avidly peruses the theatre and sees nothing which might please him; however, in one of the box seats he thinks he sees the mother accompanied by the cause of his torment. He goes upstairs, walks through the corridors, he peeks through the door of the box; there is no doubt—it is they— Maurice wears himself out with signals and grimaces, but he accomplishes nothing; finally the opera ends, he awaits their descent, and in the darkest part of the stairway, he comes up to the girl and says to her :

—Señorita, pardon my blunder. If you come out upon your balcony later I will tell you—in the meantime, here is the handkerchief.

—Sir, what are you saying?—a strange voice answered him at the very moment that a miserable lantern (one of the lanterns which so weakly light our theatre stairways) suddenly revealed to him that he was speaking to another person, although she greatly resembled his idol.

—Madam—

—Why, this handkerchief is my sister's !

—What's this, child?

—Nothing, Mamá; just this gentleman who is giving me Matilda's handkerchief.

—And how is it that this gentleman has Matilda's handkerchief?

—Madam, I—pardon me, the other day, the other night, I mean—at the ball of the Marquesa of—

—That's true, Mamá; this gentleman danced with my sister, and it is not strange that she should have forgotten her handkerchief.

—Yes, that's it, señorita; she forgot it, forgot—

—Truly it is odd; but nevertheless, sir, we thank you.

A thunderbolt fallen at his feet could not have upset poor Maurice more, and what most aggravated him was that in a corner of the handkerchief he had tied a note in which he spoke of his love, of the mistake of the house address, of the protestations at the ball, in short, he detailed the whole exposition of the drama, and he did not know to what fate that paper would come.

Trembling and uncertain, he followed the ladies at a distance, until they entered their house and left him in the street in the most utter abandonment. In vain he cocked his ear to see if he could hear some animated dialogue; the distant voice of the night watchman who was calling midnight, or the sonorous march of the dirty cleaning wagons were the only things which struck his ears and his nostrils; until, tired of waiting fruitlessly, he went home to lie awake and ponder his unhappy love.

In the meanwhile, what was happening inside the other house? Mama, who took the handkerchief in order to scold her daughter, had discovered the note, had read its contents, and after the first moments of wrath, had resolved, on the sister's advice, not to make a scene but quietly to write a short-worded and decisive answer to the young gallant—with the purpose that he should have no desire to return; they did this, and the note was written, signed in a woman's handwriting (they all look alike), sealed with sealing-wax and paste, and as a stronger proof, pricked with a pin. This undertaking completed, they went to bed, certain that the next morning the hapless lover would pass through the street. Actually, this was not asking for much; for it was not even 8 a.m. when he was already at the entrance across the way, not daring to look. As he waits thus, he hears a balcony open—and—o joy! a white hand throws out a small paper; the happy youth runs to catch it and he finds—the balcony has already closed and with it the hope of his heart.

In vain one might attempt to describe the effect which that series of misadventures had upon Maurice; let it suffice to say that he renounced love *forever*; but after all, he was a young man, and at the end of two weeks he thought differently, and out he one of those pleasant July nights which invite one to enjoy the agreeable surroundings beneath the leafy trees and, both comrades seated, they began the usual discussion of their respective love affairs. Maurice, with his accustomed frankness, related his last adventure to his friend, with all the intrigues and sudden changes in fortune which it involved, even unto the bitter farewell to which his hapless blunders had brought him; but upon finishing his tale, he perceived a rapid movement on the next benches, where among other persons he saw seated a military man and a young lady; he moves a little closer, he pulls out his eyeglass (Stupid! why didn't you take it out from the very beginning?) and he learns that the young lady seated at his back listening to his conversation is none other than the beautiful Matilda.

—Ingrate!—was all he was able to say, while the father called a boy to light his cigar.

—I did not write that letter. (This answer he received after a quarter of an hour.)

—Well then, who?

—I don't know. Bring it. At twelve I will be on the balcony.

Hope again poured its healing balm on poor Maurice's heart, and filled with pleasing thoughts he awaited the appointed hour; he runs swiftly to the balcony, and indeed, she is there; now he sees her lovely eyes shining, now he glimpses her white hand, now—But oh, how wisely says Shakespeare that *when sorrows come, they come not single spies, but in battalions*! That night it had occurred to Papa to enjoy some fresh air after dinner, and it was *he* who was stretched out there, feet on the balcony rail, notwithstanding the agitation of Matilda, who begged him to retire and avoid the night dew.

—My darling—said Maurice, in honeyed tones—is it you?

—Daughter, Matilda (said the father in a low voice), is that for you?

—Me, Papa? No sir, I don't have any idea—

—No? Well, these things are either yours or your sister's.

—So that you may see (continues the smitten young gallant) whether I had reason to be angry, there is the letter.

—Let me see it, let me see it, girl, now get away, get away, and bring a light, I'm going to read it!

No sooner said than done; glaring at his daughter with threatening eyes, he enters the parlour, opens the letter, and reads : 'Sir, if the night of the Marquesa's ball I, in my indiscretion, inspired in you wild expectations . . .'

—Heavens! But what do I see—this handwriting is my wife's!

—Oh, father!

—Infamous one! At forty you go about inspiring wild expectations!

—But, Papa—

—Just let me wake her up and let the whole house explode!

And indeed, he did just that, and for an hour the outcries, the sobs, the weepings interested the entire neighbourhood, with no small fright on the part of the Phantom Lover, who from the street came to half-understand the extraordinary *quid pro quo*.

His nobility and punctiliousness did not allow him to permit that all should suffer any longer on his account, and strongly determined, he knocks at the door; the father appears on the balcony :

—Sir, please be so kind as to listen to an explanatory word of my conduct.

The father grabs two pistols and hurriedly descends; he opens the door.

—Choose!—he tells him.

—Calm yourself, answers the young man;—I am a gentleman; my name is ——, and my family is well-known; an unfortunate combination of events has made me disturb the tranquillity of your family, and I cannot permit this without explaining it to you.

At this point he gave a detailed and truthful account of all the happenings, which the mother and the girls successively confirmed, with which the agitation of the jealous colonel was calmed.

The next day the Marquesa formally presented Maurice in the home of Matilda, and the father, informed of the circumstances, did not object.

From here on, the history of these amours followed a more tranquil path; and those who wish to rush things to their conclusion may relax, knowing that Maurice and his beloved were married, in spite of that fact that she, seen at close range in a good light, and through eyeglasses, appeared to him not so beautiful, by reason of smallpox pits and a few other little defects; nevertheless, her moral qualities were very creditable, and Maurice overlooked the physical, for all he had to do in order to forget these was one simple operation, which was—take off his glasses.

JEANNE PASMANTIER

FRANCISCO MARTÍNEZ DE LA ROSA
[1787–1862]

Martínez de la Rosa, distinguished diplomat, dramatist and poet, came into contact with French romanticism while an exile in France. His prose drama, La conjuración de Venecia (*1834*), *was the first great triumph of romanticism on the Spanish stage. He continued, however, to write poetry in his favoured neo-classic style.*

THE ALHAMBRA

Come to my bidding, gentle damsels fair,
　That haunt the banks of Douro and Genil!
Come, crowned with roses in your fragrant hair,
　More fresh and pure than April balms distil!

With long, dark locks adown your shoulders straying;
　With eyes of fire, and lips of honeyed power;
Uncinctured robes, the bosom bare displaying,
　Let songs of love escort me to the bower.

With love resounds the murmur of the stream;
　With love the nightingale awakes the grove;
O'er wood and mountain love inspires the theme,
　And Earth and Heaven repeat the strain of love.

Even there, where, 'midst the Alcazar's Moorish pride,
　Three centuries of ruin sleep profound,
From marble walls, with gold diversified,
　The sullen echoes murmur love around.

Where are its glories now?—the pomps, the charms,
　The triumph, the emprise of proud display,
The song, the dance, the feast, the deeds of arms,
　The gardens, baths, and fountains,—where are they?

Round jasper columns thorns and ivy creep;
　Where roses blossomed, brambles now o'erspread:
The mournful ruins bid the spirit weep;
　The broken fragments stay the passing tread.

Ye nymphs of Douro! to my words give heed;
  Behold how transient pride and glory prove;
Then, while the headlong moments urge their speed,
  Taste happiness, and try the joys of love.

                  HENRY WADSWORTH LONGFELLOW

ANACREONTIC

Let thunder burst,
  Pour out and drink the wine!
Thou never saw'st a thunderbolt
  Strike the tender vine.

Vesuvius himself
  To Bacchus tribute pays,
And spares the vineyard flourishing
  Where his lava sways.

In Italy in vain
  I hero sought or sage;
Mine eyes but dusty ruins found,
  Mouldering with age.

Of Rome the image scarce
  Remains to be portrayed;
A tomb is Herculaneum,
  Pompeii is a shade.

But I found Falernum,
  His nectar rich remained,
And in memory of Horace
  A bottleful I drained.

                            JAMES KENNEDY

DUQUE DE RIVAS
[1791–1865]

Though he was later to hold posts as an honoured statesman and diplomat of his country, Angel de Saavedra, Duque de Rivas, spent many years banished from Spain. While an exile in Malta he read the works of the great English romantics, and turned wholeheartedly to that school in his own writings.

Rivas is most famous for his sensational romantic melodrama, Don Alvaro o La fuerza del sino (1835). Composed in prose and verse, disregarding the unities, combining fantastic, violent and passionate elements, Don Alvaro enjoyed overwhelming acclaim. It served as the basis for Verdi's opera La Forza del Destino.

Besides his success as a dramatist, Rivas was Spain's outstanding romantic poet in the early years of the nineteenth century. His verse legends and historical ballads are among his best works.

ODE TO THE LIGHTHOUSE AT MALTA

The world in dreary darkness sleeps profound;
   The storm-clouds hurry on, by hoarse winds driven;
And night's dull shades and spectral mists confound
    Earth, sea, and heaven!

King of surrounding Chaos! thy dim form
   Rises with fiery crown upon thy brow,
To scatter light and peace amid the storm,
    And life bestow.

In vain the sea with thundering waves may peal
   And burst beneath thy feet in giant sport,
Till the white foam in snowy clouds conceal
    The sheltering port:

Thy flaming tongue proclaims, 'Behold the shore!'
   And voiceless hails the weary pilot back,
Whose watchful eyes, like worshippers, explore
    Thy shining track.

Now silent night a gorgeous mantle wears,—
   By sportive winds the clouds are scattered far,
And lo! with starry train the moon appears
    In circling car:

While the pale mist, that thy tall brow enshrouds,
    In vain would veil thy diadem from sight,
Whose form colossal seems to touch the clouds
    With starlike light.

Ocean's perfidious waves may calmly sleep,
    Yet hide sharp rocks,—the cliff, false signs display,—
And luring lights, far flashing o'er the deep,
    The ship betray.

But thou, whose splendour dims each lesser beam,—
    Whose firm, unmoved position might declare
Thy throne a monarch's,—like the North Star's gleam,
    Reveal'st each snare.

So Reason's steady torch, with light as pure,
    Dispels the gloom, when stormy passions rise,
Or Fortune's cheating phantoms would obscure
    The soul's dim eyes.

Since I am cast by adverse fortunes here,
    Where thou presidest o'er this scanty soil,
And bounteous Heaven a shelter grants to cheer
    My spirit's toil.

Frequent I turn to thee, with homage mute,
    Ere yet each troubled thought is calmed in sleep,
And still thy gem-like brow my eyes salute
    Above the deep.

How many now may gaze on this seashore,
    Alas! like me, as exiles doomed to roam!
Some who, perchance, would greet a wife once more,
    Or children's home!

Wanderers, by poverty or despots driven
    To seek a refuge, as I do, afar,
Here find, at last, the sign of welcome given,—
    A hospitable star!

And still, to guide the bark, it calmly shines,—
    The bark that from my native land oft bears
Tidings of bitter griefs, and mournful lines
    Written with tears.

When first thy vision flashed upon my eyes,
　And all its dazzling glory I beheld,
O, how my heart, long used to miseries,
　　With rapture swelled !

Inhospitable Latium's shores were lost,
　And, as amid the threatening waves we steered,
When near to dangerous shoals, by tempests tossed,
　　Thy light appeared.

No saints the fickle mariners then praised,
　But vows and prayers forgot they with the night,
While from the silent gloom the cry was raised,
　　'Malta in sight !'

And thou wert like a sainted image crowned,
　Whose forehead bears a shower of golden rays,
Which pilgrims, seeking health and peace, surround
　　With holy praise.

Never may I forget thee ! One alone
　Of cherished objects shall with thee aspire,
King of the Night ! to match thy lofty throne
　　And friendly fire :

That vision still with sparkling light appears
　In the sun's dazzling beams at matin hour,
And is the golden angel memory rears
　　On Córdova's proud tower.

ANONYMOUS

JUAN EUGENIO HARTZENBUSCH
[1806–1880]

Hartzenbusch, Director of the National Library in his later years, was a literary scholar of international eminence. His tragedy Los amantes de Teruel (1837), based on a well-known legend, ranks as one of the most technically perfect of the romantic dramas.

THE LOVERS OF TERUEL

Act I

SCENE IV

Marsilla, Zulima.

MARSILLA. My name is Diego Marsilla. I was born
In Teruel, which, founded but yesterday,
Is now a mighty city, whose proud walls
Amid the horrors of atrocious strife
Were fashioned, and cemented with the blood
Of her brave citizens. I think when God
Decreed my birth, His purpose was to form
A man and woman, patterns of pure love;
So, to maintain in perfect equipoise
Their mutual affection, first He shared
The twin halves of a single radiant soul
Between them both, and then said 'Live and love'.
And at the sound of that creative voice
My Isabel and I came into being:
Both saw the light the selfsame day and hour.
Already from our earliest years were we
Devoted lovers. The very day we met,
Before we met indeed, we loved each other.
For love began to inflame our souls when God
Moulded them from mere nothing, and they felt
The quickening touch of the Creator's hand.
And so the miracle of our young love,
Of love made flesh before we both were born,
Destined my Isabel and me to love,
And to love with all our heart, as first
With all our soul.
ZULIMA.   A passion so well matched
Presages nought but happiness.

MARSILLA.   I am poor.
   And Isabel is rich.
ZULIMA (*aside*).   I breathe again.
MARSILLA. I had a rival.
ZULIMA.   Yes?
MARSILLA.   A man of wealth.
ZULIMA. What then . . . ?
MARSILLA.   He boasted of his riches . . .
ZULIMA.   Well?
   Did he o'ercome the lady's constancy?
MARSILLA. For one who loves, gold has but little charm.
   Her father, he indeed was dazzled . . .
ZULIMA.   And
   Refused thy suit, and robbed thee of her sight.
MARSILLA. I saw him, told him of my love, and he,
   Moved by my passionate appeal, at length
   Put off their marriage, granting me a space
   Wherein I should with my unaided arm
   Win for myself an honourable fortune.
ZULIMA. And has the time appointed now expired?
MARSILLA. Ah, lady, as thou seest . . . I am still alive.
   Six years, and six days more, were granted me.
   Today the years come to an end; tomorrow
   Ends one of six days only.
ZULIMA.   Tell me more.
MARSILLA. I bade my love farewell, who is the light
   Of my adoring eyes, went to the wars,
   And at Las Navas de Tolosa fought
   Against the Crescent. There by my brave bearing
   I won repute for a most gallant soldier.
   Next I was made a prisoner in France
   By Count de Montfort. I escaped from him.
   Then, in the Holy Land, a refugee
   From the Albigensian wars, whose life I saved
   By Béziers, dying soon, left me his heir.
   But coming back to Spain with great increase
   Of fame and fortune, I fell into the hands
   Of Moorish pirates, and was brought by them
   A captive to Valencia. With my own hands
   I burst the iron bonds that held me fast,
   And for my pains was buried dead-alive,
   Deep in a dungeon, where a mysterious guard,
   Unseen, unheard, in pity or in hate,

Prolonged my wretched life. From that foul den
You rescue me. Fair lady, I can feel
And can be grateful. Tell me, how can I
Repay the debt I owe?
ZULIMA.   Bear well in mind
What thou hast rightly offered, and give heed
To this strange story thou shalt hear. One day
A youth from Aragon was brought in chains
To this harem. No need to give his name
And quality. Thou knowest whom I mean.
A woman grieves to see a noble youth
Exposed to insult and indignity.
Zulima set her eyes upon the slave,
And pity soon gave place to ardent passion.
With us, the heart's a mass of flaming fire;
With you, a lump of snow. He tried to escape.
He is caught, and by his master doomed to die.
Zulima, ever heedful for his good,
Blinded by her mad passion, saves him, nay,
She even offers him her heart and hand.
In such a vital issue, she deserves
An answer. So, do thou speak for the slave,
I will speak for Zulima.
MARSILLA.   In all my life,
In poverty and in prosperity,
Deceit did never yet defile my lips.
This heart belongs to Isabel de Segura.
ZULIMA. Reflect awhile, and thou wilt grant that Time
Takes tribute from us all. How dost thou know
If she still loves thee? Art thou sure that thou
Wilt ever see her?
MARSILLA.   My own constancy
Is my assurance of her steadfast love.
My life I'll gladly give, if so I must.
My soul—our souls once given in exchange—
I keep for one who claims it.
ZULIMA.   'Tis rash indeed.
To mock thy royal mistress, when thou knowest
The blood of Africa runs in her veins,
And makes her prompt alike to love and hate.
And if she knows I offer thee her heart,
And suffer for her sake the bitter pain
Of seeing thee coolly tread it underfoot,

Thou soon wilt find thyself back in thy chains
And in thy gloomy prison. There shall I,
With pleasure that shall deepen thy distress,
Bring thee the news that Isabel is married.

MARSILLA. And in so horrible a den, how long
Shall I remain alive?

ZULIMA.   Ye heavens! The wretch
Brings all my plans to nought. He hides behind
The menace of the tomb, and mocks my rage.
But soon I'll change thy laughter into tears :
They shall bring Isabel from Teruel
A captive here to me.

MARSILLA.   And who art thou
To dare so much?

ZULIMA.   Beware my wrath.

MARSILLA.   Thy wrath
Is all in vain.

ZULIMA.   Thou fool! She whom thou seest
Is not the daughter of Mervàn, she is
Zulima.

MARSILLA. You, the Sultana!

ZULIMA.   I, the Queen.

ACT II

SCENE VI

Doña Margarita, Isabel.

ISABEL (*following her mother*).   O mother,
For heaven's sake, hear me.

MARGARITA.   No : 'tis mad of you
To show this great aversion for a match
That promises such profit for us all.
You are noble, true; but then, remember well
That he who offers you his life and love
Is Don Rodrigo de Azagra, who
Holds higher rank and boasts of greater wealth.
In Aragon his family and friends
Respect him, and he shows, towards you at least,
A friendly disposition.

ISABEL.   To me he seems
Proud and revengeful.

MARGARITA.   Your father thinks him fit
To be your husband. 'Tis not right a maid
Herself should choose her lover. Her will should be
No other than her father's. That is how,
These days, a marriage is arranged. And thus
We all are wed; and thus was I.
ISABEL.   Have you
No other comfort then for my distress?
MARGARITA. I cannot listen to your stupid talk
Of childish love. I hold no brief for folly.
Leave me.
ISABEL.   My hopes were vain.
        (*Sobbing as she goes to withdraw.*)
MARGARITA.   What! are you weeping?
ISABEL. You have not yet denied me that relief.
MARGARITA. If I refuse to hear you, Isabel,
    You must not think me cruel. I understand
    Your grief, and feel for you indeed. But, child . . .
    For four long years Marsilla has not written.
    If he is dead . . .
ISABEL.   No, Mother, he still lives! . . .
    But how? Perchance he toils in chains for me,
    Weeping in Zion, or perchance he groans
    On Libyan sands. He has not wished to grieve me
    With such sad tidings. I often dwell on this,
    And fain would deem it true. I once resolved
    To train myself to banish him from mind,
    Thinking he was unfaithful, and enjoyed
    The raptures of another woman's love.
    I listened to his rival's hateful pleas,
    And steeled myself to fancy even they
    Did not offend my ears. But then, alas,
    When reason was about to rise supreme
    In boastful triumph o'er rebellious passion,
    Fond memory would recall a single sigh
    Of my long-absent lover, and suddenly
    My vaunted stronghold fell, and once again,
    The battle lost and over, Love surged in
    With all the greater force of blood and fire
    Through the defenceless tangle of my senses.
    Then I called virtue a deceitful jade,
    And weeping bitter angry tears, I swore

In my mad passion I would sooner lie
Dead in my grave than yield to this man's will,
This murderer, this my evil genius.

MARGARITA. For heaven's sake, Isabel, restrain yourself.
You little know what torture you inflict
With these wild words on your poor mother.

ISABEL.   What!
You marvel at my boldness? But when the heart
Is so exceeding full of rancour, it needs
Must burst its bounds. Not you, but the dull stone
Of these bare walls, this roof that mutely heard
The cry of my despair, this earth my tears
Might well impress, were it not even as hard
And cold as some that tread it—these, all these
I call to witness my profound distress,
For if they give no comfort, they at least
Take no offence.

MARGARITA (aside). I cannot bear to hear her.—
Oh, grieve no more, come to thy mother's arms,
Rest on this loving bosom. Learn to know me.
Let not my harsh appearance frighten thee :
'Tis a forced mask that grief fixed on my face;
But behind that, to comfort thy distress,
There lies the tender and indulgent love
Of a true mother.

ISABEL.   Mother!   (They embrace.)

MARGARITA.   I hid my love,
My tenderness, from thee . . . because I must. . . .
For fifteen years I have kept hidden here
Such store of bitterness. Oh, I have yearned
For mutual love; yet must I yearn in vain
For love, for happiness, since I put on
Horse-hair and sackcloth.

ISABEL.   Mother!

MARGARITA.   I was afraid—
I feared I might encourage thy young love,
And only to prevent it, showed myself
Severe towards thee; but night after night
Hearing thee lying groaning on thy bed,
Cursing my harshness even in thy despair,
I offered, weeping floods of silent tears,
My life to God to purchase thy repose.

ISABEL. Oh, what a happy revelation! Heavens!
  How unjust I have been to you! How much
  You must have loved me, mother of my heart!
  Forgive me. . . . What a thrill of joy I feel,
  Although you see me weep! I have not known
  Such happiness for six long years and more.
  Consider what my sufferings must have been,
  When I count it happiness to feel
  This momentary respite from my pain.
  Surely you will not let this ray of light,
  That has illumined my afflicted soul,
  Fade into blacker darkness than before.
  Mother, O my dear mother, at your feet
  A suppliant I kneel, and here I'll yield   *(Kneels.)*
  My life's last breath, unless you heed my prayers.
MARGARITA. Rise up, dear Isabel; come, dry these tears,
  And trust me. . . . Yes, so far as in me lies. . . .
ISABEL. You see the allotted time runs to its close.
  But three days more, three only, and the rest
  Are nought to me, when every hope is dead.
  My father to fulfil his solemn pledge,
  Will at the altar freely offer him
  The sacrifice of my enforced consent.
  Your pleading has the power to convey
  Conviction to his heart, whereas in me
  Reluctance would be disrespect, a crime.
  Mother, I see it clearly. He may well
  Force me to wed, but let him furnish then,
  Instead of bridal dress and jewels rare,
  A simple shroud and cross : this is the dress,
  This is the only jewel I shall need.
MARGARITA. No, Isabel, no, no! Not one word more!
  I pledge myself to speak for thee. Azagra
  Shall never be thy lord and master. I
  Will urge thy father to withdraw his pledge,
  And he will heed my voice, and will prevent
  So great a tragedy. Today I'll be—
  What I've not been these many years—thy mother.

ACT IV

SCENE VII

Marsilla, Isabel.

MARSILLA. Merciful Heaven!

ISABEL.   Dear God!

MARSILLA.   Is it not she?

ISABEL. 'Tis he!

MARSILLA.   O my belovèd, my adored! . . .

ISABEL. Marsilla!

MARSILLA.   O my glorious love!

ISABEL.   Alas! . . .
How did you dare to set foot in this house?
If they have seen you . . . Oh, why did you come?

MARSILLA. By heaven . . . I had forgot. But, for Marsilla
To fly to Isabel, is it not enough
To wish, to long, to need to see her? Oh,
How beautiful thou seemest in my sight!
I never saw thee so magnificent. . . .
And yet these jewels and this brave attire
Fill me with vague misgiving. Cast them off,
My love; let modest woollen frocks, and flowers
Of purest white, gathered in my own garden,
Once more set off thy maiden charm : my heart
Is troubled at the sight of so much wealth.

ISABEL (aside). Unhappy man! He is beside himself.
I cannot bear his sad bewildered glance.—
Do you not understand this rich attire,
Which you can only view with loathing, means
Our separation?

MARSILLA.   God in heaven! Ah, yes,
The awful truth!

ISABEL.   I am married.

MARSILLA.   Yes, I know.
I came too late. In sight of happiness,
I reached my hand to grasp it. At my touch,
It flew away.

ISABEL.   They lied to me. They thought
That you were dead, unfaithful.

MARSILLA.   Horrible!
Infamous!

ISABEL.   I believed that you were dead.

MARSILLA. Since you were living, and your life and mine
  Are both but one, how could the life that lives
  In me be parted from you, without you?
  Together on our earthly pilgrimage
  He exiled us who with discerning hand
  Apportions joy and grief; when at the end
  Our mortal course is run, it shall be ours
  To win together our celestial home.
ISABEL. Oh, if God heard me . . .
MARSILLA.   Listen, Isabel,
  I come not to complain : 'tis useless now.
  Nor have I come to say that I might well
  Have looked for greater constancy in you,
  Better fulfilment of those tender vows
  Which, calling on the Immaculate Mother's name,
  You swore so lovingly on that last night
  When dawn forced me to leave your balcony.
  'Thy bride', you said between sobs, 'or Christ's.'
  Sweet words, that never failed to comfort me
  In all my sorrows, on the burning plains
  Of Asia, and in my captivity!
  Today, you are not my bride, nor yet the bride
  Of Christ. Tell me—'tis all I ask to know—
  Whence this amazing, this disastrous change?
  There must have been some cause.
ISABEL.   There was indeed.
MARSILLA. Great cause.
ISABEL.   Most powerful, irresistible :
  One who has loved as I have does not wed,
  Unless compelled by the most potent force
  That man can wield.
MARSILLA.   Tell me then what it is;
  Come, tell me, quickly.
ISABEL.   No. Impossible.
  You must not know it.
MARSILLA.   Yes.
ISABEL.   No.
MARSILLA.   Everything.
ISABEL. Nothing. But in my place you would have bent
  Your neck as meekly to the yoke.
MARSILLA.   Not I.
  No, Isabel. Marsilla had the strength
  To scorn a royal hand, defying death,

For one who sells her own, and hides from him
The cause.

ISABEL (*aside*). O mother, mother!

MARSILLA. Answer me.

ISABEL (*aside*). What shall I tell him?—Yes, I must confess. . . .
I am guilty. What else can I do? You see
I am another's. Forgive me. . . . Punish me (*Weeping.*)
For being faithless.. . . . Kill me, if you will. . . .
Here on my knees I await the fatal blow.

MARSILLA. My angel, no; rather it is for me
To kiss the ground thou treadest. Oh, rise up.
The tears that dim with sadness those bright eyes
Are not tears of repentance, they are tears
Of love, full well I know, of constant love,
Love without guile, love without spot or blemish,
Ardent, passionate love, matching my own.
O Isabel, is it not true? Come, tell me
In all sincerity : my life depends
Upon thy answer.

ISABEL. Will you promise then
To obey your Isabel?

MARSILLA. Unkind, unkind!
When did I once rebel against thy pleasure?
Is not thy will mine too? Speak; I'll obey thee.

ISABEL. Swear it.

MARSILLA. I swear.

ISABEL. Well then . . . I love thee.—Go now.

MARSILLA. Ah, cruel! Didst thou fear such happiness
Would kill me at thy feet, unless the sweet
Were tempered with the poisoned touch of gall?
How couldst thou link in this strange brotherhood
Such enemies as love and banishment?

ISABEL. I am not my own mistress, as thou seest;
I am wedded to a husband now who leaves
His honour in my keeping, and I must
Be faithful to him. Virtue kept our love
Free from the stain of sin : let us preserve
Its ermine purity. Here we shall win
A cross, in heaven a crown of victory.
Thine is my love, and ever will be thine,
And in my heart I'll treasure and adore
Thy most dear likeness. That I promise thee.

I swear it, Oh, but leave me. Go at once,
And save me from the danger of thy presence.
Be generous : save me from myself. . . .

MARSILLA.   No more!
So thou wouldst have me gone. Well then, I'll leave thee.
Courage . . . and we will part. In recompense,
In memory at least of so much pain
Borne gladly for the sake of thy dear love,
Let me, my Isabel, clasp thee this once
Within my arms. . . .

ISABEL.   Oh, let the slave fulfil
Her duty to her lord.

MARSILLA.   The embrace shall be
That of a loving brother and his sister,
Our kiss shall be such as with childlike love
In happy innocence on our mothers' laps
We exchanged so oft.

ISABEL.   Do not recall it.

MARSILLA.   Come. . . .

ISABEL. No, never.

MARSILLA.   'Tis vain to oppose me.

ISABEL.   Hold, or I call. . . .

MARSILLA. For whom? For Don Rodrigo? Do not think
He will come forward at your summons. No!
He does not feed his pride in solemn state,
Filling his ears with flattering compliment.
Far from the city walls he bites the dust
Now moistened with his blood.

ISABEL.   Oh, horrible!
You have killed him?

MARSILLA.   Faithless creature! You regret it?
If I thought that, what power on earth could save him?

ISABEL. He lives then?

MARSILLA.   Yes. Thanks to my generous folly,
He lives. We both had scarce crossed swords, ere mine
Had fleshed itself so furiously in him,
That in a moment his o'erweening pride
Sank to the ground. His sword was in my power.
O cursèd skill in arms! Thrice cursèd he
Who scatters virtues that produce a crop
Of nothing but misfortunes! Away with kindness!
Henceforth I must have crimes. Your cruel words
Have goaded me to cruelty, and I

Must practise it on you. You must leave here
At once with me.

ISABEL. No, no!

MARSILLA. Yes, Isabel.
I mean to save you. Do you know what he—
This coward you bewail so tearfully—
Said as he fell? 'The victory is yours;
And yet my blood shall cost someone full dear.'

ISABEL. What did he mean? Oh, what ...?

MARSILLA. 'I'll be revenged
On Pedro, on his wife, ay, on all three.
The letters still are in my hands.'

ISABEL. Ah, God!

MARSILLA. What letters did he mean?

ISABEL. You have ruined me!
Misfortune dogs your steps. Where is my husband?
Tell me at once, that as a faithful wife
I may make haste to help him, and o'ercome
His anger with my prayers.

MARSILLA. God help me! And,
She said she loved me!

ISABEL. What! You dare reproach
Azagra's wife, vengeful Azagra's wife,
With her unhappy love? Oh, I hate you! (*Exit.*)

SCENE VIII

MARSILLA. Good God! From her own lips! In anger too!
I am not deceived. There is no love left here.
The deadly poisonous words she flung at me
Sink in my tortured bosom and consume
My throbbing, bursting heart. With her, through her,
For her sweet sake I lived. . . . Oh, without her,
Without her love, I cannot breathe. To me
Her love became the very breath of life!
She has refused it, she has taken it from me:
I cannot breathe, I cannot live.

VOICES (*within*). In there!
Surround the house.

SCENE IX

Isabel, *hurrying back in great agitation.* Marsilla.

ISABEL. Fly, they are coming, fly.

MARSILLA (*quite overcome*). I cannot.

VOICES (*within*). Death to him, death!
ISABEL. Come quick, come quick.
MARSILLA. God help me!
(Isabel *seizes his hand and drags him through the door at the*
back of the stage.)

SCENE X

Adel, *pursued by various Gentlemen with drawn swords;* Don
Pedro, Doña Margarita. *Servants.* Isabel *and* Marsilla *within.*

GENTLEMEN. Death to him!
Death to him!
PEDRO and MARGARITA. Listen.
ADEL. Men of Aragon,
I slew the Moorish Queen; but know, the King,
Her lord and master, sent me from Valencia
To take and kill her. She, a faithless wife,
A wicked trafficker in love, conspired
Marsilla's death, Isabel's too. . . .
ISABEL (*within*). Ah, woe
Is me!
ADEL. In proof behold this poisoned blade.
(*Showing Zulima's dagger.*)
Marsilla will confirm what I have said:
He must be somewhere here.

(*The door at the back opens, and* Isabel *comes forward and*
throws herself in her mother's arms. Marsilla *is seen lying*
across a couch.)

ISABEL. My darling mother!
ADEL. Behold him there. . . .
MARGARITA. Ah, God!
PEDRO. Motionless. . . .
ISABEL. Dead!
ADEL. Zulima then has wreaked her cruel vengeance.
ISABEL. No! Not the vengeance of the Moorish Queen
Has killed him. I being there, who would have dared
To touch him? No! My ill-starred love, that was
His very life . . . his own disastrous love . . .
'Twas this that killed him. Beside myself with wrath,
I said to him 'I hate you'. He believed
That sacrilegious word, and died of grief.
MARGARITA. Merciful Heaven!

ISABEL.   Yes, Heaven that parted us
   In life, will re-unite us in the grave.
PEDRO. My daughter!
ISABEL.   See, Marsilla signifies
   My place is by his side.
MARGARITA.   Isabel!
PEDRO.   Isabel!
ISABEL. My love, forgive those fatal angry words.
   I loved thee. I was thine. Thine I remain.
   In quest of thee my loving spirit hies.

   (*Goes towards* Marsilla's *body, but before reaching it, falls
   lifeless, with her arms outstretched towards her lover.*)

                                        HENRY THOMAS

JOSÉ DE ESPRONCEDA
[1808–1842]

The stormy life of José de Espronceda, the greatest lyric poet of the romantic period, in itself exemplified the spirit of romanticism. A tortured soul, ever rebelling, he battled his way through exile from Spain for political activity, the Parisian barricade fighting of 1830, Spanish revolutionary struggles in 1835 and 1836, and a host of other freedom-seeking causes. His brief, trouble-streaked years—he died at thirty-four—held one great love: Teresa Mancha, who deserted husband and family for him. Their frequent separations brought bitterness to both; their raptures inspired some of Espronceda's most gripping poetry.

Himself a social outcast by choice and romantic inclination, he often in his short poems describes others beyond the pale of society: the beggar, the criminal, the executioner, the pirate. His two longest works are El estudiante de Salamanca, on the Don Juan theme, and El diablo mundo, an extraordinary attempt to synthesize the struggle of humanity.

Espronceda's poetry is generally tinged by rebellion, melancholy and despair. But every line sings with innate rhythm. This musical quality is most evident in his famous Canción del pirata.

PIRATE'S SONG

With cannon ten on port and starboard,
Wind just aft and strong,
Flying the sea, not ploughing through,
A brigantine skims along.
She is called the *Dreaded* by a host
And feared on every side,
From the eastern to the western coast,
Wherever she may ride.

Across the sea the moonlight shines,
The wind goes wailing through,
Shrill in the canvas, ruffling waves
Of silver and of blue.
There on the poop the captain sings
By whom the band is led,
With Asia left and Europe right
And Istambul ahead.

Sail on, swift bark, at my command,
  So brave and bold,
No warship by your foemen manned,
Nor storm, nor calm, nor any force
Shall turn you from your chosen course
Nor daunt your hardy soul.

A score of ships
We've seized aright
And this despite
The English fleet.
And I have forced
A hundred lords
To lay their swords
Beneath my feet.

My only treasure a pirate ship,
My god but liberty,
My law, brute force and a hearty wind,
My land, the open sea.

Kings are plunging into war,
  Unseeing fools,
To fight for land, for a trifle more,
While anything that sails the sea
Belongs by my own laws to me,
Unchecked by others' rules.

There nowhere lies
A foreign land
Or distant strand
That does not feel,
Whate'er its flag,
My crushing might,
Admit my right,
And to me yield.

My only treasure a pirate ship . . .

The cry, 'A ship !' is a sudden threat.
  Watch them veer.
See how fast, full canvas set,
In desperate fright they try to flee :
I am king of all the sea,
My wrath inspires their fear.

The spoils of war
That raids provide
I then divide
With justice fine,
Unless I claim
Some damsel rare,
Surpassing fair,
And make her mine.

My only treasure a pirate ship . . .

And I have been condemned to die !
  I laugh at that.
Upon good fortune I rely,
And hope to hang him by the neck,
Perhaps from a yardarm on his deck,
Who sentenced me to die.

    If I should fall,
    If life's the cost?
    I'd count well lost
    The life I gave.
    I knew the risk
    Yet with one stroke
    Cast off the yoke
    That held me slave.

My only treasure a pirate ship . . .

Melodies in the winds abound :
  I love to hear
The cables' splashing, scraping sound,
The roar and bark of the loud Black Sea,
The crash of the cannon's battery,
Delightful to my ear.

    Rolls of thunder
    Snap and growl
    And seawinds howl
    Across the deep.
    I am calmed
    As sounds grow dulled,
    And by them lulled
    I drift to sleep.

My only treasure a pirate ship,
My god but liberty,
My law, brute force and a hearty wind,
My land, the open sea.

ALICE JANE M^cVAN

THE CONDEMNED TO DIE

I

His form upon the ground reclined,
  With bitter anguish inward drawn,
Full of the coming day his mind
  That soon will sadly dawn,
The culprit waits, in silence laid,
  The fatal moments hastening now,
In which his last sun's light display'd
  Will shine upon his brow.

O'er crucifix and altar there,
  The chapel cell in mourning hung,
From the dim candle's yellow glare
  A funeral light is flung;
And by the wretched culprit's side,
  His face with hood half cover'd o'er,
The friar, with trembling voice to guide,
  Is heard his prayers implore.

His brow then raises he again,
  And slowly lifts to heaven his eyes;
Perhaps a prayer for mercy fain
  May in his grief arise.
A tear flows : whence had that release?
  Was it from bitterness or fear?
Perhaps his sorrows to increase
  Some thought to memory dear?

So young ! and life, that he had dream'd
  Was full of golden days to glide,
Is pass'd, when childhood's tears it seem'd
  As scarcely yet were dried.
Then on him of his childhood burst
  The thought, and of his mother's woe,
That he whom she so fondly nursed
  Was doom'd that death to know.

And while that hopelessly he sees
  His course already death arrest,
He feels his life's best energies
  Beat strongly in his breast;
And sees that friar, who calmly now
  Is laid, with sleep no more to strive,
With age so feebly doom'd to bow,
  Tomorrow will survive.

But hark! what noise that silence breaks
  This hour unseasonably by?
Some one a gay guitar awakes
  And mirthful songs reply;
And shouts are raised, and sounds are heard
  Of bottles rattling, and perchance
Others, remember'd well, concurr'd
  Of lovers in the dance.
And then he hears funereal roll,
  Between each pause in accents high,
'Your alms, for prayers to rest the soul
  Of him condemn'd to die.'

And so combined the drunkard's shout,
  The toast, the strifes, and fancies wild
Of all that Bacchanalian rout,
  With wanton's songs defiled,
And bursts of idle laughter, reach
  Distinct into the gloomy cell,
And seem far off ejected each
  The very sounds of hell.
And then he hears, funereal roll
  Between each pause, those accents high,
'Your alms, for prayers to rest the soul
  Of him condemn'd to die.'
He cursed them all, as one by one
  The impious echoes each express'd;

He cursed the mother as a son
  Who nursed him at her breast :
The whole world round alike he cursed,
  His evil destiny forlorn,
And the dark day and hour when first
  That wretched he was born.

II

The moon serene illumes the skies,
And earth in deepest stillness lies;
No sound is heard, the watchdog's mute,
And even the lover's plaintive lute.

Madrid enveloped lies in sleep;
    Repose o'er all its shade has cast,
And men of him no memory keep
    Who soon will breathe his last.
Or if perchance one thinks to wake
    At early dawn, no thoughts whate'er
Rise for the wretched being's sake,
    Who death is waiting there.
Unmoved by pity's kind control,
    Men hear around the funeral cry,
'Your alms, for prayers to rest the soul
    Of him condemn'd to die.'

Sleeps in his bed the judge in peace;
    And sleeps and dreams of how his store,
The executioner, to increase;
    And pleased he counts it o'er.
Only the city's silence breaks,
    And destined place of death portrays,
The harden'd workman who awakes
    The scaffolding to raise.

III

Confused and mad his heated mind,
With raving feverish dreams combined,
The culprit's soul exhaustion press'd,
His head sunk heavy on his breast.

And in his dreams he life and death
    Confounds, remembers, and forgets;
And fearful struggling every breath,
    And sigh he gives besets.

And in a world of darkness seems
  As now to stray; feels fear and cold,
And in his horrid madness deems
  The cord his neck infold :
And so much more, in desperate fight,
  In anguish to escape his lot,
He strives, with so much more the might
  He binds the fatal knot :
And voices hears, confused the whole,
  Of people round, and then that cry,
'Your alms, for prayers to rest the soul
  Of him condemn'd to die !'

Or fancies now that he is free;
  And breathes the fresh pure air, and hears
Her sigh of love, the maid whom he
  Had loved in happier years :
Beauteous and kind as e'er of old,
  Sweet flower of spring-time's gay resort,
As could for love the meads behold,
  Or gallant April court.

And joyful he to see her flies,
  And seeks to reach her, but in vain;
For as with anxious hands he tries
  His hoped-for bliss to gain,
The illusion suddenly to break,
  He finds the dream deceitful fled !
A cold stiff corpse the shape to take,
  And scaffold in its stead.
And hears the mournful funeral knoll,
  And hollow voice resounding nigh,
'Your alms, for prayers to rest the soul
  Of him condemn'd to die !'

                              JAMES KENNEDY

TO HARIFA, IN AN ORGY

Thy hand, Harifa ! bring it me;
  Come near, and place it on my brow;
As on some lava's boiling sea
  I feel my head is burning now.

Come, bring with mine thy lips to meet,
    Though they but madden me astray,
Where yet I find the kisses beat,
    There left thy loves of yesterday.
What is virtue, what is joy,
    Or love, or purity, or truth?
The false illusions of a boy,
    The cherish'd flatteries of my youth.
Then bring me wine; there let me try
    Remembrance drown'd to hold repress'd,
Without a pang from life to fly;
    In frenzy death may give me rest.

O'erspreads my face a burning flood,
    And red and glaring wildly start
My eyes forth out in heated blood,
    And forth leaps restlessly my heart.
Woman! I hate thee; fly thee—go :
    I feel thy hands my hands infold,
And feel them freezing, cold as snow,
    As snow thy kisses are as cold.

Ever the same, try, tempters weak!
    Other endearments to enthral;
Another world, new pleasures seek,
    For such your joys I curse them all.
Your kisses are a lie; a cheat
    Is all the tenderness you feign;
Your beauty ugly in deceit,
    The enjoyment suffering and pain.

I wish for love, ethereal, high,
    For some diviner joy my lot;
For such my heart will imaged sigh,
    For such as in the world is not.
And 'tis that meteor light afar,
    The phantom that deceived my mind,
The treacherous guide, the vapour star,
    That leads me wandering and blind.

Why is my soul for pleasure dead,
    And yet alive to grief and care?
Why doom'd in listless stupor laid
    This arid loathing still to bear?

Why this consuming wild desire,
  This restless passion vague and strange?
That well I know I rave, 'tis fire,
  Yet plunge in its deceitful range.

Why do I dream of love and joy,
  That I am sure a lie will prove?
Why where fantastic charms decoy,
  Will thus my heart delirious move,
If soon it finds for meads and flowers,
  But arid wastes and tangled thorns,
And soon a loathing rage o'erpowers
  The mad or mournful love it scorns?

Flung as a rapid comet wide,
  On ardent fancy's wings I flew,
Where'er my wayward mind espied
  Or joys or triumphs to pursue.
I launch'd myself, in daring flight,
  Beyond the world through heavenward space,
And found but doubt, and all so bright
  That seem'd, illusive proved the chase.

Then on the earth I anxious sought
  For virtue, glory, love sublime;
And my worn spirit found there nought
  But fetid dust and loathsome slime.
Mid clouds with heavenly hues o'ercast
  Women of virgin lustre shone;
I saw, I touch'd them, and they pass'd,
  And smoke and ashes left alone.

I found the illusion fled; but rife,
  Unquench'd desires their longings crave;
I felt the real, I hated life,
  And peace believed but in the grave.
And yet I seek, and anxious seek,
  For pleasures still I ask and sigh,
And hear dread accents answering speak,
  'Unhappy one! despair, and die.

'Die : Life is a torment, joy a cheat,
  Hope not for good on earth for thee,
But fruitless struggles look to meet
  In thy vain longings endlessly!

For so God punishes the soul
    That in its madness dares espy
The unfathom'd secrets of the scroll
    Of truth, denied to mortal eye!'

O! cease : no more I ask to know,
    No more to see : my soul oppress'd
Is humbly bow'd, and prostrate low,
    Now only asks, and longs for rest.
In me let feeling then lie dead,
    Since died my hopes of happiness,
Nor joys nor griefs be o'er me spread
    My soul returning to depress.

Pass, as in magic optic glass,
    And other youthful hearts deceive,
Bright images of glory! pass,
    That crowns of gold and laurel weave.
Pass, ye voluptuous fair ones, on!
    With dance and mirthful songs attuned,
Like vaporous visions, pass, begone!
    No more my heart to move or wound.
And let the dance, and festal din,
    O'er my revolted fancy reign,
And fled the night, see morn begin,
    Surprised in senseless stupor's chain.

Harifa, come! Like me this woe
    Thou too hast borne! Thou ne'er dost weep!
But, ah! how wretched 'tis to know
    Feelings so bitter and so deep!
The same our sufferings and care;
    In vain thou hold'st thy tears apart;
Like me thou also hast to bear
    A wounded and an aching heart!

JAMES KENNEDY

JOSÉ ZORRILLA
[1817–1893]

José Zorrilla, Spain's exceedingly popular romantic poet, wrote with an easy and instinctive brilliance; words cascaded from his pen in a stunning melodic flow. His excellent leyendas, *stemming from Spanish traditions and tales, helped earn for him the title 'el poeta nacional'. Zorrilla is equally famous for his religious-romantic drama* Don Juan Tenorio *(1844), based on Tirso de Molina's often-imitated* El burlador de Sevilla *(1630). The success of Zorrilla's play, in which Don Juan attains salvation, has exceeded that of any other Spanish dramatic work. For more than a century it has been unfailingly presented during the first week of November in almost all Spanish theatres.*

BOABDIL

Lady of the dark head-dress,
    And monkish vest of purple hue,
Gladly would Boabdil give
    Granada for a kiss of you.

He would give the best adventure
    Of the bravest horseman tried,
And with all its verdant freshness
    A whole bank of Darro's tide.

He would give rich carpets, perfumes,
    Armours of rare price and force,
And so much he values you,
    A troop, ay, of his favourite horse.

'Because thine eyes are beautiful,
    Because the morning's blushing light
From them arises to the East,
    And gilds the whole world bright.

'From thy lips smiles are flowing,
    From thy tongue gentle peace,
Light and aerial as the course
    Of the purple morning's breeze.

'O ! lovely Nazarene, how choice !
  For an Eastern harem's pride,
Those dark locks waving freely
  Thy crystal neck beside.

'Upon a couch of velvet,
  In a cloud of perfumed air,
Wrapp'd in the white and flowing veil
  Of Mahomet's daughters fair.

'O, Lady ! come to Cordova,
  There Sultana thou shalt be,
And the Sultan there, Sultana,
  Shall be but a slave for thee.

'Such riches he will give thee,
  And such robes of Tunisine,
That thou wilt judge thy beauty,
  To repay him for them, mean.'

.   .   .

O ! Lady of the dark head-dress !
That him a kiss of thee might bless,
  Resign a realm Boabdil would !
But I for that, fair Christian, fain
Would give of heavens, and think it gain,
  A thousand if I only could.

JAMES KENNEDY

THE CHRISTIAN LADY AND THE MOOR

Hastening to Granada's gates,
  Came o'er the Vega's land,
Some forty Gomel horsemen,
  And the Captain of the band.

He, entering in the city,
  Check'd his white steed's career;
And to a lady on his arm,
  Borne weeping many a tear,

Said, 'Cease your tears, fair Christian,
  That grief afflicting me,
I have a second Eden,
  Sultana, here for thee.

'A palace in Granada,
    With gardens and with flowers,
And a gilded fountain playing
    More than a hundred showers.

'And in the Henil's valley
    I have a fortress grey,
To be among a thousand queen
    Beneath thy beauty's sway.

'For over all yon winding shore
    Extends my wide domain,
Nor Cordova's, nor Seville's lands,
    A park like mine contain.

'There towers the lofty palm-tree,
    The pomegranate's glowing there,
And the leafy fig-tree, spreading
    O'er hill and valley fair.

'There grows the hardy walnut,
    The yellow nopal tall,
And mulberry darkly shading
    Beneath the castle wall;

'And elms I have in my arcades
    That to the skies aspire,
And singing birds in cages
    Of silk, and silver wire.

'And thou shalt my Sultana be,
    My halls alone to cheer;
My harem without other fair,
    Without sweet songs my ear.

'And velvets I will give thee,
    And eastern rich perfumes,
From Greece I'll bring thee choicest veils,
    And shawls for Cashmere's looms :

'And I will give thee feathers white,
    To deck thy beauteous brow,
Whiter than ev'n the ocean foam
    Our eastern waters know.

'And pearls to twine amid thy hair,
    Cool baths when heat's above,
And gold and jewels for thy neck,
    And for thy lips be—love!'

'O! what avail those riches all,'
    Replied the Christian fair,
'If from my father and my friends,
    My ladies, me you tear?

'Restore me, O! restore me, Moor,
    To my father's land, my own;
To me more dear are Leon's towers
    Than thy Granada's throne.'

Smoothing his beard, awhile the Moor
    In silence heard her speak;
Then said as one who deeply thinks,
    With a tear upon his cheek,

'If better seem thy castle there,
    Than here our gardens shine,
And thy flowers are more beautiful,
    Because in Leon thine;

'And thou hast given thy youthful love
    One of thy warriors there,
Houri of Eden! weep no more,
    But to thy knights repair!'

Then giving her his chosen steed,
    And half his lordly train,
The Moorish chieftain turn'd him back
    In silence home again.

                        JAMES KENNEDY

ORIENTAL

Seen in moonlight's silver ray,
Far away,
Gleams an Arab tower tall,
And the Darro's water clear,
Flowing near,
Break against its wall.

Elms that murmur o'er the river,
Leaves aquiver,
Restful solace bring.
In the reeds and in the cane,
Soft refrain
Fleeting breezes sing.

Flowers on the yellow sand
Along the strand
Perfumes sweet exhale.
Hovering with plumage rare,
O'er flowers fair
Wings the nightingale.

Dewdrops falling brightly shine,
Crystalline,
Silvery pearls aglimmer.
Mirrored in the drops of dew,
Rainbow hue,
Moorish turrets shimmer.

Jalousies are opened wide
While inside
The fair Sultana sings.
From her fretted tower's height,
Through the night,
Clear the music rings.

Freely through the ambient air,
Everywhere,
Floats her mournful song.
Lost in grasses far below
Strong winds blow
Bearing it along.

And in time to her soft cry,
Lilting high,
A linnet's answer rings
Flitting through the garden's maze,
Where ablaze,
Many a tulip springs.

To the sound of that sweet trill,
Echoing still,
Of beauty, bird, and lyre,

Elm and field and lovely flower,
Lofty tower,
Listening never tire.

To the Moorish maid's lament
The linnet sent
Answering reply.
This the jealous Moor could hear,
Listening near,
Where dark shadows lie.

'A Moorish heart is mine to hold,
Pearls and gold,
Crowns that richly gleam.
Tell me, flower, what I miss
Of loveliness
In this sad hareem.

'Rugs the Caliphs give and shawls;
In these vast halls
Garlands rare are seen.
Tell me, garden, what I miss
Of loveliness
In this sad hareem.

'Festivals and gardens gay,
Where waters play,
In Eden false I dream.
Tell me, river, what I miss
Of loveliness
In this sad hareem.

'Feathers light as foam on sea
They give to me,
Veils that cobwebs seem.
Tell me what I still bewail,
Nightingale,
In this sad hareem.

'Smooth my forehead is from care,
And unaware
My eyes of sorrow's theme.
Tell me, pale moon, what I miss
Of loveliness
In this sad hareem.'

Where the lamplight's fitful glow
Burns most low,
A shadow passes by.
She hears the Sultan softly glide
To her side,
Murmuring reply.

'You have gold and towers bright,
Pearls so white,
Wreaths for your forehead pale.
Say what in this pleasant bourne
You still mourn,
In what gift I fail.

'Dusky garden, flying bird,
River heard
Swiftly flowing on,
What do all of these possess
Of happiness
That I'd not bring at dawn?

'What mad fancies are there still
To fulfil,
What lacks your beauty fair?'
'Alas, my Lord, these nightingales
In flowery vales
Have *liberty and air*.'

ELIZABETH DU GUÉ TRAPIER

MANUEL BRETÓN DE LOS HERREROS
[1796–1873]

Bretón de los Herreros was a facile, light poet and a prolific author of popular comedies of manners. Like his contemporary, Hartzenbusch, he served at one time as Director of the National Library.

SATIRICAL LETRILLA III

Such is, dear girl, my tenderness,
   Naught can its equal be!
If thou a dowry didst possess
The charms to rival of thy face,
   I would marry thee.

Thou wert my bliss, my star, my all!
   So kind and fair to see;
And me thy consort to install,
At once for witness Heaven I call,
   I would marry thee.

Thou dost adore me? yes, and I,
   Thy love so raptures me,
If thou wouldst not so anxious try
To know my pay, and what I buy,
   I would marry thee.

If thou wert not so always coy,
   Ne'er listening to my plea,
But when I, fool! my cash employ
To bring thee sweets, or some fine toy,
   I would marry thee.

If thou must not instructions wait,
   As may mamma agree,
To write or speak to me, or state
When thou wilt meet me at the gate,
   I would marry thee.

If 'twere not when to dine, the most
   Thy meagre soup bouillie
Thou givest, as many airs thou show'st,
As Roderic at the hanging-post
   I would marry thee.

If for my punishment instead
  Of ease and quiet, we
Might not three hungry brothers dread,
And mother too, to keep when wed,
  I would marry thee.

If 'twere not when these plagues combine
  With thy tears flowing free,
The virtues of a heavenly sign
I see must solace me, not thine,
  I would marry thee.

Go, get another in thy chain,
  And Heaven for you decree
A thousand joys, for me 'tis vain;
I know thee cheat, and tell thee plain,
  I will not marry thee.

JAMES KENNEDY

SATIRICAL LETRILLA IV

Whene'er Don Juan has a feast at home
I am forgotten as if at Rome;
But he will for funerals me invite,
To kill me with the annoyance quite;
Well, be it so!

Cœleste, with a thousand coy excuses
Will sing the song that set she chooses,
And all about her that environ,
Though like an owl, call her a siren;
Well, be it so!

A hundred bees, without reposing,
Work their sweet combs, with skill composing;
Alas! for an idle drone they strive,
Who soon will come to destroy the hive;
Well, be it so!

Man to his like moves furious war,
As if he were too numerous far;
Alone the medical squadrons wait
The world itself to depopulate;
Well, be it so!

There are of usurers heaps in Spain,
Of catchpoles, hucksterers, heaps again,
And of vintners too, yet people still
Talk about robbers in the hill;
Well, be it so!

In vain may the poor, O Conde, try
Thy door, for the dog makes sole reply;
And yet to spend thou hast extollers,
Over a ball two thousand dollars;
Well, be it so!

Enough today, my pen, this preaching;
A better time we wait for teaching;
If vices in vain I try to brand,
And find I only write on sand,
Well, be it so!

JAMES KENNEDY

FERNÁN CABALLERO
[1796–1877]

Fernán Caballero is the pseudonym of Cecilia Böhl de Faber, daughter of a famous German Hispanist and a Spanish mother. Though born in Switzerland and educated in Germany, she spent most of her life in Andalusia and made a careful study of its traditions and customs. This background of folklore constitutes one of the chief merits of her many novels and short stories.

She is generally considered to have initiated the revival of the realistic novel in Spain. Her first and finest novel, La Gaviota, *appeared in 1849. The title, which means 'Seagull', was a term applied to the heroine, María, because of her temperamental character.*

LA GAVIOTA

THE DEATH OF PEPE VERA

. . . Maria began to weep.

'Come!' replied Pepe, 'dry your tears, the *refugium peccatorum* of women. You know the proverb which says, "Make a woman weep, and you vanquish her"; but, my beautiful, there is another proverb, "Confide not either in the barking of dogs, or in the tears of women." Keep your tears for the theatre; here we do not play comedy. Look well to yourself. If you deceive me, you make me incur the danger of death; I do not prove my love by the recipes of the apothecary, nor by dollars. I am not satisfied with grimaces, I must have acts. If you do not come this afternoon to the bull-fight you will repent of it.'

And Pepe Vera went away, without even saying *Adios* to his mistress. He was at that moment borne down by two opposite feelings which required iron nerves to conceal them, as he did, under appearances the most tranquil, under a countenance the most calm, and the most perfect indifference.

He had studied the bulls he was about to fight with; never had he seen any so ferocious. One of them strangely preoccupied him; as often happens to men of his profession, who, without caring for the other bulls, believe themselves saved if they can conquer the one which causes their anxiety. Besides, he was jealous. Jealous! he who knew only how to vanquish, and be cheered by bravos. He was told that they mocked him, and in a few hours he went to find himself between life and death, between love and treason. At least he believed so.

When he had quitted Maria, she tore the lace trimmings of her bed, unjustly scolded Marina, and shed abundance of tears. Then she dressed herself, called one of her maids, and went with her to the bull-fight, where she seated herself in the box which Pepe had reserved for her.

The noise and the heat increased her fever. Her cheeks, ordinarily pale, were inflamed, and a feverish ardour shone in her large black eyes. Anger, indignation, jealousy, offended pride, terror, anxiety, physical pain, combined in vain to force a complaint, even a sigh, from that mouth closed like a tomb. Pepe Vera perceived her : he smiled; but his smile in no way moved the Gaviota, who, under her icy countenance, swore to revenge her wounded vanity.

One bull had already bitten the dust, under the blow of another *toreador*. This bull had been *good* : he had been well fought.

The trumpet again sounded. The *toril* opened its narrow and sombre door, and a bull, black as night, dashed into the arena.

'It is *Medianoche* !' cried the crowd.

Medianoche was the *bull of the corrida*; that is to say, the king of the *fête*.

Medianoche was in no way like an ordinary bull, who at once seeks his liberty, his fields, and his deserts. He would, before every thing, show them they were not playing with a contemptible enemy; he would revenge himself, and punish. At the noise made by the cries of the crowd, he stopped suddenly.

There is not the least doubt of the bull being a stupid animal. Nevertheless, whether it be the sharp anger, or intelligence the most rebellious, whether it be that he has the faculty to render clear instincts the most blind; it is the fact that some bulls can divine and baffle the most secret ruses of the course. The *picadores* attracted, at first, the attention of the bull. He charged the one he found nearest to him, and felled him to the earth; he did the same with the second, without leaving the spot, without the lance being able to arrest him, and which inflicted but a slight wound. The third *picador* shared the fate of his comrades.

Medianoche, his horns and front bloody, raised his head towards the seats whence came cries of admiration at such bravery.

The *chulos* conveyed the *picadores* outside the arena. One of them had a broken leg; they took him to the infirmary, and the other two changed their horses.

A new *picador* replaced the wounded, and while the *chulos* occupied the attention of the bull, the three *picadores* resumed their places, their lances in rest.

The bull divided them, and after a combat of two minutes all three were overthrown. One had fainted from having his head cut open; the furious animal attacked the horse, whose lacerated body served as a shield to the unfortunate cavalier.

There was then a moment of profound stupefaction. The *chulos* searched in vain, at the risk of their lives, to turn aside *Medianoche*, who appeared to have a thirst for blood, and quenched his rage upon his victim.

At this terrible moment a *chulo* rushed towards the animal, and covered his head with his cloak. His success was of short duration. The bull disengaged himself promptly; he made the aggressor fly, and pursued him; but, in his blind fury, he passed him; the *chulo* had thrown himself on the ground. When the animal suddenly turned round, for he was one of those who never abandon their prey, the nimble *chulo* had already risen, and leaped the barrier amid the acclamations of the enthusiastic crowd for so much courage and agility.

All this had passed with the rapidity of light. The heroic devotion with which the *toreros* aid and defend each other, is the only thing really noble and beautiful displayed in these cruel, immoral, inhuman *fêtes*, which are a real anachronism in our times, so much vaunted as an age of light.

The bull, full of the pride of triumph, walked about as master of the arena. A sentiment of terror pervaded all the spectators.

Various opinions were expressed. Some wished that the *cabestro* (the bull who leads the troop . . .) be let into the arena, to lead out the formidable animal, as much to avoid new misfortunes as to preserve the propagation of his valiant race. They sometimes have recourse to this measure; but it frequently happens that the bull withdrawn does not survive the inflammation of blood which had provoked the fight. Others insisted that his tendons be cut, thus killing the bull easily. Unfortunately the greatest number cried out that it would be a crime not to see so beautiful a bull killed according to all the rules of art.

The alcalde did not know which party to side with. To preside over a bull-fight is not an easy thing.

At last, that which happens in all similar cases occurred in this : victory was with those who cried the loudest, and it was decided that the powerful and terrible *Medianoche* should die according to rule, and in possession of all his means of defence.

Pepe Vera then appeared in the arena, armed for the combat. He saluted the authorities, placed himself before Maria, and offered her the *brindo*—the honour of the bull. He was pale.

Maria, her countenance on fire, her eyes darting from their sockets, breathed with difficulty. Her body bent forward, her nails forced into the velvet cushions of her box, she contemplated this young man, so beautiful, so calm before death, and whom she loved. She felt a power in his love which subjugated her, which made her tremble and weep; because that this brutal and tyrannical passion, this exchange of profound affection, impassioned and exclusive, was the love which she felt : as with certain men of a special organization, who require in place of sweet liqueurs and fine wines the powerful excitement of alcoholic drinks.

Everywhere reigned the most profound silence. A gloomy presentiment seemed to agitate every soul. Many arose and left the place.

The bull himself, now in the middle of the arena, appeared valiant; he proudly defied his adversary.

Pepe Vera chose the spot which seemed to him the most favourable, with his habitual calm and self-possessed manner; and designated it to the *chulos*, by pointing with his finger.

'Here !' he said to them.

The *chulos* sprang out like rockets in a display of fireworks; the bull had not for an instant the idea of pursuing them. They disappeared. *Medianoche* found himself face to face with the *matador*.

The situation did not last long. The bull precipitated himself with a rapidity so sudden, that Pepe had not time to put himself on guard. All he could do was to dodge the first attack of his adversary. But the animal, contrary to the habits of those of his species, took a sudden spring, and turning suddenly, he came like a clap of thunder on the *matador*, caught him on his horns, furiously shook his head, and threw at a distance from him the body of Pepe Vera, which fell like an inert mass upon the ground of the arena.

A cry, such as the imagination of Dante alone could conceive, broke forth from a thousand human breasts, a cry profound, mournful, prolonged, and terrific.

The *picadores* rushed towards the bull to prevent his returning to his victim. The *chulos* also surrounded him.

'The *medias lunas* ! the *medias lunas* !' (long partisans by which sometimes the tendons are cut) cried the crowd.

The alcalde repeated the cry of the crowd.

Then were seen to appear these terrible weapons, and soon

Medianoche had his tendons cut; he was red with rage and with pain.

At last he fell under the ignoble poniard of the horse-killer.

The *chulos* raised up the body of Pepe Vera.

'Dead!'

Such was the cry which escaped from the lips of the group of *chulos*; and which, passing from mouth to mouth throughout the vast amphitheatre, brought mourning to all hearts. . . .

J. LEANDER STARR

MANUEL TAMAYO Y BAUS
[1829–1898]

Manuel Tamayo y Baus, one of the best Spanish dramatists of the nineteenth century, wrote many successful plays on a variety of themes—classic, romantic, historical, realistic. His masterpiece is the tragedy Un drama nuevo *(1867). This work, in one sense, is of special interest to English-speaking readers since William Shakespeare and his acting troupe are the characters.*

A NEW DRAMA

Characters

Yorick, comedian in Shakespeare's company.
Alice, his wife.
Edmund, his foster-son.
Shakespeare.
Walton, tragedian.

The scene is London, 1605

ACT I

A room in Yorick's house.

SCENE II

YORICK. 'It is so easy to cause laughter,' they said to me last night —Walton and the rest. They'll see right soon that when the time comes I can bring tears as well. They'll see it and they'll storm; when I, no more with mirth, but now with tragic passions, compel the public's bravos and applause. (*He takes from the top of the table the manuscript.*) None the less, one must proceed with plentiful caution, because the blessed rôle of Count Octavio is just a trifle difficult, and at the slightest stumbling one might take a fall and destroy himself.

'Tremble, thou faithless spouse! . . .'

(*Reading in the manuscript.*) Here's where the big scene comes. One Signor Rodolfo or Pandolfo . . . Landolfo, Landolfo is his name,—(*Finding this name in the manuscript*),—a sly knave, delivers to the Count a letter which proves that Manfredo, to whom he has been a father, is the lover of his wife, the enchanting Beatrice. The Count was jealous of every living creature except this fine young squire; and when at last his house of cards comes tumbling about his ears, he is left, poor fellow, as stupefied as if the world were falling on him.

'Tremble, thou faithless spouse! thou ingrate, tremble!

Destroyer of my honour and my peace!

Vain was thy craft—behold the damning proof!

(*He opens the letter.*)

My blood is freezing.

(*Without daring to look at the letter.*)

Let it flame with wrath!

Woe be to him—the infamous wretch—for whom

Thou blindly dost defile me.

Alas! what do I see! A thousand devils!'

(*He fixes his glance on the letter, gives a horrible cry, and falls on a bench as though struck by lightning.*) (*From 'Tremble, thou faithless spouse' up to this point, reading in the manuscript; the stage directions in a tone different from that of the verses.*) Now to see how I manage that yell. (*He takes an affectedly tragic attitude, doubles up the manuscript so that it may serve as a letter, and declaims stupidly with ridiculous intonation.*)

'Woe be to him—the infamous wretch—for whom

Thou blindly dost defile me.

Alas! what do I see! . . .'

(*Giving a discordant yell.*) No . . . 'tis true, I do it less than perfectly yet.—'Oh!' (*Giving a yell worse than before.*) Bad, unconscionably bad; 'tis thus one yells when someone treads upon his foot.—'Oh!' (*Yelling again.*) Nay, no human noise that—'tis the croaking of some great bird. Bah! Later with the heat of the situation . . . Let's see here . . .

'So then, 'tis thou who art the villain. . . .'

Too weak.

'So then, 'tis thou who art the villain. . . .'

Too strong.
                'So then, 'tis thou who art the villain. . . .'
Nay, the villain I, the madman I, at my age to insist on going
counter to my nature and old custom.—Perhaps now the fault's not
altogether mine. . . . Perhaps the author is somewhat to blame. . . .
These poets sometimes write the veriest stuff. . . .
                'So then, 'tis thou who art the villain. . . .'
Beshrew me, how to say't aright! What if William's prophecy be
fulfilled, and they hiss me. . . . No, I'll not consider that. I should
die of rage and shame. Well, we'll see what happens. Away with
fear! Set on! (*Pause, during which he reads in a low tone from
the manuscript, making facial expressions and gestures.*) Ay, now I
begin to like my rendering. I perceive that in a low tone everything
I say sounds wondrous fine. Oh, I'll carry it off triumphantly!
Faith, I'll do it to suit the Queen's taste!

SCENE V

Edmund, *and shortly afterward* Alice.

EDMUND. What must I think? Does Walton know my secret? God
forbid! Was he speaking without malice, or with base intent?
Always to fear, to tremble at every whisper! How timorous is guilt!
Oh, what a life the guilty lead! (*He sits near the table, on which
he leans his arms, allowing his head to fall upon them. Alice
comes from the door at left and on seeing him in that attitude
shudders and runs toward him, terrified.*)
ALICE. Edmund, what's this? What has happened to you? What is
the matter?
EDMUND. You too, poor girl, forever trembling, even as I!
ALICE. What can I do but tremble? One struggles not with conscience without fear.
EDMUND. And must we always live thus? Tell me, in pity's name,
is this life?
ALICE. You ask me this? It may be one could count the moments
of the day; but not the griefs and frights I suffer in the day. If
someone looks at me, I say: He knows it. If one draws near my
husband, I say: He is about to tell him. In every face methinks I
find a threatening look; the innocentest word re-echoes in my
bosom like a threat. The light makes me afraid; I fear it will
expose my conscience. The darkness frightens me; for in its midst
my conscience seems a still more shadowy thing. At times I would
take oath that here upon my brow I feel the brand of sin; I want

to touch it with my hand, and hardly can I ban the fixed illusion by looking on myself within the glass. Now all my strength's exhausted; my heart no longer wills to go on suffering. Even the hour that's welcomed by the weary brings me new terrors. What torment! Alas, if I sleep, perchance I'll dream of him; perchance his name will escape my lips; perhaps I'll cry aloud that I love him! And if at last I sleep despite myself, then I am still more wretched, for the vague fears of my waking hours take on in sleep the vivid form of dread reality. And again it is day; and the bitterness of yesterday which seemed so limitless is outdone by today's; and the bitterness of today, seeming to crowd upon the infinite, is ever outdone by tomorrow's. To weep, oh, how much I have wept! How sighed! I have no longer tears nor sighs to console me. You come?—what fear! What longing to have you gone! You leave me? What disquietude, what longing for your coming! You come again, and when as now I talk with you alone, it seems my words resound so loud that they can everywhere be heard. The flutter of an insect stops my blood; everywhere, meseems, are ears that hear, eyes that see, and I know not where to turn mine own . . . (*Looking with terror in one direction and another.*) and . . . Oh! (*Cries out.*)

EDMUND. What? Speak! (*With fear and anxiety, looking in the same direction as* Alice.)

ALICE. Nothing! My shadow—my shadow, which seemed to me an accusing witness. And you would ask me if this be life? Edmund, how can it be? It is not life—not life. It is but death on death.

EDMUND. Alice, be calm, and think on this : had you but more of guilt, you would believe yourself less guilty. For sin seems ever horrible when virtue gleams beside it still.

ALICE. Oh, tell me not of virtue. Merely by loving you I trample every duty under foot; I offend earth and heaven. Save me! O save me as a strong man saves a helpless woman.

EDMUND. Oh, yes, we must both be saved! But how? To see my Alice, my heart's idol, and not to speak with her; to speak with her and tell her not I love her; to cease to love her, having loved her once! . . . What folly! what madness! Still every day I cheer myself in forming high resolves with no intention of fulfilling them; thus does one give the devil cause for laughter. I set myself the task that everyone proposes in such straits : to turn love into friendship. And love that strives to abate itself, grows ever greater. Love is not to be turned to friendship; forsooth it may be changed to odium as deep and active as itself. To love you with delirium, or to hate with frenzy, there is no other way. Let us face it. Tell me, how could I come to hate you?

ALICE. Whole days I, too, spend planning means to break this tyrant of my will. If only Edmund loved another woman, I tell myself, 'twould settle all. And at the mere thought of seeing you at the side of another woman, I tremble with anger; nay, compared with that grief there's none which does not in my eyes seem joy. I set myself to asking God that you'll forget me, and presently I find myself imploring Him to make you love me. No longer can I fight this losing battle. I know myself an ingrate to the best of men —I love you. I know my vileness—yet I love you. Save me, I said —when my salvation's only this—to love you not. You can not save me.

EDMUND. Alice! Alice, my darling!

ALICE. Edmund! (*They are about to embrace, and stop, hearing a noise in the background.*) Oh, stay!

SCENE VI

The same and Shakespeare.

Later, Yorick *and* Walton.

SHAKESPEARE. Blessed be God that I find you alone. I was seeking you.

EDMUND. Whom . . . me? (*With suspicion.*)

SHAKESPEARE. You, and her.

ALICE. Both of us?

SHAKESPEARE. Both.

EDMUND. Heavens! (*Aside.*)

ALICE. Dear God! (*Aside.*)

SHAKESPEARE. Can I speak without fear of being overheard?

EDMUND. So secret, then, is what you have to tell us?

SHAKESPEARE. Would I were deaf to it myself!

ALICE. What's to come? (*Aside.*)

EDMUND. Speak, but have a care what 'tis you speak.

SHAKESPEARE. Nay, it is for you to have a care. (*Fixing him with a look.*)

EDMUND. I cannot tolerate . . .

SHAKESPEARE. Silence, and listen. (*Imperiously.*)

EDMUND. Oh! (*Lowering his head, dominated by the tone and attitude of* Shakespeare.)

SHAKESPEARE. I should long since have ventured what today I do from hard compulsion. I was a coward. These curst conventions that turn good men to cowards! I no longer hesitate : I regard nothing. Edmund, you love that woman.

EDMUND. I? ...

SHAKESPEARE. Alice, you love him.

ALICE. Ah! (*With fright and grief.*)

EDMUND. By what right dare you ... ?

SHAKESPEARE. By the right that's given me as the friend of your father, the friend of her husband.

EDMUND. And if it is not true—if they've deceived you?

ALICE. They have deceived you, doubt it not.

SHAKESPEARE. Hypocrisy and guilt are twin sisters. Come here. (*Seizing* Alice *by one hand and drawing her near.*) And you. (*Seizing* Edmund, *and placing him opposite her.*) Raise your head, Edmund. You, yours. (*Lifting their heads.*) Look at each other face to face with the calmness of innocence. Look!—Ah! you were pale : why blush you now? Before, the colour of remorse; and now of shame.

ALICE. Pity!

EDMUND. Enough! (*With profound grief.*)

ALICE. So sudden were your words ...

EDMUND. The charge has fallen on us like a thunderbolt.

ALICE. We were afraid.

EDMUND. I'll tell you all the truth.

ALICE. Ay, it is truth—he loves me, I love him.

EDMUND. You are noble and generous.

ALICE. You will have pity on two unhappy beings.

EDMUND. Nor wish to increase our misery.

ALICE. Nay, so, you will protect us, you will defend us against our very selves.

SHAKESPEARE. Come, my children, be calm.

ALICE. Children he calls us. Do you hear?

EDMUND. We'll throw ourselves at your feet.

ALICE. (*Starting to kneel.*) Yes!

SHAKESPEARE. (*Opening his arms.*) No, better be ye in my arms.

EDMUND. (*Restraining himself with shamefaced diffidence.*) William! ...

ALICE. (*With joy.*) Is it possible?

SHAKESPEARE. Come.

EDMUND. (*Throwing himself into his arms.*) Save us!

ALICE. (*Throwing herself also into* Shakespeare's *arms.*) Save us, in pity's name!

SHAKESPEARE. Yes, with God's aid I will save you.

(*A pause during which one hears the sobs of* Edmund *and* Alice.)
ALICE. But what's this? You are weeping?
SHAKESPEARE. Seeing tears, what can one do but weep?
ALICE. Edmund, it is a protector that Heaven sends us. And we
wanted to deceive him, we wanted to reject him! How blind are
the wretched! To have a friend to comfort us, to take upon him-
self some of our woe—protected by the one who best can cure the
ills of the soul because 'tis he who knows them best. . . . Oh, what
unexpected joy! Who would have told me a moment ago that
happiness was so near? Once more I begin to breathe. Ah,
Edmund, this is life indeed!
SHAKESPEARE. There is no time to lose. Speak. I must know everything. (*Pause.*)
EDMUND. Two years ago, Alice joined your company. 'Twas then
I met her. Would I never had!
ALICE. Would I had ne'er met him!
EDMUND. I saw her from a distance; a mysterious force drew me
toward her. I reached her side. My vision was enrapt—'twas no
mere look I gave her. I spoke, but no one heard my words. I
trembled : I loved her!
ALICE. And I loved him!
EDMUND. Love, even rightful, inclines to live hidden in the depths
of the heart. Days passed . . . I resolved at last to declare myself.
. . . Impossible!
ALICE. Yorick had already told me of his affection.
EDMUND. My rival was the man to whom I owed everything.
ALICE. My mother fell dangerously sick; we lacked resources. To
our eyes, Yorick seemed as one sent by the Infinite Pity.
EDMUND. Could I prevent my benefactor's doing good to others?
ALICE. And one day, 'Alice,' saith my mother, 'thou wilt be left
abandoned; marry Yorick—he loves thee so, and is so worthy.'
EDMUND. Yorick had picked me up, naked and starving, from the
gutter, to give me shelter and love and happiness and a place in the
world.
ALICE. 'Twas Yorick cheered the last days of my mother's life with
all manner of comforts.
EDMUND. For me to destroy his happiness would have been the
depth of meanness.
ALICE. My mother on her death-bed begged me . . .
EDMUND. I did but pay the tribute that gratitude demands.
ALICE. And I but gave the answer that one gives a dying mother.
EDMUND. I swore to forget her.
ALICE. And I, in striving to love him less, but loved him more.

EDMUND. Vain resistance!

ALICE. Yes, thought I, Edmund is his son.

EDMUND. Yorick is my father, so I told myself.

ALICE. And when I marry Yorick, 'twill end the love that Edmund has inspired.

EDMUND. The instant Yorick's bound to her in wedlock, my love for her is ended.

ALICE. To love my husband's son? How horrible—Nay, impossible!

EDMUND. So I—to love my father's wife? What madness! It cannot be.

ALICE. And how I longed and waited for my marriage-hour!

EDMUND. For me, each minute seemed a century, till then.

ALICE. At last the hour was here!

EDMUND. At last she married him!

ALICE. And love, its one hope lost, instead of fleeing from our breast . . .

EDMUND. Arose therein, with outcries like a wild beast at bay.

ALICE. Silent we, still silent.

EDMUND. In spite of Yorick's prayers and tears, I would no longer live with him.

ALICE. Yet here he often had to come.

EDMUND. So Yorick bade.

ALICE. We saw each other daily—silent.

EDMUND. Hour after hour we passed alone together—silent.

ALICE. At last one day while playing Romeo and Juliet . . .

EDMUND. Animated by the flame of the beautiful fiction . . .

ALICE. Mingling with the flame of the fiction the burning flame of reality . . .

EDMUND. With all eyes fixed on us . . .

ALICE. And all ears hanging on our words . . .

EDMUND. Then my lips—nay, my heart—asked her gently, very gently : 'Dost thou love me?'

ALICE. And my lips—nay, my heart—softly, very softly, answered : 'Yes.'

EDMUND. Such is our guilt.

ALICE. Our punishment, at every hour to dread and tremble.

EDMUND. A cankering remorse.

ALICE. Without a single solace.

EDMUND. One remedy alone.

ALICE. To die.

EDMUND. There's nothing more to tell you.

ALICE. We swear it.

EDMUND. By the soul of Yorick!

ALICE. By his soul!

EDMUND. This is what has come to pass.

ALICE. Just this.

SHAKESPEARE. Poor human nature! In thee the noble enterprise begun with strength unequal to the task, becomes a well of evil. Poor human nature. Thou dost recoil before the smaller bar, and dost leap o'er the greater. You love each other; 'Tis imperative you shall not love.

EDMUND. Who says so knows not that the soul enslaved by love cannot free itself from its tyrant.

SHAKESPEARE. Who says so knows the soul is free, as being the child of God.

ALICE. Explain it to me, in the name of pity! What must be done when one who loves would cease to love?

SHAKESPEARE. *Will.*

EDMUND. To will is not enough.

SHAKESPEARE. 'Tis enough, if the willing be not feigned.

ALICE. Who assures that?

SHAKESPEARE. A witness not to be denied.

EDMUND. What witness?

SHAKESPEARE. Your conscience. If it were not responsible for the guilt, why these starts, these tears, and this remorse. You will flee from Alice forever.

EDMUND. That thought has come to me a thousand times already. Don't demand the impossible.

SHAKESPEARE. On the downward slope of sin one must advance, or make retreat; you will retreat despite yourself.

EDMUND. You'll force me to go away?

SHAKESPEARE. If 'tis the only means, by force must right prevail.

ALICE. Edmund will obey you. At last with some one to protect us, you shall see how faith and courage are reborn in our hearts.

EDMUND. Ah, yes: with you to aid, no deed can seem impossible. We are soldiers of duty.

ALICE. You, our captain.

EDMUND. Lead us to victory!

SHAKESPEARE. Could I but bring to pass this one good deed, I'd laugh at my Othello and Macbeth and all that foolery. (*With inner joy.*) I trust in the promise of a man. (*Taking* Edmund's *hand.*) And in the promise of a woman (*Taking hers.*)

EDMUND and ALICE. Yes!

SHAKESPEARE. Now then, until the day shall come when Edmund leaves us, you must not be alone; never in the presence of others look at each other, not even by a glance. Duty asks this, necessity demands it. I thought myself the sole possessor of the secret . . . fool that I was! Love never could stay hidden.

ALICE. What say you?

EDMUND. Explain yourself!

SHAKESPEARE. This awful secret's known as well by one quite capable of villainy.

EDMUND. What's he?

SHAKESPEARE. By getting his assignment in the new drama, Yorick has maddened Walton.

EDMUND. (*With terror.*) Walton!

SHAKESPEARE. I have it from the author of the piece, who came just now from Walton's house to mine, and told me of their recent discourse. He saw not Walton's thoughts, but he did echo certain words of his, as these: 'The rôle of outraged husband divinely fits this Yorick, and no one should dispute his having it.'

ALICE. God of my soul!

SHAKESPEARE. 'If now neglect or blindness should make him miss the fine points of the rôle, 'tis I shall open his eyes.'

ALICE. Ah, 'tis certain. That man's a wicked wretch; he'll ruin us!

EDMUND. (*With profound anxiety.*) Yes, Alice, we are ruined, ruined utterly.

SHAKESPEARE. Not yet. I go at once in search of him, and finding him—there is no longer anything to fear. (*Going toward the rear.*)

EDMUND. (*Going to her, seizing her hand.*) Alice! Alice!

ALICE. What is it? Why so moved?

SHAKESPEARE. (*From the rear.*) Courage, Edmund. I shall return at once to calm you both.

EDMUND. Leave us not, for God's sake!

SHAKESPEARE. (*Taking a few steps toward the front.*) Not leave you? What's the reason?

EDMUND. Walton's no longer there—not at his house.

SHAKESPEARE. (*Coming to* Edmund's *side.*) How know you this?

EDMUND. 'Tis I who say to you, Courage! (*To* Shakespeare.) Courage, poor girl! (*To* Alice.)

ALICE. Nay, end this horrible suspense.

SHAKESPEARE. Where is he?

EDMUND. Here.

SHAKESPEARE. Heavens!

ALICE. With him?

EDMUND. With him!

SHAKESPEARE. You have seen him, then?

EDMUND. Even in my presence he began to explain the object of his coming.

ALICE. Ah! what shall I do now—my God, what shall I do?
EDMUND. Earth hates me, else would she open at my feet!
SHAKESPEARE. Ill fortune!
ALICE. Do not abandon me; defend me, shield me. . . .
EDMUND. In pity's name, a way, a hope!
SHAKESPEARE. If we lose our heads . . . Calm . . . quiet. . . . (*Pondering.* Yorick *appears in the door at right, followed by* Walton; *he gives* Walton *the manuscript that he holds in his hand, and with joyous countenance, makes signs for him to keep silence, putting his finger on his lips. He then approaches his wife rapidly on tip-toe.*)
EDMUND. (*With great anxiety, to* Shakespeare.) What make you of it?
ALICE. Speak.
YORICK. (*Seizing his wife with one arm, with a tragically affected attitude, and declaiming with exaggerated emphasis.*) 'Tremble, thou faithless spouse! thou ingrate . . .'
ALICE. Christ! (*Shuddering with fright.*) Pardon! (*Falling to the floor in a faint.*)
YORICK. Eh? . . .
EDMUND. (*Trying to hurl himself at* Walton.) Damned villain!
SHAKESPEARE. (*In a low tone to* Edmund, *holding him back.*) Fool!
YORICK. (*Confused and stunned.*) 'Pardon!'
WALTON. (*Aside, ironically.*) Such a coincidence!
YORICK. 'Pardon!' . . . (*Trying to explain to himself what has happened.* Shakespeare *goes to help* Alice.)

JOHN D. FITZGERALD and THACHER GUILD

RAMÓN DE CAMPOAMOR
[1817–1901]

Ramón de Campoamor, an extremely popular poet in his own day, has not been treated kindly by many recent critics. Few dispute, however, the deftness of his wit or the wisdom of his observations. These qualities are most evident in the series which he called humoradas *(epigrams in verse) and* doloras *(poetic vignettes expressing a simple truth or philosophy). In the latter group,* Quién supiera escribir *is his best-known poem.*

DOLORAS

BOREDOM

Grievous is the hermit's plight;
Lone, he know not love's delight :
But Solitude's more dreadful far,
When two together lonely are.

J. D. M. FORD

AFTER TWENTY YEARS

Now after twenty years have passed; again he's here,
And meeting, they exclaim, both she and he :
Good Lord ! is this the man I once held dear?
Good God ! and can this woman here be she?

J. D. M. FORD

THE GREAT BANQUET

Cast from a rush, into a running stream
 A worm once chanced to fall;
And then a trout, darting with silvery gleam,
 Seized it and ate it all.

The bird king-fisher came and caught the trout,
 Its appetite to sate;
And then this bird, after a savage bout,
 A hawk o'ercame and ate.

Such carnage to avenge, a hunter shot,
 With his unerring aim,
The hawk that with rapacious claw had got
 King-fisher as his game.

Alas! the luckless hunter who had slain
The hawk, with cunning wont,
A guard now killed, for failing to obtain
A privilege to hunt.

To other worms his corpse will soon give life,
As it must rot away;
And now again this circle fierce of strife
Will have its ceaseless play.

And love? and happiness? and all men born,
What other end have they?
Unless to eat, and in their turn adorn
Earth's cruel banquet on their fated day.

J. D. M. FORD

IF ONLY I COULD WRITE!

I

'I pray you, reverend Sir, this letter write.'
'To whom then? Ah, I know.'
'You know, because that dark and starless night
You saw us meet?' 'E'en so.'

'O Sir, forgive us.' 'Nay, 'twas no great sin,
The hour to love did lend;
Give me a pen and paper, I'll begin :
Raymond, beloved friend!'

'Beloved? Well, 'tis written.' 'You're not vext?
Do you approve it?' 'Yes.'
'*I am so sad alone.* (Should that come next?)
More sad than you can guess.

Such sorrow fills me since we two did part!'
'How do you know my pain?'
'To these old eyes is every young maid's heart
Like crystal, free from stain.

*What without you is life? A vale of woe.
With you? The promised land.*'
'Ah, Señor Cura! Make your writing so
That he may understand.'

'*The kiss I gave you when you left me, sweet—*'
'What! Know you of my kiss?'
'Ever when lovers part, and when they meet—
    Oh, take it not amiss.

*Oh, if your love should never bring you more,
    How should I grieve and sigh!*'
'What grieve, and nothing more? Nay, good Señor,
    Say, I were like to die.'

'To die! My child, such word were blasphemy.'
    'Yet die full well I might.'
'I'll not put "die".' 'Your heart is ice. Ah me!
    If only I could write!'

II

'Ah, Señor Cura, 'tis in vain you seek
    My sorrow thus to still;
Unless, indeed, to make my whole heart speak
    These pen-strokes have the skill.

For God's sake write, my soul would fain be free
    From all its weary grief,
Which day by day would even stifle me,
    But that tears bring relief.

Tell him these rosy lips he loved, that met
    His own dear lips erewhile,
Are now for ever closed, and fast forget
    Even what 'tis to smile.

Tell him, these eyes, that won from him such praise,
    Are drooping and dejected,
Even because therein his well-loved face
    No longer is reflected.

Tell him, of all the torments life can bring,
    Be absence my last choice;
Tell him, that ever in my ears will ring
    The echo of his voice.

Yet say, that since for him so sad I stay,
I count my sorrow light,
O God, how many are the things I'd say,
If I could only write!

END *

Now Sir, 'tis done. I trace these words for end :
"*To Raymond*", and bestow
Upon it this my mark, the which to send,
Small Latin need I know.'

IDA FARNELL

HUMORADAS

You wave your fan with such a graceful art,
You brush the dust off from the oldest heart.

The children of the mothers I loved, ah see,
They kiss me as though they kissed a saint in me!

No woman yet, since they were made all
Has ever got quite outside of the cradle.

If too easy she should be,
I, beholding, quit her;
If the thing's too hard for me,
Trying proves too bitter.
Girls, now see,
Best it is to love with easy
Difficulty.

Have I not seen you? Yes, but where and when?
Ah, I remember : I was dreaming then.

She's faithless, and you love her? As you will :
Hope I adore, and hope is faithless still.

ARTHUR SYMONS

* A more precise translation of the epilogue would show a change of speaker and that it is the priest who says the last four lines. The editors offer the following substitution :

'Well, now, I'll copy what you've said and add
To Raymond . . . for you speak
More clearly with love's fire than if you had
All my Latin and my Greek.'

GUSTAVO ADOLFO BÉCQUER
[1836–1870]

A poverty-stricken orphan, dogged by poor health, unhappily married, Gustavo Adolfo Bécquer spent the few years of his life in a stranglehold of financial and emotional difficulties. But from the depths of his personal grief, Bécquer composed lyric poetry of such breath-taking artistry and bittersweet sentiment that his name is today immortal in Spanish literature. Hardly a Spaniard exists who cannot recite at least one of his seventy-six Rimas, the exquisite poems for which he is most famous.

Besides the small collection of Rimas and other short poems, Bécquer wrote a brief series of literary letters, and twenty-two leyendas. The latter are dream-like legends of Spain, especially of Toledo, written in prose as haunting and delicate as his poetry.

THE GOLDEN BRACELET

I

She was beautiful, beautiful with that beauty which turns a man dizzy; beautiful with that beauty which in no wise resembles our dream of the angels, and yet is supernatural; a diabolical beauty that the devil perchance gives to certain things to make them his instruments on earth.

He loved her—he loved her with that love which knows not check nor bounds; he loved her with that love which seeks delight and finds but martyrdom; a love which is akin to bliss, yet which Heaven seems to cast on mortals for the expiation of their sins.

She was wayward, wayward and unreasonable, like all the women of the world.

He, superstitious, superstitious and valiant, like all the men of his time.

Her name was Maria Antúnez.

His, Pedro Alfonso de Orellana.

Both were natives of Toledo, and both had their homes in the city which saw their birth.

The tradition which relates this marvellous event, an event of many years since, tells nothing more of these two central actors.

I, in my character of scrupulous historian, will not add a single word of my own invention to describe them further.

II

One day he found her in tears and asked her :
'Why dost thou weep?'

She dried her eyes, looked at him searchingly, heaved a sigh and began to weep anew.

Then, drawing close to Maria, he took her hand, leaned his elbow on the fretted edge of the Arabic parapet whence the beautiful maiden was watching the river flow beneath, and again he asked her : 'Why dost thou weep?'

The Tajo, moaning at the tower's foot, twisted in and out amid the rocks on which is seated the imperial city. The sun was sinking behind the neighbouring mountains, the afternoon haze was floating a veil of azure gauze, and only the monotonous sound of the water broke the profound stillness.

Maria exclaimed : 'Ask me not why I weep, ask me not; for I would not know how to answer thee, nor thou how to understand. In the souls of us women are stifling desires which reveal themselves only in a sigh, mad ideas that cross the imagination without our daring to form them into speech, strange phenomena of our mysterious nature which man cannot even conceive. I implore thee, ask me not the cause of my grief; if I should reveal it to thee, perchance thou wouldst reply with peals of laughter.'

When these words were faltered out, again she bowed the head and again he urged his questions.

The radiant damsel, breaking at last her stubborn silence, said to her lover in a hoarse, unsteady voice :

'Thou wilt have it. It is a folly that will make thee laugh, but be it so. I will tell thee, since thou dost crave to hear.

'Yesterday I was in the temple. They were celebrating the feast of the Virgin; her image, placed on a golden pedestal above the High Altar, glowed like a burning coal; the notes of the organ trembled, spreading from echo to echo throughout the length and breadth of the church, and in the choir the priests were chanting the *Salve, Regina.*

'I was praying; I was praying, all absorbed in my religious meditations, when involuntarily I lifted my head, and my gaze sought the altar. I know not why my eyes from that instant fixed themselves upon the image, but I speak amiss—it was not on the image; they fixed themselves upon an object which until then I had not seen—an object which, I know not why, thenceforth held all my attention. Do not laugh; that object was the golden bracelet that the Mother of God wears on one of the arms in which rests her divine Son. I turned aside my gaze and strove again to pray. Impossible. Without my will, my eyes moved back to the same point. The altar lights, reflected in the thousand facets of those diamonds, were multiplied prodigiously. Millions of living sparks, rosy, azure, green and golden, were whirling around the jewels like a storm of fiery atoms, like a dizzy round of those spirits of flame which fascinate with their brightness and their marvellous unrest.

'I left the church. I came home, but I came with that idea fixed in imagination. I went to bed; I could not sleep. The night passed, a night eternal with one thought. At dawn my eyelids closed and —believest thou?—even in slumber I saw crossing before me, dimming in the distance and ever returning, a woman, a woman dark and beautiful, who wore the ornament of gold and jewel work; a woman, yes, for it was no longer the Virgin, whom I adore and at whose feet I bow; it was a woman, another woman like myself who looked upon me and laughed mockingly. "Dost see it?" she appeared to say, showing me the treasure. "How it glitters! It seems a circlet of stars snatched from the sky some summer night. Dost see it? But it is not thine, and it will be thine never, never. Thou wilt perchance have others that surpass it, others richer, if it be possible, but this, this which sparkles so piquantly, so bewitchingly, never, never." I awoke, but with the same idea fixed here, then as now, like a red-hot nail, diabolical, irresistible, inspired beyond a doubt by Satan himself.—And what then?—Thou art silent, silent, and dost hang thy head.—Does not my folly make thee laugh?'

Pedro, with a convulsive movement, grasped the hilt of his sword, raised his head, which he had, indeed, bent low and said with smothered voice :

'Which Virgin has this jewel?'

'The Virgin of the Sagrario,' murmured Maria.

'The Virgin of the Sagrario!' repeated the youth, with accent of terror. 'The Virgin of the Sagrario of the cathedral!'

And in his features was portrayed for an instant the state of his mind, appalled before a thought.

'Ah, why does not some other Virgin own it?' he continued, with a tense, impassioned tone. 'Why does not the archbishop bear it in his mitre, the king in his crown, or the devil between his claws? I would tear it away for thee, though its price were death or hell. But from the Virgin of the Sagrario, our own Holy Patroness,—I—I who was born in Toledo! Impossible, impossible!'

'Never!' murmured Maria, in a voice that scarcely reached the ear. 'Never!'

And she wept again.

Pedro fixed a stupefied stare on the running waves of the river

—on the running waves, which flowed and flowed unceasingly before his absent-thoughted eyes, breaking at the foot of the tower amid the rocks on which is seated the imperial city.

III

The cathedral of Toledo! Imagine a forest of colossal palm trees of granite, that by the interlacing of their branches form a gigantic, magnificent arch, beneath which take refuge and live, with the life genius has lent them, a whole creation of beings, both fictitious and real.

Imagine an incomprehensible fall of shadow and light wherein the coloured rays from the ogive windows meet and are merged with the dusk of the nave; where the gleam of the lamps struggles and is lost in the gloom of the sanctuary.

Imagine a world of stone, immense as the spirit of our religion, sombre as its traditions, enigmatic as its parables, and yet you will not have even a remote idea of this eternal monument of the enthusiasm and faith of our ancestors—a monument upon which the centuries have emulously lavished their treasures of knowledge, inspiration and the arts.

In the cathedral-heart dwells silence, majesty, the poetry of mysticism, and a holy dread which guards those thresholds against worldly thoughts and the paltry passions of earth.

Consumption of the body is stayed by breathing pure mountain air; atheism should be cured by breathing this atmosphere of faith.

But great and impressive as the cathedral presents itself to our eyes at whatsoever hour we enter its mysterious and sacred precinct, never does it produce an impression so profound as in those days when it arrays itself in all the splendours of religious pomp, when its shrines are covered with gold and jewels, its steps with costly carpeting and its pillars with tapestry.

Then, when its thousand silver lamps, aglow, shed forth a flood of light, when a cloud of incense floats in air, and the voices of the choir, the harmonious pealing of the organs, and the bells of the tower make the building tremble from its deepest foundations to its highest spires, then it is we comprehend, because we feel, the ineffable majesty of God who dwells within, gives it life with His breath and fills it with the reflection of His glory.

The same day on which occurred the scene we have just described, the last rites of the magnificent eight-day feast of the Virgin were held in the cathedral.

The holy feast had attracted an immense multitude of the

faithful; but already they had dispersed in all directions; already the lights of the chapels and of the High Altar had been extinguished, and the mighty doors of the temple had groaned upon their hinges as they closed behind the last departing worshipper, when forth from the depth of shadow, and pale, pale as the statue of the tomb on which he leant for an instant, while he conquered his emotion, there advanced a man, who came slipping with the utmost stealthiness toward the screen of the central chapel. There the gleam of a lamp made it possible to distinguish his features.

It was Pedro.

What had passed between the two lovers to bring him to the point of putting into execution an idea whose mere conception had lifted his hair with horror? That could never be learned.

But there he was, and he was there to carry out his criminal intent. In his restless glances, in the trembling of his knees, in the sweat which ran in great drops down his face, his thought stood written.

The cathedral was alone, utterly alone, and drowned in deepest hush.

Nevertheless, there were perceptible from time to time suggestions of dim disturbance, creakings of wood maybe or murmurs of the wind, or—who knows?—perchance illusion of the fancy, which in its excited moments hears and sees and feels what is not; but in very truth there sounded, now here, now there, now behind him, now even at his side, something like sobs suppressed, something like the rustle of trailing robes, and a muffled stir as of steps that go and come unceasingly.

Pedro forced himself to hold his course; he reached the grating and mounted the first step of the chancel. All along the inner wall of this chapel are ranged the tombs of kings, whose images of stone, with hand upon sword-hilt, seem to keep watch night and day over the sanctuary in whose shade they take their everlasting rest.

'Onward!' he murmured under his breath, and he strove to move and could not. It seemed as if his feet were nailed to the pavement. He lowered his eyes, and his hair stood on end with horror. The floor of the chapel was made of wide, dark burial slabs.

For a moment he believed that a cold and fleshless hand was holding him there with strength invincible. The dying lamps, which sparkled in the hollow aisles and transepts like lost stars in the dark, wavered before his vision, the statues of the sepulchres wavered and the images of the altar, all the cathedral wavered, with its granite arcades and buttresses of solid stone.

'Onward!' Pedro exclaimed again, as if beside himself; he approached the altar and climbing upon it, he reached the pedestal of the image. All the space about clothed itself in weird and frightful shapes, all was shadow and flickering light, more awful even than total darkness. Only the Queen of Heaven, softly illuminated by a golden lamp, seemed to smile, tranquil, gracious and serene, in the midst of all that horror.

Nevertheless, that silent, changeless smile, which calmed him for an instant, in the end filled him with fear, a fear stranger and more profound than what he had suffered hitherto.

Yet he regained his self-control, shut his eyes so as not to see her, extended his hand with a spasmodic movement and snatched off the golden bracelet, pious offering of a sainted archbishop, the golden bracelet whose value equalled a fortune.

Now the jewel was in his possession; his convulsed fingers clutched it with superhuman force; there was nothing left save to flee—to flee with it; but for this it was necessary to open his eyes, and Pedro was afraid to see, to see the image, to see the kings of the sepulchres, the demons of the cornices, the griffins of the capitals, the blotches of shadow and flashes of light which, like ghostly, gigantic phantoms, were moving slowly in the depths of the nave, now filled with confused noises, unearthly and appalling.

At last he opened his eyes, cast one glance about him, and from his lips escaped a piercing cry.

The cathedral was full of statues, statues, which, clothed in strange, flowing raiment, had descended from their niches and were thronging all the vast compass of the church, staring at him with their hollow eyes.

Saints, nuns, angels, devils, warriors, great ladies, pages, hermits, peasants surrounded him on every side and were massed confusedly in the open spaces and about the altar. Before it there officiated, in presence of the kings who were kneeling upon their tombs, the marble archbishops whom he had seen heretofore stretched motionless upon their beds of death, while a whole world of granite beasts and creeping things, writhing over the paving-stones, twisting along the buttresses, curled up in the canopies, swinging from the vaulted roof, quivered into life like worms in a giant corpse, fantastic, distorted, hideous.

He could resist no longer. His brows throbbed with terrible violence; a cloud of blood darkening his vision; he uttered a second scream, a scream heart-rending, inhuman, and fell swooning across the altar.

When the sacristans found him crouching on the altar steps the next morning, he still clutched the golden bracelet in both hands and on seeing them draw near, he shrieked with discordant yells of laughter :

'Hers ! hers !'

The poor wretch had gone mad.

CORNELIA FRANCES BATES
and KATHARINE LEE BATES

RIMA II

Flitting arrow, speeding onward,
    To the air at random cast,
Ne'er divining where now trembling
    It shall fix itself at last.

Leaf which from the branch now withered
    By the wind is snatched away,
And no one can mark the furrow
    Where at last it falls to stay.

Giant wave urged by a tempest,
    Curling, tumbling o'er the sea,
Rolling, passing, never knowing
    Of what strand its quest must be.

Light in wavering circles gleaming,
    To exhaustion nearing now,
And each circle all unwitting
    Which shall be the last to glow.

This am I, who, aimless roving,
    O'er this earth my way must wend;
Ne'er reflecting whence I came, nor
    To what goal my footsteps tend.

J. D. M. FORD

RIMA IV

Say not that, its treasure exhausted,
    The lyre is mute, lacking a melody :
There may be no poets, but forever
    Poesy will be.

As long as the waves quiver glowingly
    At dawning's caress;
As long as the sun doth, with fire and gold,
    The flying clouds dress;

As long as the breezes are laden with
Fragrance and harmony;
As long as the springtide comes to the earth,
Poesy will be!

As long as by science the well of life
Has not been found,
And in seas or in heavens an abyss remains
That men cannot sound;

While ignorant whither, but forward yet,
Goes humanity;
As long as one mystery remains for man,
Poesy will be!

As long as the soul joys and yet no smile
Without doth appear;
As long as there's sorrow when from the eye
There falls no tear;

As long as mankind is still left with hope
And memory;
As long as the heart and head battle still,
Poesy will be!

As long as eyes mirror the tender gaze
Of other eyes;
As long as a sighing mouth still responds
To a mouth that sighs;

As long as two souls in a kiss can feel
One unity;
As long as one beautiful woman is . . .
Poesy will be!

YOUNG ALLISON

RIMA VII

In the room, in a corner all darkened,
By its owner perhaps now forgotten,
Mute-voiced and covered over with dust,
    The harp was seen.

What notes lay slumbering in its chord-strings—
As the bird sleeps in the branches—
Awaiting the snow-white fingers
    Which know how to wake them!

Oh! thought I—how often does genius
Thus sleep in the deep of soul's vault,
And, like Lazarus, a voice await, anxious,
That will bid it : 'Arise and walk!'

JEANNE PASMANTIER

RIMA X

The particles invisible of air
   Around me quiver and vehemently glow;
The heavens burst forth in rays of golden light;
   All earth doth tremble in a joyous throe.
Floating in waves of harmony I hear
   A stir of kisses and of wings on high;
Mine eyelids close themselves. . . . What passes now?
   ' *'Tis love goes by!*'

YOUNG ALLISON

RIMA XI

I am black and comely; my lips are glowing;
I am passion; my heart is hot;
The rapture of life in my veins is flowing.
For me thou callest?—I call thee not.

Pale is my forehead and gold my tresses;
Endless comforts are locked in me,
Treasure of hearthside tendernesses.
'Tis I whom thou seekest?—Nay, not thee.

I am a dream, afar, forbidden,
Vague as the mist on the mountain-brow,
A bodiless glory, haunting, hidden;
I cannot love thee.—Oh, come! come thou!

KATHARINE LEE BATES

RIMA XXI

What is poetry, you say,
Holding my eyes with yours of blue,
What is poetry? . . . *You* ask that?
   Poetry . . . It is you!

INA DUVALL SINGLETON

RIMA XXXVIII

Sighs are air, and go to the air.
Tears are water, and to the sea flow.
Tell me, woman : when love's forgot,
Knowest where it doth go?

YOUNG ALLISON

RIMA LII

O waves gigantic that roaring break
And hurl yourselves on a desert strand,
Wrapt in a sheet of the foam you make
 Drag me below with you, bear me on high.

O hurricane, driving with whips of wind
The faded leaves from the forest grand,
Dragged along by the whirlwind blind
 Goad me to go with you, prone as I lie.

O clouds of the tempest, by lightning kiss'd,
Your edges shot with the fire of its love,
Whirled along in the sombre mist
 Bear me away with you, bear me above.

O bear me away with you, bear me away
Where frenzied with vertigo mad I may slay
My reason and memory, for I fear
 To be left all alone with my sorrow here.

MASON CARNES

RIMA LIII

The dusky swallows will hang their nests
In your balcony once again,
And with their wings they will lightly tap,
As they flit past your window-pane;
But those who paused in their eager flight
And lingered our names to learn,
That viewed your beauty and my delight. . . .
Ah! these will not return!

Dense honeysuckle will scale the walls
Of your garden, and there once more
Will show its blossoms when evening comes,
Even lovelier than before;

But those, dew-laden, whose drops we watched
Now tremble and fall, alack!
That we saw fall like the tears of day. . . .
Ah! these will not come back!

The burning passionate words of love
Once again in your ears will sound;
And then your heart will perhaps awake,
Will be roused from its sleep profound;
But as one kneels at His altar, mute,
Adoring, with head bent low,
As I have loved you . . . be undeceived,
Ah! they'll not love you so!

MRS. W. S. HENDRIX

RIMA LXXIII

They closed her eyes
That were still open;
They hid her face
With a white linen,
And, some sobbing
Others in silence,
From the sad bedroom
All came away.

The nightlight in a dish
Burned on the floor;
It threw on the wall
The bed's shadow,
And in that shadow
One saw sometime
Drawn in sharp line
The body's shape.

The dawn appeared.
At its first whiteness
With its thousand noises
The town awoke.
Before that contrast
Of light and darkness,
Of life and strangeness
I thought a moment.

My God, how lonely
The dead are!

On the shoulders of men
To church they bore her,
And in a chapel
They left her bier.
There they surrounded
Her pale body
With yellow candles
And black stuffs.

At the last stroke
Of the ringing for the Souls,
An old crone finished
Her last prayers.
She crossed the narrow nave,
The doors moaned,
And the holy place
Remained deserted.

From a clock one heard
The measured ticking,
And from a candle
The guttering.
All things there
Were so dark and mournful,
So cold and rigid,
That I thought a moment :
My God, how lonely
The dead are!

From the high belfry
The tongue of iron
Clanged, giving out
A last farewell.
Crêpe on their clothes,
Her friends and kindred
Passed in a line
In homage to her.

In the last vault
Dark and narrow,
The pickaxe opened
A niche at one end;

They laid her away there.
Soon they bricked the place up,
And with a gesture
Bade grief farewell.

Pickaxe on shoulder
The gravedigger,
Singing between his teeth,
Passed out of sight.
The night came down,
It was all silent.
Alone in the darkness
I thought a moment,—
*My God, how lonely
The dead are!*

In the dark nights
Of bitter winter,
When the wind makes
The rafter creak,
When the violent rain
Lashes the windows,
Lonely I remember
That poor girl.

There falls the rain
With its noise eternal,
There the northwind
Fights with the rain.
Stretched in the hollow
Of the damp bricks,
Perhaps her bones
Freeze with the cold.

Does the dust return to dust?
Does the soul fly to heaven?
Or is all vile matter,
Rottenness, filthiness?
I know not, but
There is something—something—
Something which gives me
Loathing, terror,—
To leave the dead
So alone, so wretched.

JOHN MASEFIELD

GASPAR NÚÑEZ DE ARCE
[1834–1903]

The poetry of Gaspar Núñez de Arce, an important figure in the politics of his day, often reflects his activities. Gritos del combate (*1875*) *contains some of his most impressive verses, generally on social, political and philosophical themes. He also wrote a number of plays; the best is* El haz de leña, *an historical drama in verse which deals with the imprisonment and death of Prince Don Carlos in the sixteenth century.*

DEJECTION

Whene'er my mind the dawn of life recalls,
How once within the walls
Of our cathedrals, lost in prayer, I knelt,
And, kneeling, saw the blessed Rood before me,
While God's own peace came o'er me,
And dreams of Paradise within dwelt;

My heavy brow I beat, and all afire
With feverish desire
Would seek the vanished bliss of childhood tender;
To hold once more that faith without alloy
Alas, with what great joy
This weary length of life I would surrender!

Ah me! The ardent love I mind me now,
Wherewith I bent my brow
E'en to the flagstones of the holy shrine,
Steeping, the while I prayed, my fantasy
In light and poetry,
Mingled with reverent awe for things divine.

The soaring arches, that to heaven raised
My spirit as I gazed,
Their majesty serene, sublime, and grave,
The slow and cadenced psalm, that, mounting high,
Seeming half groan, half sigh,
Reverberated in the spacious nave;

The splendour dimly seen in twilight gloom
Of many an ancient tomb,
Whose art austere the infinite proclaims,
The light that set the painted windows glowing,
Which, soft reflections throwing,
Lit up grey columns with their coloured flames;

Those clustered shafts, from whence in graceful flight
To build the arch aright,
United yet apart, each branch ascends,
As when the multitude in prayer is found,
And from one wave of sound
Each heart distinct its own petition sends;

The Gothic altar with the Cross above,
Whereon in wondrous love
Hangs the Redeemer—Christ the Crucified,
Wresting in agony, with failing breath,
'Gainst sin, our foe, and Death,
His arms to all that sorrow opening wide;

And the wild clamour of the pealing bell,
That to the soul would tell
Its heavenly story from the belfry-tower,
While strange, sweet promises appear to float
Around each winged note
To all who sigh in dark and lonely hour;

These bore me upwards into regions fair,
Where in serener air
Religion fed my soul with rapture mute,
All, all, that in the sanctuary I saw,
Made me with holy awe
To tremble like the strings of harp or lute.

Led by that voice that he alone can hear
Who with a holy fear
And fervent faith and love is all aflame,
Arrayed in floating garments, dazzling white,
Up to the zenith's height
My infant prayer like some pure virgin came.

.   .   .

O breath that givest life to all our being!
O glory past our seeing!
O thirst unquenchable, divine and pure!
O heaven, whose azure vault in days of old
Meseemed o'erlaid with gold,
But now hangs shrouded, gloomy, and obscure!

My inner heart Thou dost no longer chasten,
No longer do I hasten
As once in childhood to Thy holy altar;

Alas! to reach Thee I have lost the way,
And, miserably astray,
Ever in darkness and despair I falter.

Onward I go 'mid bitter tears and sighs,
I call, no voice replies,
Distractedly I cast mine eyes around,
Yet may not pierce the gloom, so, reft of hope,
Full timorously I grope
Along a weary path where thorns abound.

Child of the age, I strive, O Christ, in vain
Against its impious reign;
Its demoniac greatness lays me low;
An age it is of wonders and of fears,
That amid ruin rears
Its god of dull dejection, doubt, and woe.

Not such art Thou, for with Thy gracious face
Vain terrors dost Thou chase;
Thou to the wanderer art light and guide;
But this one is a god from the Unknown,
Chaos his only throne,
His law supreme, blind chance and naught beside.

. . .

A helmless, broken vessel is this Age!
Round it the billows rage,
The lightning burns, the furious tempests beat,
As, drifting on a wide and heaving sea,
In its immensity
It flames resplendent 'mid devouring heat.

Ah me! The mystic shore so distant seems,
And wondrously it gleams,
As the great Sun sinks sadly in the West;
The vessel burns, above the storm-winds pass,
Too late, too late, alas,
To reach the far-off haven of our rest!

What then is Science when our faith is cold?
A war-horse none may hold,
That, by delirium seized, outstrips the wind,
Till, plunging into thick and tangled brakes,
His random course he takes,
And struggling ever, still no goal may find.

. . .

Save us, O Christ, who once for men didst bleed,
Oh, save us in our need!
Haply less guilty than infirm our race;
O'erwhelmed by very pride, a heavy weight,
We rush upon our fate,
Saviour, if yet Thou livest, grant us grace.

When science rashly from Thy way departs,
It plants within our hearts
Full many an evil germ of hidden powers;
E'en as the insect, when it takes its flight,
Leaves, like a poisonous blight,
Its larva in the calyx of the flowers.

If in this dreary maze, profound and dark,
Dwell yet the enkindling spark,
Source of all life and hope—Thy holy Word,
Speak to our faith long dead, and cry aloud :
'Awake, put off thy shroud,'
E'en as when Lazarus Thy summons heard.

IDA FARNELL

JOSÉ MARÍA DE PEREDA
[1833–1906]

José María de Pereda, native of the province of Santander, is a leading author among the great realist-regionalist novelists of the nineteenth century. His first publication, a collection of sketches and poems, was entitled Escenas montañesas *(1864). With its realistic descriptions of character types and landscapes of the Montaña region, the work forecast the pattern of his numerous novels.*

Throughout his writings, Pereda defends the conservative, traditional viewpoint in religious, political and social doctrines. His language and style are vigorous, enriched by an abundance of regional expressions.

La leva *('The Conscription'), part of which is presented here, is taken from* Escenas montañesas, *and is regarded as one of the best short stories of the century.*

THE CONSCRIPTION

TUERTO'S FAMILY LIFE

. . . So now we continue.

Tuerto ('Cross-Eyes') enters his house. He tosses off his sou'-wester, or serviceable tarpaulin hat, throws down upon an old chest his duck waterproof, which he had carried on his shoulder, and hangs up on a nail a basket with an oilskin covering, and full of fishing-tackle. His wife dishes up in an old broken pan a mess of beans and cabbage, badly cooked and worse seasoned, sets it on the chest, and puts alongside it a big piece of coarse brown bread. Tuerto, without letting fall a word, waits till his children have got around the board also, and then begins to eat the mess with a pewter spoon. His wife and children accompany him, taking turns with another spoon, of wood. The beans and cabbage are finished. Tuerto has the air of expecting something next, which does not come; he looks at the dish, then into the bottom of the empty stew-pan, then finally at his wife. The woman turns pale.

'Where is the meat?' he at length inquires, with the chronic hoarse voice of the fisherman.

'The meat?' stammers his wife. 'As the butcher's shop was closed when I went to get it, I did not bring any.'

'That's a lie. I gave you the two reals and a half to buy it yesterday noon, and the butcher's doesn't close till four. What have you done with the money?'

'The money?—the money?—It's in my pocket.'

'You thieving jade, if you've been drinking again, I swear I'll let daylight through you,' roared the enraged Tuerto, on observing the continually increasing confusion of his wife. 'Let me see that money, and be quick about it, I say.'

The woman pulls forth tremblingly a few small coins from her pocket, and holds them out to her husband, without fully opening her hand.

'It's only eight coppers you've got there, and I gave you twenty-one. Where's the rest?'

'I must have lost—have lost them. I had twenty-one this morning.'

'Don't tell me such a thing as that; the two reals I gave you were in silver.'

'Yes, but I changed them at the market.'

'What has your mother done this morning?' quickly demands Tuerto, clutching his eldest child by the arm.

The child trembles in affright, looks alternately at father and mother, and remains silent.

'Speak out, I say.'

'Mother will go and beat me if I do,' replies the poor little brat, snivelling.

'And if you don't answer me, I'll give you a crack that will spoil your face.'

The boy, who knows by hard experience that his father never deals in vain threats, now, despite the signals his mother makes him to keep still, shuts his eyes, and speaking as rapidly as if he feared the words would burn his mouth, says :

'Mother brought home a pint of brandy this morning, and has the bottle hidden in the straw mattress.'

Tuerto no sooner hears these words than he fells his culprit spouse to the floor with a resounding whack, rushes to the bed, rummages amid the contents of the poor mattress, pulls out from it a small bottle which contains the remainder of the contraband liquor, and returning with it towards his wife, hurls it at her head at the moment when she is just getting up from the floor. It knocks her down anew, and the children are sprinkled with the flying spirits. The wretched woman, sorely hurt, laments and groans; the frightened children weep; and the irate mariner sallies forth to the balcony, cursing his wife and the day that he was ever born.

Uncle Tremontorio, who arrived from the sea at the same time with his mates Bolina and Tuerto, had been on his balcony knitting away at his fishing-nets (his customary occupation when at home) from the beginning of the dispute between his neighbours. From time to time he would take a bite out of a hunk of bread, and another of dried codfish, the provision that constituted his usual dinner. Though he is perfectly well posted about what has just taken place, it is not his way to mix himself up in what does not concern him. But the furious husband, who needs an outlet for the venomous rage that still half chokes him, calls to his neighbour, and the pair shout from one balcony to the other the following dialogue :

'Uncle Tremontorio, I can't stand this devil of a woman any longer. One of these days you'll hear of some desperate deed on my part; I suppose that's the way it will all end.'

'I have told you that it was your own fault, from the beginning. She tacked your way a little, and you let her go your whole cable and thought your voyage was over.'

'What could I do? I thought then she was one of heaven's own saints.'

'What could you do? Do? Why, what I've always told you : haul her taut, and make fast with a double turn. Rough wind astern? All right, ahead you go.'

'But there's not a bone in her body I haven't already tinkered at with a cudgel, as you might mend the ribs of a boat.'

'You waited till the wood was rotten, my friend.'

'As God is my witness she's the worst villain unhung. What is going to become of those poor brats of mine when I am taken away from them? . . . for the devil will never take that woman : he has no place to put her. Last week I handed her twenty-four reals to dress the children with. Have you laid eyes on that money? Well, neither have I. The drunkard spent them for drink. I gave her a walloping that left her for dead, and yet what does she do? Three days after that she sells a sheet from our bed for a quart of rum. Yesterday I gave her twenty-one cents for meat, and she drank them also. And with all this the young ones are naked, I haven't a shirt to my back, and I never dare think of treating myself to an honest glass of wine of a fête-day.'

'Why don't you get an exorcism said over her? Maybe she's bewitched by evil spirits, and that's the cause of it.'

'I've spent a small fortune in those very tomfooleries, Tremontorio. I took her to more than three leagues from here, to get a parson that they said had the gift of such things, to chuck the gospels at her. Well, he did; then he gave me a little card he had said a prayer over, and a sprig of rue, sewed it all up in a bag, hung it round her neck, charged me nearly four dollars for it, and that was all the good it did—not the first blessed thing. The very next day she had a jag on worse than ever, and wanted to paint the town red. I've given her brandy with gunpowder in it,—a thing, they say, that creates a distaste for liquor,—but that beast, did it affect her that way? Not much! She seemed to like the drink after that better than ever. I've laid out a treasure in candles alone, setting them up before the Holy Martyrs, to see if they'd rid her of the vice; and it was just the same as if I had not spent a farthing. I swear to you, I don't know what to do, Uncle Tremontorio, unless it is to kill her; there are no bounds to this vice of hers. Just tell me what you say of this : When I gave her the brandy with powder in it, she was taken with such a colic I thought she'd burst. I had heard that flannels soaked in spirits, applied good and hot, was a cure for that sort of pains in the stomach; so I heated up about half a pint of liquor in a saucepan. When it was blazing hot, I took it over to the bedside, where the thief of the world was writhing about in contortions. I had to leave the saucepan with her a minute while I went to the chest to get out some rags; I turned around, and, man, what do you think I saw? She was just swallowing down the last drops of the spirits from the saucepan, almost ablaze as it was. Man, man, was there ever a worse curse of God?'

'Well, friend—in regard to that—ahem! what can I say to you? When a woman chooses to take the crooked path, like yours, give her the stick, and plenty of it. If with that she doesn't mend her ways and float off in good style, then either sink her to the bottom, once for all, or string yourself up to a yard-arm.'

'I've told you already—what's the matter with you?—that I've covered every inch of her body with the welts of a stick, and I've decorated her face all over with bruises till there's hardly room for another.'

'Then go hang yourself, and leave me in peace to finish these meshes. And you may as well know that the reason I never married is to keep out of the devil's own scrape that you are in.'

WILLIAM HENRY BISHOP

PEDRO ANTONIO DE ALARCÓN
[1833–1891]

An inspired and skilful teller of tales, the Andalusian Pedro Antonio de Alarcón wrote what has been termed the most perfect short story in all Spanish literature—El sombrero de tres picos (*1874*). Closer to a novelette in length, it is based on the popular legend of the mayor and the miller's wife. The picaresque story is related in graceful, humorous style against a glowing Andalusian background; its characters are so vividly delineated that they seem alive.

Besides the charming Sombrero de tres picos, Alarcón wrote many excellent short stories and a number of long novels, of which the best is El escándalo.

THE THREE-CORNERED HAT

CHAPTER XI

THE BOMBARDMENT OF PAMPELUNA

'God save you, Frasquita,' said the Corregidor, in a low tone, appearing under the grapevine and walking on tip-toe.

'Oh, Señor Corregidor, how good of you,' she replied in her usual tone of voice, making a deep curtsy. 'You Honour here at this time of day, and when it is so very warm! Well, well, please sit down here, Your Honour. It is cool here; why did not your Lordship wait for the other gentlemen. I have their seats all ready for them. We expect the Lord Bishop himself this afternoon, who has promised my Luke to come to taste some of the first grapes off the vine. And how do you do? and how is your lady?'

The Corregidor was confused. He did desire to find Frasquita alone, but it seemed to him now like a dream, or else a snare spread by treacherous fate to decoy him into a yawning gulf of deception. He therefore only answered :

'It is not so early as you imagine it is. It is certainly half-past three.' Just then the parrot squawked the hour.

'It is exactly a quarter-past two!' said the Navarrese, staring at the Corregidor full in the face.

He kept silent like a convicted criminal who renounces his defence.

'And Luke? is he asleep?' he inquired after a short pause.

Now just at this point, we must tell you that the Corregidor, like all who have no teeth, spoke with a drivelling, hissing sound, as though he were chewing his own lips.

'Of course,' replied Señá Frasquita, 'usually at this time he falls asleep, wherever he may be, even if it were on the edge of a precipice.'

'Well, just let him sleep on,' exclaimed the Corregidor, turning even paler than usual. 'And you, my dear Frasquita, listen to me; hark ye, come here. Sit down by my side. I have a great deal to say to you.'

'There now, I'm ready,' replied the miller's wife, bringing a low chair, and putting it in front of the Corregidor at a very short distance from his own.

As soon as she was seated, Frasquita crossed one leg over the other, leaned forward, resting her elbow on her knee, which she kept trotting up and down; and leaning her fresh and lovely face on one of her hands; and so with her head bent a little to one side, a smile on her lips, her bodice provocatively gaping, the five dimples in full play, and her clear eyes fixed on the Corregidor, she waited to hear what he would say. You might have compared her, figuratively, to Pampeluna waiting for the bombardment.

The poor man tried to speak, but remained dumbfounded, with his mouth wide open, before the superb beauty of that formidable woman, with her exuberant charms, her alabaster-like complexion, her magnificent form, her overwhelming bosom, her lovely smiling lips, her deep, unfathomable blue eyes, and looking altogether like one of Rubens' creations.

'Frasquita,' the King's Delegate murmured, at last in a faint voice, while his wrinkled face, covered with perspiration rising above his hump, expressed the greatest anguish, 'Frasquita.'

'That's my name,' replied the daughter of the Pyrenees. 'Well, what is it?'

'Whatever you like,' replied the old man most tenderly.

'Well, your Honour already knows what I want. I want you to appoint my nephew in Estella as Secretary of the City Corporation, so that he may get away from those mountains where he is having such a hard time of it.'

'I told you, Frasquita, that it is quite impossible. The Secretary who now holds that office——'

'Is a thief, a drunkard, and a beast!'

'Yes, I know it, but he has a good hold on the Perpetual Alderman, and I cannot appoint a new one without the sanction of the City Corporation. If I did, I would run the risk of——'

'Would run the risk of! Would run the risk of! What wouldn't we risk for your Honour? yes, even to the cats in the house.'

'Would you like me at that price?' stuttered the old Corregidor.
'No, sir, for I love your Lordship gratis.'

'Child, do not treat me with so much formality, say simply—
you—do not say your Lordship. Call me what you please. So you
will like me? Say now.'

'Have I not already told you that I like you?'

'But.'

'But—there's no but worth a button. You'll see how handsome
my nephew is, what an honest fellow he is!'

'You, indeed, are handsome, Frasquita.'

'Do you really like me?'

'Do I like you? There is no woman equal to you.'

'Well, see here, there's nothing false here,' replied Frasquita,
rolling up her sleeve of her bodice, and displaying to the Corregidor
the rest of her arm whiter than a lily, and a fit model for a
sculptor.

'Do I like thee?' continued the Corregidor. 'By day and by night,
at all hours, wherever I may be, I am thinking of thee.'

'How's that? Don't you like the Lady Mayoress?' inquired Señá
Frasquita, with such poorly feigned compassion that it would have
moved even a hypochondriac to mirth. 'What a pity! My Luke
says that he had the pleasure of meeting her and talking with her,
when he went to regulate the clock in your sleeping chamber,
and that she is very beautiful, very good, and has very sweet
manners.'

'Not quite, not quite,' murmured the Corregidor, with a certain
degree of bitterness.

'On the other hand, some say,' added the miller's wife, 'that she
has a bad temper, and is very jealous, and that you fear her more
than a green switch.'

'Not quite, my girl,' replied Don Eugene de Zuñiga Ponce de
Leon, turning red. 'Not so much, nor so little. My lady has her
whims, it's true, but that she makes me quake with fear is a very
different matter. I am the Corregidor.'

'But, in short, do you love her or not?'

'I'll tell you the truth. I love her a great deal, or I should say,
I did before I knew you. But since I saw you I don't know what
is the matter with me, and she herself knows that something ails
me. You must know, for instance, to caress my wife's face would
not affect me more than if I touched my own. So you see, I cannot
like her more, nor feel less, while just to touch your hand, your
arm, your waist, I would give what I have not got.'

So saying the Corregidor attempted to seize the bare arm which Frasquita was actually rubbing into his eyes, but she, without losing her self-possession in the least, extended her hand, just touched his Lordship's chest with the pacific force and incomparable rigidity of an elephant's trunk, and threw him sprawling on the ground, chair and all.

'Ave Maria Purisima!' exclaimed the Navarrese, laughing until she could laugh no longer. 'It seems that chair must have been broken.'

'What's going on down there?' just at this moment exclaimed Uncle Luke, with his homely face looming out among the leaves and the tendrils of the grapevine. The Corregidor was still lying on his back on the ground, and looked up with unutterable fear at the man who now appeared suspended in the air face downward. One might say that his Honour was the devil conquered not by St. Michael, but by some fiend from the infernal regions.

'What's going on?' answered Frasquita briskly. 'Why, the Señor Corregidor went to balance his chair on nothing, went to rock on it, and over he fell!'

'Jesus, Mary and Joseph!' piously exclaimed the miller. 'And has his Honour hurt himself? Do you want some vinegar and water?'

'Oh, no, I have not hurt myself,' said the Corregidor, getting up as well as he could, while he added in a low tone, but so that Frasquita could hear him :

'You'll pay for this.'

'But, then, on the other hand, his Honour saved my life,' added the miller, without moving from his perch, 'Just imagine, wife, I was seated up here, gazing at the grapes, when I fell asleep on a network of twigs and stalks, which left an opening big enough for my body to fall through. So if you had not awakened me by your fall, just as you did, I might have broken my head against those stones.'

'Is that so? Eh,' replied the Corregidor; 'well, I am glad of it, I assure you. I am really glad that I fell down.'

'I'll pay you up for this,' he added immediately after, addressing the miller's wife.

He pronounced these words with such an expression of concentrated rage that Frasquita immediately became serious. She perceived that the Corregidor had got frightened at first, thinking that the miller had overheard all, but since he was convinced now that he had not, for Uncle Luke's dissimulation would have disarmed the most suspicious being, he began to give way to his passion and try to devise some means of revenging himself.

'Come now, get down from there and help me brush his Honour, for he is covered with dust,' exclaimed Frasquita.

While Uncle Luke was getting down from the trellis, she remarked to the Corregidor, brushing his coat with her apron and, in her zeal, occasionally giving him some hard cuffs over the ears :

'The poor fellow did not hear anything. He was as sound asleep as a log.' The very fact that she uttered these words in a low tone, more than the words themselves, pretending to have a secret understanding with him, produced a most marvellous effect.

'You rogue, you sly kitten,' stammered Don Eugene de Zuñiga, with his mouth watering, but still grunting.

'Do you still feel angry with me?' asked Frasquita coaxingly.

As the Corregidor noticed that his severity produced a good effect, he tried to look at her with anger; but when he met her bewitching smile, her heavenly eyes gazing at him so imploringly, his ire melted at once, and he said with a drivelling and hissing accent, displaying more than ever his total lack of teeth :

'It all depends on you, my darling—' Now at this particular moment, down dropped Uncle Luke from the grapevine trellis.

CHAPTER XX

DOUBT AND REALITY

It was now open, and yet when he left he had heard his wife close and fasten it with key, bolt, and bar. Consequently only his own wife could have opened it. But how? Why? When? Had it been the result of some treachery? Or was it in consequence of a command? Or had she opened it deliberately and voluntarily by virtue of a previous understanding with the Corregidor? What was he about to see? What awaited him at home? Had Frasquita eloped? Had she been carried off? Was she dead, or was she in the arms of his rival? 'The Corregidor was sure that I could not possibly get back tonight,' said Uncle Luke gloomily, 'and the village Alcalde had orders even to chain me up before letting me come home, without doubt. Was Frasquita aware of all this? Was she in the plot? Or has she been the victim of some deceit, some violent act of villainy?'

The time it took for these cruel reflections to pass through the wretched man's brain was just while he was crossing the square under the grapevine. The front door of the house was also open, and the front room was the kitchen as in all rustic dwellings. There was no one in the kitchen. Nevertheless an enormous fire of faggots blazed away in the fireplace—the fireplace which he had left bare; for they never built a fire until way into the middle of December. Lastly, on one of the hooks on the rack a lighted lamp was hanging.

What was the meaning of all this? And how could such a sign of company and watchfulness tally with the death-like stillness which reigned in the house? What had become of his wife?

Then and only then did uncle Luke notice that some clothes were hanging on the backs of two or three chairs placed around in front of the hearth.

He fixed his gaze on the apparel and then gave a hoarse cry, as though it strangled in his throat and was turned into a dumb and suffocating sob. The unhappy man thought that he was choking, and put his hand to his throat, while pale, convulsed, with his eyes starting from their sockets, he gazed at the apparel, filled with as much horror as a criminal about to be executed, to whom they bring the black shroud of death. Because what he beheld was the red cloak, the three-cornered hat, the dove-coloured coat and waistcoat, the black silk breeches, the white stockings, the shoes with buckles, and even the cane, the small sword, and the gloves of the execrable Corregidor. What he saw there was the robe of his ignominy, the shroud of his honour, the winding sheet of his happiness.

The formidable blunderbuss was in the same corner still, where the Navarrese had left it two hours ago.

Uncle Luke gave a leap like a tiger and seized it. He tried the barrel with the ramrod, and found that it was loaded. He looked at the flint and found it in its proper place. Then he turned toward the staircase which led to the bedroom which he and his wife had shared so many years together, while he murmured hoarsely : 'They are there!' He advanced a step in that direction, but immediately stopped to look round about him to see whether anyone was watching him. 'Nobody,' he murmured mentally, 'only my Heavenly Father—God—and He has allowed this to happen!'

The sentence thus pronounced, he was going to advance a step forward, when his wandering gaze alighted on a document which was lying on the table. To see it, fall on it, and seize it in his grasp, was but the work of a second.

That document was the appointment of Frasquita's nephew, signed by Don Eugene de Zuñiga Ponce de Leon.

'So this was the price of the transaction,' muttered Uncle Luke, stuffing the paper into his mouth in order to stifle his cries and to feed his rage. 'I always feared that she cared more for her family than for me! Alas, we never had any children! This is the cause of it all!'

And the unhappy man almost burst into tears again. But he again became infuriated, and expressed it by a terrible gesture, but without words.

'Up, up!' and he began to creep up the stairway on all fours, feeling around with one hand, while carrying the blunderbuss in the other, and the infamous paper between his teeth. To corroborate his reasonable suspicions, on arriving at the door of the room, which was closed, he saw some rays of light issuing through the cracks in the door, and through the keyhole.

'There they are!' he repeated, stopping a moment as though to swallow this new dose of bitterness.

Then he went on until he reached the very door of the bedroom; no noise was to be heard from within.

'Suppose that there is nobody there!' hope suggested timidly, but at that very moment the unfortunate man heard someone cough in the room.

It was the Corregidor's asthmatic cough!

There was no longer any doubt about it! No plank was left on which to save himself from the wreck.

The miller smiled in the darkness in a horrible manner. How is it that such lightning flashes do not shine out in the dark? what is all the fire of the infernal regions compared to that which sometimes rages in the heart of man?

Notwithstanding, Uncle Luke's temperament was so peculiar, as we have already stated that as soon as he heard his enemy's cough he became calmer. Reality did him less harm than doubt. As he had told Frasquita that afternoon, from the very moment and the hour that he lost the faith which was the very life of his soul, he was transfigured into another man. Like the Moor of Venice, with whom we compared him at the beginning of this tale in describing his peculiar temperament, disenchantment killed his love at one blow, causing him to look on the world like a strange region in which he had just arrived. The only difference was that Uncle Luke's temperament was less tragic, less austere, and more selfish than that of Desdemona's stupid destroyer.

It was very singular, indeed, but the natural result of such situations!

Doubt, or hope, which in that case is perchance the same, began to torment him again, for a moment. 'Suppose I was mistaken,' he thought. 'Suppose it were Frasquita who coughed.'

But, in the midst of his unfortunate tribulation, he forgot for a moment that he had seen the Corregidor's apparel in front of the hearthstone, that he had found the door of the mill open, and that he had read the credential of his dishonour. Then, stooping down, he peered through the keyhole, trembling with doubt and anxiety. But his visual range could only discern a small corner of the couch, just by the headpost, and exactly within that limited range he saw one end of the pillows, and resting there was the Corregidor's head !

Another diabolical smile disfigured the miller's face. It might be said that he was beginning to be happy again.

'I have mastered the truth,' he said. 'Let me think,' he added, drawing himself up proudly.

And he descended the stairs as cautiously as he had ascended, and while he went on his way, he reflected, 'This is a delicate affair, but I have time and to spare for all !'

When he reached the kitchen, he sat down in the middle of the room, and covered his face with his hands. He remained so for some time, till he was startled from his meditation by a slight blow on his foot. It was the blunderbuss, which had slipped off his knees and made him this sort of signal.

'No, I tell you no !' murmured Uncle Luke, facing the weapon. 'You don't suit me ! All the world would pity them, and they would hang me ! This affair treats with a mayor, and it is still an unpardonable offence in Spain to kill a mayor. They would say that I killed him for unfounded jealousy, and afterward undressed him, and put him in my bed. Furthermore they'd say that I killed my wife on simple suspicion—and they'd hang me ! Of course they'd hang me ! Besides, I'd be very mean-spirited if the end of my life should inspire pity ! Everybody would laugh at me ! They'd say that my misfortune was only natural, I being a humpback and Frasquita a beauty ! No, indeed ! what I need is to avenge myself, and, after I have avenged myself, to triumph over them, loathe them, and laugh, laugh till I can laugh no longer; laugh at all of them; and so prevent anyone from ever making sport of this hump, which I have succeeded in making even enviable, and which would look so grotesque on the scaffold !'

Thus reasoned Uncle Luke, and perhaps unconsciously; and as the result of his pondering he put the weapon in its place, and commenced to pace up and down, with his head bowed, and his hands behind his back, as though seeking for some means of vengeance, on the floor, in the earth, in the baseness of life; for some way of inflicting a ludicrous and ignominious vengeance on his wife and the Corregidor, far from seeking redress from the law, or in a duel, in forgiveness, or in heaven; as some other man, less rebellious against the restraints of nature and society, or his own sentiments, might have done in his place.

Suddenly his eyes alighted on the Corregidor's clothes. Then his face began to express, little by little, joy, pleasure, and an inexpressible triumph, until at last he began to laugh in a frightful manner; that is, shaking with uncontrollable laughter, but without making any noise. So none should overhear him upstairs, he held on to his sides as though not to split, shaking all over as if with an epileptic fit; and at last threw himself into a chair, until this sardonic burst of merriment passed off. It was like the satanic glee of Mephistopheles.

As soon as he became calmer, he began to undress with feverish haste, and put all his clothes on the same chairs where the Corregidor's were. Then he put on all his apparel, from the shoes with buckles to the three-cornered hat; buckled on the small sword; wrapped himself in the red cloak, took the cane and gloves and left the mill, going toward the city with the very same swaggering gait characteristic of Don Eugene de Zuñiga, and muttering once in a while these words, which gave an inkling to his purpose :

'The mayor's wife is very luscious also.'

CHAPTER XXXI

LEX TALIONIS

'Mercedes !' exclaimed the Corregidor, appearing before his wife, 'I must know immediately——'

'Ah, Uncle Luke! so you are here?' interrupted the mayoress. 'Has anything happened at the mill?'

'Madame, I am in no mood for jesting!' replied the infuriated Corregidor. 'Before entering into explanations on my part, I must know what has become of my honour.'

'That is not my affair. Did you perchance leave it in my keeping?'

'Yes, madame, in yours,' replied Don Eugene. 'The wife is the keeper of her husband's honour.'

'Well, then, my dear Uncle Luke, ask your wife there; she is listening to us now.'

Señá Frasquita, who was standing at the door of the apartment, gave a sort of hoarse cry.

'Come in, madame, and sit down,' continued the mayoress, addressing the miller's wife with queenly dignity, and going toward the sofa herself. The generous and high-minded Navarrese knew how to understand all the grandeur of the wronged wife's attitude, doubly wronged, perchance. Thus raising herself to the same level, and restraining her natural impetuosity, she preserved a decorous silence; all the more so, as Dame Frasquita, sure of her own innocence and strength, was in no haste to defend herself.

She was most certainly prepared to make accusations, and heavy ones too, but not against the mayoress. The person with whom she wanted to settle accounts was Uncle Luke, and Uncle Luke was not there !

'Señá Frasquita,' repeated the noble dame, perceiving that the miller's wife had not moved from her place, 'I have told you that you might come in and sit down.'

This second invitation was given in a kinder and more affectionate manner than the first. It appeared as though the mayoress instinctively perceived, on looking at that woman's noble beauty, that she was not about to deal with a vulgar and despicable being; but perchance another as unfortunate as herself; unfortunate, surely, in the mere fact of having known the Corregidor.

So those two delectable ladies, who considered each other as rivals, doubly so, exchanged peaceful and forgiving looks and were surprised to feel that their souls seemed to soothe each other, like two sisters meeting again. Somewhat in this fashion do the chaste snows of lofty mountains salute each other from afar.

In the enjoyment of these sweet emotions the miller's wife entered the room majestically, and sat down on the edge of the chair.

When she passed by the mill, foreseeing that she would have to make some important visits in the city, she had arranged her toilet a little, and put on a black flannel mantelet, trimmed with broad fringe, which was very becoming to her, so she looked just like a lady.

As for the Corregidor, he had not opened his lips during this episode. Mistress Frasquita's hoarse cry of rage, and her appearance on the scene, had startled him. He was more afraid of that woman than of his own wife.

'So now, Uncle Luke,' continued Donna Mercedes, addressing her husband. 'There you have Señá Frasquita. You may repeat your charge to her. You can now ask her about that little affair of your honour.'

'Mercedes, by the blood of Christ!' shouted the Corregidor, 'take care; you do not know of what I am capable! I again command you to stop joking, and tell me all that has transpired here during my absence! Where is that man?'

'Who, my husband? My husband is getting up and will soon be here.'

'Getting up!' roared Don Eugene.

'Are you surprised? Well, where would you expect an honest man to be at this hour of the night but in his own home, in his own room, with his own lawful wife, as God has commanded.'

'Mercedes, take care what you say! Remember that they are listening to us! Recollect that I am the Corregidor!'

'Don't dare to raise your voice to me, Uncle Luke; or I shall tell the alguazils to march you off to prison,' replied the mayoress, starting to her feet.

'Take me to jail? Me, the Corregidor of the city?'

'The Corregidor of the city, the representative of justice, the King's Delegate,' replied the noble lady with energetic severity, which drowned the voice of the fictitious miller, 'came home at the usual hour, to rest from the arduous duties of his noble office, in order to be able to continue tomorrow to protect the honour and the lives of our citizens, the sanctity of their homes, and the purity of their women, so that no one, disguised as a corregidor, or in any other disguise, shall be able to penetrate into the apartments of his neighbour's wife; that nobody shall overcome her virtue when resting secure in slumber, nor take advantage of her chaste repose.'

'Mercedes, what are you saying?' hissed the Corregidor between his lips and gums. 'If it is true that such a thing has happened in my dwelling, I shall say that you are a sly, perfidious, and abandoned woman!'

'To whom is that man talking?' burst forth the mayoress disdainfully, looking all around at the assembled company. 'Who is that lunatic? Who is that tippler? I cannot believe that he is an honest miller like Uncle Luke, in spite of his wearing a peasant's garb.

'Don Juan Lopez, believe me,' she said, facing the country alcalde, who was stupefied with fear. 'My husband, the Corregidor of the city, came home two hours ago, with his three-cornered hat, his red cloak, his knightly sword and his official staff; the alguazils and the servants, who are listening to me now, arose, and saluted him as he passed through the portico, went upstairs, and through the ante-chamber. All the doors were immediately closed, and since then, no one else has entered my dwelling, until your arrival. It is not so? Answer, all of you.'

'It is true, very true!' replied the nurse, the servants, and the attendants, who were all grouped around the door of the salon, witnessing this most extraordinary scene.

'Get out of here, every one of you!' cried Don Eugene, foaming at the mouth with rage. 'Garduña, Garduña, come and arrest all these scoundrels who are insulting me! Off to jail with them! Off to the scaffold!'

But Garduña did not make his appearance.

'Furthermore, sir,' continued Donna Mercedes, changing her tone, and condescending to look at her husband and consider him as such once more, afraid that the joke might be carried too far; 'Let us suppose that you are Don Eugene de Zuñiga y Ponce de Leon.'

'So I am!'

'Let us suppose, in addition, that I might be slightly to blame in having mistaken for you the man who entered my apartment, dressed as the Corregidor.'

'Vile wretches!' cried the old man, attempting to draw his sword, and finding only the miller's sash in place of it.

The Navarrese covered her face with one end of her mantilla, in order to conceal her jealous rage. 'Let us suppose that all you say may be true,' continued Donna Mercedes, with inexplicable calmness.

'But, answer me now, sir, would you have a right to complain? Could you accuse me as a prosecutor, could you condemn me as a judge? Do you happen to come from mass? Do you come from confession? Do you come from hearing a sermon? Or where do you come from, in that garb? Whence do you come with that lady? Where have you passed half of the night?'

'With your permission!' exclaimed Frasquita, jumping up as though moved by springs, and coming proudly between the mayoress and her husband.

The latter, who was just about to speak, remained with his mouth wide open on seeing the Navarrese open the attack. But Donna Mercedes forestalled her by saying :

'Madame, do not trouble yourself to explain anything to me. I do not require any explanations at all. Here comes the proper person to demand them, armed with the rights of a husband. Explain yourself to him.'

At the same moment, the door of the boudoir opened, and Uncle Luke made his appearance, dressed like the Corregidor, from head to foot, with his cane, gauntlets, and small sword; just as he used to present himself in the Hall of the Corporation.

CHAPTER XXXII

FAITH MOVES MOUNTAINS

'Good evening, gentlemen and ladies,' said the newcomer, taking off his three-cornered hat, and talking with his mouth drawn in, as Don Eugene de Zuñiga had the habit of doing.

Immediately afterward he advanced into the salon with his swaggering gait and proceeded to kiss the mayoress's hand.

All were astounded. The resemblance of Uncle Luke to the real Corregidor was truly marvellous, so that even the servants and Don Juan Lopez could not restrain their mirth. Don Eugene felt this new insult keenly, and sprang upon Uncle Luke like a serpent.

But Dame Frasquita came to the rescue, and with her robust arm pulled the Corregidor away, and his Honour, to avoid toppling over again and the subsequent derision this would involve, made no effort to defend himself, neither saying yea nor nay. It was plain to see that this woman was destined to be the tamer of the poor old man.

Uncle Luke turned paler than death, on seeing that his wife drew near him; but afterward restrained himself, while with a burst of laughter, so violent that he was obliged to put his hand on his heart, so that it should not burst, he said, mimicking the Corregidor :

'God keep you, Frasquita, have you already sent the appointment to your nephew?'

The Navarrese was then a sight to behold. She threw back her mantilla, raised her head as proudly as a lioness, and fixing her eyes like two daggers on the false Corregidor, thrusting her face close to his, said :

'I despise you, Luke!'

All thought that she had spat on him, for her gesture, her attitude, and her tone of voice gave force to her words.

On hearing his wife, the miller's face become transfigured. A sort of inspiration, like that of a religious belief, had penetrated his soul, inundating it with light and joy. For a moment he forgot all that he had seen, or thought he had seen in the mill, while he exclaimed with tears in his eyes and sincerity on his lips :

'So you are my own Frasquita still?'

'No!' replied the Navarrese, beside herself. 'I am not any longer your Frasquita! I am—— You may ask your exploits of tonight who I am, and they will tell you what you have done to the woman who loved you so dearly!'

So saying, she burst into tears—and seemed like an iceberg when it begins to melt, and is about to sink.

The mayoress advanced toward her, no longer able to restrain herself, throwing her arms around her with the greatest affection. Señá Frasquita began to kiss her, without being conscious either of what she was doing; saying in the midst of her sobs, like a child who seeks for shelter in her mother's arms :

'Madame, madame, how unhappy I am!'

'Not so much as you fancy you are!' answered the mayoress, shedding tears of sympathy.

'I am the unhappy one!' blubbered Uncle Luke, ramming his fists into his eyes, which were overflowing with tears, as though he were ashamed to shed them.

'Well then, and I?' burst forth at length Don Eugene, feeling himself moved by the contagious grief of the rest, and hoping to save himself also by giving full play to his lachrymal glands. 'Alas, I am a scamp, a monster, a hot-headed man who has only got what he deserved!'

And he began to bellow mournfully, clasping the ponderous waist of Don Juan Lopez, while the latter and the servants likewise cried, and it looked as though everything had ended, but notwithstanding no one had made any kind of an explanation whatever.

CHAPTER XXXV

AN IMPERIAL EDICT

Just then the Corregidor and Uncle Luke returned to the room, each dressed in his own clothes.

'It is my turn now!' said the arrogant Don Eugene de Zuñiga as he entered.

After thumping the floor with his cane, as though to regain his energy, like unto an official Antaeus, who did not feel his strength till his Indian reed touched the earth, he said emphatically to the mayoress :

'Mercedes, I am waiting to hear your explanations.'

Meanwhile the miller's wife had risen and given Uncle Luke such a playful pinch as a token of peace, that it made him see stars, although she looked at him at the same time with happy and bewitching eyes.

The Corregidor, who observed this pantomime, was bedazzled, without being able to comprehend a reconciliation which seemed so senseless to him. He therefore addressed his wife again, saying in a tone as sour as vinegar :

'Madame, they all understand one another except you and I. Relieve me of my doubts. I command you to do so as your husband and as the Corregidor.'

So saying, he thumped again on the floor with his cane.

'So you are going!' exclaimed Donna Mercedes, drawing near Mistress Frasquita, without paying any attention whatever to Don Eugene. 'Well, rest assured that all this disturbance will have no further result. Rosa, light the way for these gentlefolks, who say that they are going. Good-bye, Uncle Luke.'

'Oh, no!' cried Zuñiga, thrusting himself in the way. 'As for Uncle Luke, he shall not go! Uncle Luke is under arrest until I discover the truth! Here, ho! alguazils. In the King's name!'

Not a soul stirred to obey Don Eugene. All looked at the mayoress.

'Come now, man, clear the way!' added she, passing almost over her husband, and dismissing everybody with the greatest politeness; that is, with her head bent to one side, catching up her skirt with the tips of her fingers, and stooping down gracefully to complete the courtesy in vogue at that time, called *la pompa*.

'But I—but you—but we—but they!' cried the old man, mumbling his words, pulling at his wife's dress, and spoiling her best courtesies.

Useless labour. Nobody paid any attention to his Honour.

As soon as all had gone away, and the discordant couple were left alone, the mayoress deigned to remark to her husband at last, in a tone with which a Russian Czarina might have fulminated upon a fallen Minister the order of perpetual banishment to Siberia :

'If you live a thousand years, you shall never know what transpired tonight in my apartment. If you had been there in your proper place you would have no need to ask anybody. As for my part, there is no longer, nor never will be, any reason to oblige me to give you satisfaction; because I despise you so thoroughly that, if you were not the father of my children, I would throw you over the balcony, at once; as I now cast you out from my apartment forever. So, good night, sir !'

After pronouncing these words, which Don Eugene heard without winking, because, when he found himself alone with his wife, he dared not cope with her, the mayoress passed into her boudoir, and from that to her bedroom, closing the door behind her; while the wretched old man was left standing in the middle of the drawing-room, mumbling with unparalleled cynicism between his gums, for he had no teeth :

'Well, sir! I did not expect to get off so well. Garduña will find me another one !'

CHAPTER XXXVI

CONCLUSION, MORAL, AND EPILOGUE

The birds were saluting the dawn of day when Uncle Luke and Frasquita left the city on their way to the mill.

The married pair went afoot, while the coupled donkeys trotted on ahead.

'Sunday you must go to confession,' said the miller's wife to her husband, 'because you must clear your conscience of all your bad conclusions and wicked purposes of tonight.'

'You are right,' replied the miller. 'But, meanwhile, you must do me a favour, and that is to give away to the poor the mattress and all the bedclothes in our room, and get everything new. I will not lie down where that venomous beast has lain !'

'Don't speak of him, Luke!' replied his wife. 'Let us talk of something else. I want you to do me another favour.'

'Open your mouth and ask.'

'Next summer you must take me to the baths at the Solanillos.'

'What for?'

'To see whether we may have any children.'

'Most happy thought! I will certainly take you, if God spares our lives.'

Just then they arrived at the mill, while the rising sun was just gilding the mountain-tops.

That afternoon, much to the surprise of the worthy couple, who did not expect any distinguished visitors to come there again after a scandal like that of the preceding night, more people of rank came to the mill than ever before, the venerable prelate, a number of canons, the advocate, two priors from the convent, and several other dignitaries; and later on they found out that all had been summoned to meet there by His Grace the Bishop; and they quite filled the square in the grapevine arbour.

Only the Corregidor was wanting. When the company were all

assembled the worthy bishop took the floor, saying that for the very reason that certain things had happened in that dwelling, his canons and he would continue to frequent it the same as ever, so that neither the honest miller, nor any of the other people gathered there, should suffer from public censure, only merited by the one who had profaned by his wicked conduct, a reunion so circumspect and so orderly. He exhorted Mistress Frasquita, in a fatherly way, to be less provocative and coquettish in her sayings and doings in future; and to endeavour to wear her bodice cut higher in the neck, and to cover her arms more. He advised Uncle Luke to show more disinterestedness, greater circumspection and reserve in his demeanour toward his superiors; and concluded by bestowing his blessing on all, and adding that, as he was not fasting on that day, he would eat a couple of clusters of grapes with great gusto.

All agreed with him regarding this last point, so that the grapevine was left in a trembling condition that afternoon; and Uncle Luke calculated the cost to him at fifty pounds of grapes.

MARY J. SERRANO

JUAN VALERA
[1824–1905]

Juan Valera combined a distinguished diplomatic career with that of a dedicated littérateur. An exponent of 'art for art's sake', he excelled in the field of literary criticism. But he is most famous for his penetrating psychological novel, Pepita Jiménez (1874).

The first part of the novel consists of letters from a young seminary student, Don Luis, to his uncle. The youth's character reveals itself in the course of these letters, and Valera masterfully depicts his hero's panic as he becomes aware of his perilous situation. Valera's prose is faultless; his style, almost classic in feeling.

PEPITA JIMÉNEZ

LETTERS FROM DON LUIS TO HIS UNCLE

May 19th.

I return thanks to Heaven and to you for the letters and the counsels you have lately sent me. Today I need them more than ever.

The mystical and learned St. Theresa is right in dwelling upon the suffering of timid souls that allow themselves to be disturbed by temptation; but a thousand times worse than that suffering is the awakening from error of those who, like me, have permitted themselves to indulge in arrogance and self-confidence.

Our bodies are the temples of the Holy Spirit; but when fire is set to the walls of the temple, though they do not burn, yet they are blackened.

The first evil thought is the head of the serpent; if we do not crush it with firm and courageous foot, then will the venomous reptile climb up and hide himself in our bosom.

The nectar of earthly joys, however innocent they be, is sweet to the taste; but afterward it is converted into gall, and into the venom of the serpent.

It is true—I can no longer deny it to you—I ought not to have allowed my eyes to rest with so much complacency on this dangerous woman.

I do not deem myself lost; but I feel my soul troubled.

Even as the thirsty hart desires and seeks the water-brooks, so does my soul still seek God. To God does it turn that He may give it rest; it longs to drink at the torrent of His delights, whose gushing waters rejoice Paradise, and whose clear waves can wash us whiter than snow; but deep calleth unto deep, and my feet have stuck fast in the mire that is hidden in their abysses.

Yet have I still breath and voice to cry out with the psalmist :
'Arise, my joy! If thou art on my side, who shall prevail against
me?'

I say unto my sinful soul, full of the chimerical imaginings and
sinful desires engendered by unlawful thoughts : 'Oh, miserable
daughter of Babylon! happy shall he be who shall give thee thy
reward! Happy shall he be that dasheth thy little ones against
the stones !'

Works of penance, fasting, prayer, and penitence, are the
weapons wherewith I shall arm myself to the combat, and, with
the Divine help, to vanquish.

It was not a dream, it was not madness; it was the truth. She
lets her eyes rest upon me at times with the ardent glance of
which I have told you. There is in her glance an inexplicable
magnetic attraction. It draws me on, it seduces me, and I cannot
withdraw my gaze from her. On such occasions my eyes must
burn, like hers, with a fatal flame, as did those of Ammon when he
turned them upon Tamar, as did those of the prince of Shechem
when they were fixed upon Dinah.

When our glances thus meet, I forget even God. Her image
rises up within my soul, the conqueror of everything. Her beauty
outshines all other beauty; the joys of heaven seem to me less
desirable than her affection. An eternity of suffering would be
little in exchange for a moment of the infinite bliss with which
one of those glances which pass like lightning inundates my
soul.

When I return home, when I am alone in my room, in the
silence of the night, I realize all the horror of my position, and I
form good resolutions, only to break them again.

I resolve to feign sickness, to make use of any pretext so as
not to go to Pepita's on the following night, and yet I go.

My father, confiding to the last degree, says to me when the
hour arrives, without any suspicion of what is passing in my soul :
'Go to Pepita's; I will go later, when I have finished with the
overseer.'

No excuse occurs to me; I can find no pretext for not going,
and instead of answering, 'I cannot go,' I take my hat and depart.

On entering the room I shake hands with Pepita, and as our
hands touch she casts a spell over me; my whole being is changed;
a devouring fire penetrates my heart, and I think only of her.
Moved by an irresistible impulse, I gaze at her with insane ardour,
and at every instant I think I discover in her new perfections. Now
it is the dimples in her cheeks when she smiles, now the roseate

whiteness of her skin, now the straight outline of her nose, now the smallness of her ear, now the softness of contour and the admirable modelling of her throat.

I enter her house against my will, as though summoned there by a conjurer, and no sooner am I there than I fall under the spell of her enchantment. I see clearly that I am in the power of an enchantress whose fascination is irresistible.

Not only is she pleasing to my sight, but her words sound in my ears like the music of the spheres, revealing to my soul the harmony of the universe; and I even fancy that a subtle fragrance emanates from her, sweeter than the perfume of the mint that grows by the brookside, or the woodlike odour of the thyme that is found among the hills.

I know not how, in this state of exaltation, I am able to play *ombre*, or to converse rationally, or even to speak, so completely am I absorbed in her.

When our eyes meet, our souls rush forth in them and seem to join and interpenetrate each other. In that meeting a thousand feelings are communicated that in no other way could be made known; poems are recited that could be uttered in no human tongue, and songs are sung that no human voice could sing, and no guitar accompany.

Since the day I met Pepita by the Pozo de la Solana I have not seen her alone. Not a word has passed between us, yet we have told each other everything.

When I withdraw myself from this fascination, when I am again alone at night in my chamber, I set myself to examine coolly the situation in which I am placed; I see the abyss that is about to engulf me yawning before me; I feel my feet slip from under me, and that I am sinking into it.

You counsel me to reflect upon death—not on the death of this woman, but on my own. You counsel me to reflect on the instability, on the insecurity of our existence, and on what there is beyond it. But these considerations, these reflections neither terrify nor daunt me. Why should I, who desire to die, fear death? Love and death are brothers. A sentiment of self-abnegation springs to life within me, and tells me that my whole being should be consecrated to and annihilated in the beloved object. I long to merge myself in one of her glances; to diffuse and exhale my whole being in the ray of light shot forth from her eyes; to die while gazing on her, even though I should be eternally lost.

What is still to some extent efficacious with me against this love is not fear, but love itself. Superior to this deep-rooted love with which I now have evidence that Pepita inspires me, Divine love exalts itself in my spirit in mighty uprising. Then everything is changed within me, and I feel that I may yet obtain the victory. The object of my higher love presents itself to my mental vision, as the sun that kindles and illuminates all things, and fills all space with light; and the object of my inferior love appears but as an atom of dust floating in the sunbeam. All her beauty, all her splendour, all her attractions are nothing but the reflection of this uncreated sun, the brilliant, transitory, fleeting spark that is cast off from that infinite and inexhaustible fire.

My soul, burning with love, would fain take itself wings and rise to that flame, in order that all that is impure within it might be consumed therein.

My life, for some days past, is a constant struggle. I know not how it is that the malady which I suffer does not betray itself in my countenance. I scarcely eat, I scarcely sleep; and if by chance sleep closes my eyelids, I awake in terror, as from a dream in which rebel angels are arrayed against good angels, and in which I am one of the combatants. In this conflict of light against darkness I do battle for the right, but I sometimes imagine that I have gone over to the enemy, that I am a vile deserter; and I hear a voice from Patmos saying, 'And men loved darkness rather than light'; and then I am filled with terror, and I look upon myself as lost.

No recourse is left me but flight. If, before the end of the month, my father does not go with me, or consent to my going alone, I shall steal away like a thief, without a word to any one.

May 23rd.

I am a vile worm, not a man; I am the opprobrium and disgrace of humanity. I am a hypocrite.

I have been encompassed by the pangs of death, and the waters of iniquity have passed over me.

I am ashamed to write to you, and yet I write. I desire to confess everything to you.

I can not turn away from evil. Far from abstaining from going to Pepita's, I go there each night earlier than the last. It would seem as if devils took me by the feet and carried me there against my will!

Happily, I never find Pepita alone; I do not desire to find her alone. I almost always find the excellent vicar there before me, who attributes our friendship to similarity of feeling in religious matters, and bases it on piety, like the pure and innocent friendship he himself entertains for her.

The progress of my malady is rapid. Like the stone that is loosened from the mountain-top and gathers force as it falls, so is it with my spirit.

When Pepita and I shake hands, it is not now as at first. Each one of us, by an effort of the will, transmits to the other, through the handclasp, every throb of the heart. It is as if, by some diabolical art, we had effected a transfusion and a blending together of the most subtle elements of our blood. She must feel my life circulate through her veins, as I feel hers in mine.

When I am near her, I love her; when I am away from her, I hate her. When I am in her presence she inspires me with love; she draws me to her; she subjugates me with gentleness; she lays upon me a very easy yoke.

But the recollection of her undoes me. When I dream of her, I dream that she is severing my head from my body, as Judith slew the captain of the Assyrians; or that she is driving a nail into my temple, as Jael did to Sisera. But when I am near her, she appears to me the Spouse of the Song of Songs, and a voice within me calls to her and I bless her, and I regard her as a sealed fountain, as an enclosed garden, as the flower of the valley, as the lily of the fields, my dove and my sister.

I desire to free myself from her, and I cannot. I abhor, yet I almost worship her. Her spirit enters into me and takes possession of me as soon as I behold her; it subjugates me, it abases me.

I leave her house each night, saying, 'This is the last night I shall return here'; and I return there on the following night!

When she speaks, and I am near, my soul hangs, as it were, upon her words. When she smiles, I imagine that a ray of spiritual light enters into my heart and rejoices it.

It has happened, when playing *ombre*, that our knees have touched by chance, and then I have felt a thrill run through me impossible to describe.

Get me away from this place. Write to my father and ask him to let me return to you. If it be necessary, tell him everything. Help me! Be my refuge!

May 30th.

God has given me strength to resist, and I have resisted.

It is now many days since I have been in the house of Pepita, many days since I have seen her.

It is scarcely necessary that I should feign sickness, for I am in reality sick. I have lost my colour, and dark circles begin to show themselves under my eyes; and my father asks me, full of affectionate anxiety, what the cause of my suffering is, and manifests the deepest concern.

The kingdom of Heaven is said to yield to violence, and I am resolved to conquer it. With violence I call at its gates that they may open to me.

With wormwood am I fed by the Lord, in order to prove me; and in vain do I supplicate Him to let this cup of bitterness pass away from me. But, as I have passed and still pass many nights in vigil, delivered up to prayer, a loving inspiration from the Supreme Consoler has come to sweeten the bitterness of my cup.

I have beheld with the eyes of the soul the new country; and the new song of the heavenly Jerusalem has resounded within the depths of my heart.

If in the end I should conquer, glorious will be the victory; but I shall owe it to the Queen of Angels, under whose protection I place myself. She is my refuge and my defence; the tower of the house of David, on whose walls hang innumerable shields and the armour of many valiant champions; the cedar of Lebanon, which puts the serpent to flight.

The woman who inspires me with an earthly love, on the contrary, I endeavour to despise and abase in my thoughts, remembering the words of the sage, and applying them to her.

'Thou art the snare of the hunter,' I say of her; 'thy heart is a net of deceit, and thy hands are bands that imprison; he who fears God will flee from thee, and the sinner shall be taken captive by thee.'

In my meditations on love I find a thousand reasons for loving God, and against loving her.

I feel, in the depths of my heart, an indescribable enthusiasm that convinces me that for the love of God I would sacrifice all things—fame, honour, power, dominion. I feel myself capable of imitating Christ, and if the Tempter should carry me off to the mountain-top, and should there offer me all the kingdoms of earth if I consented to bow the knee before him, yet would I not bend it. But were he to offer me this woman if I should do so, I feel that I should waver, that I could not reject his offer. Is this woman, then, worth more in my eyes than all the kingdoms of the earth? More than fame, honour, power, and dominion?

Is the virtue of love, I ask myself at times, always the same, even when applied to divers objects? Or are there two species and qualities of love? To love God seems to me to be the giving up of self and selfish interest. Loving Him, I desire to love, and I can love, all things through Him, and I am not troubled or jealous because of His love toward all things. I am not jealous of the saints, or of the martyrs, or of the blessed, or even of the seraphim. The greater I picture to myself to be the love of God for His creatures, and the graces and gifts He bestows upon them, the less am I troubled by jealousy; the more I love Him, the nearer to me do I feel Him to be, and the more loving and gracious does He seem toward me. My brotherhood, my more than brotherhood, with all creatures, stands forth then in a most pleasing light. It seems to me that I am one with all things, and that all things are bound together in the bonds of love, through God and in God.

Very different is it when my thoughts dwell upon Pepita, and on the love with which she inspires me. This love is a love full of hatred, that separates me from everything but myself. I love her for myself, altogether for myself, and myself altogether for her. Even devotion to her, even sacrifices made for her sake, partake of the nature of selfishness. To die for her would be to die of despair at not being able to possess her in any other manner— from the fear of not enjoying her love completely, except by dying and commingling with her in an eternal embrace.

By these reflections I endeavour to render the love of Pepita hateful to me. I envest my love in my imagination with something diabolical and fatal; but, as if I possessed a double soul, a double understanding, a double will, and a double imagination, in contradiction to this thought, other feelings rise up within me in its train, and I then deny what I have just affirmed, and insanely endeavour to reconcile the two loves. Would it not be possible, I ask myself, to fly from Pepita, and yet continue to love her, without ceasing therefore to consecrate myself with fervour to the love of God? For, as the love of God does not exclude love of country, love of humanity, love of learning, love of beauty in Nature and in Art, neither should it exclude another love, if it be spiritual and immaculate. I will make of her, I say to myself, a symbol, an allegory, an image of all that is good, of all that is beautiful. She shall be to me, as Beatrice was to Dante, the image and the symbol of country, of knowledge, and of beauty.

This intention suggests to me a horrible fancy, a monstrous thought. In order to make of Pepita this symbol, this vaporous and ethereal image, this sign and epitome of all that I can love under God, in God, and subordinate to God, I picture her to myself dead, as Beatrice was dead when Dante made her the subject of his song.

If I picture her to myself among the living, then I am unable to convert her into a pure idea; and if I convert her into a pure idea, I kill her in my thoughts.

Then I weep; I am filled with horror at my crime, and I draw near to her in spirit, and with the warmth of my heart I bring her back to life again; and I behold her, not errant, diaphanous, floating in shadowy outline among roseate clouds and celestial flowers, as the stern Ghibelline beheld his beloved in the upper sphere of Purgatory; but coherent, solid, clearly defined in the pure and serene air, like the masterpieces of Greek art, like Galatea already animated by the love of Pygmalion, and descending from her pedestal of marble, full of fire, exhaling love, rich in youth and beauty.

Then I exclaim in the depths of my perturbed heart : 'My virtue faints ! My God, do not Thou forsake me ! Hasten to my help; show Thy countenance, and I shall be saved !'

Thus do I recover strength to resist temptation. Thus again does the hope spring to life within me, that I shall regain my former tranquillity when I shall have left this place.

The Devil longs with ardour to swallow up the pure waters of Jordan, by which are symbolized the persons who are consecrated to God. Hell conspires against them, and lets loose all her monsters upon them. St. Bonaventure says : 'We should not wonder that these persons have sinned, but rather that they have not sinned.'

Notwithstanding, I shall be able to resist and not sin. The Lord will protect me.

June 6th.

Pepita's nurse—now her housekeeper—is, as my father says, a good bag of wrinkles; she is talkative, gay, and skilful, as few are. She married the son of Master Cencias, and has inherited from the father what the son did not inherit—a wonderful facility for the mechanical arts, with this difference : that while Master Cencias could set the screw of a wine-press, or repair the wheels of a wagon, or make a plough, this daughter-in-law of his knows how to make sweetmeats, conserves of honey, and other dainties. The father-in-law practised the useful arts; the daughter-in-law those that have for their object pleasure, though only innocent, or at least lawful pleasure.

Antoñona—for such is her name—is permitted, or assumes, the greatest familiarity with all the gentry here. She goes in and out of every house as if it were her own. She uses the familiar 'thou' to all young people of Pepita's age, or four or five years older; she calls them 'child', and treats them as if she had nursed them at her breast.

She behaves toward me in this way; she comes to visit me, enters my room unannounced, has asked me several times already why I no longer go to see her mistress, and has told me that I am wrong in not going.

My father, who has no suspicion of the truth, accuses me of eccentricity; he calls me an owl, and he, too, is determined that I shall resume my visits to Pepita. Last night I could no longer resist his repeated importunities, and I went to her house very early, as my father was about to settle his accounts with the overseer.

Would to God I had not gone!

Pepita was alone. When our glances met, when we saluted each other, we both turned red. We shook hands with timidity and in silence.

I did not press her hand, nor did she press mine, but for a moment we held them clasped together.

In Pepita's glance, as she looked at me, there was nothing of love; there was only friendship, sympathy, and a profound sadness.

She had divined the whole of my inward struggle; she was persuaded that Divine love had triumphed in my soul—that my resolution not to love her was firm and invincible.

She did not venture to complain of me; she had no reason to complain of me; she knew that right was on my side. A sigh, scarcely perceptible, that escaped from her dewy, parted lips, revealed to me the depth of her sorrow.

Her hand still lay in mine; we were both silent. How was I to tell her that she was not destined for me, nor I for her; that we must part forever?

But though my lips refused to tell her this in words, I told it to her with my eyes; my severe glance confirmed her fears; it convinced her of the irrevocableness of my decision.

All at once her gaze was troubled; her lovely countenance, pale with a translucent pallor, was full of a touching expression of melancholy. She looked like Our Lady of Sorrows. Two tears rose slowly to her eyes, and began to steal down her cheeks.

I know not what passed within me, nor how to describe it, even if I knew.

I bent toward her to kiss away her tears and our lips met.

Rapture unspeakable, a faintness full of peril, invaded us both. She would have fallen, but that I supported her in my arms.

Heaven willed that we should at this moment hear the step and the cough of the reverend vicar, who was approaching, and we instantly drew apart.

Recovering myself, and summoning all the strength of my will, I brought to an end this terrible scene, that had been enacted in silence, with these words, which I pronounced in low and intense accents :

'The first and the last!'

I made allusion to our profane kiss; but, as if my words had been an invocation, there rose before me the vision of the Apocalypse in all its terrible majesty. I beheld Him who is indeed the First and the Last, and with the two-edged sword that proceeded from His mouth He pierced my soul, full of evil, of wickedness, and of sin.

All that evening I passed in a species of frenzy, an inward delirium, that I know not how I was able to conceal.

I withdrew from Pepita's house very early.

The anguish of my soul was yet more poignant in solitude.

When I recalled that kiss and those words of farewell, I compared myself with the traitor Judas, who made use of a kiss to betray; and with the sanguinary and treacherous assassin Joab, who plunged the sharp steel into the bowels of Amasa while in the act of kissing him.

I had committed a double treason; I had been guilty of a double perfidy. I had sinned against God and against her.

I am an execrable wretch.

June 11th.

Everything may still be remedied.

Pepita will in time forget her love and the weakness of which we were guilty.

Since that night I have not returned to her house. Antoñona has not made her appearance in ours.

By dint of entreaties I have obtained a formal promise from my father that we shall leave here on the 25th, the day after St. John's day, which is here celebrated with splendid feasts, and on the eve of which there is a great vigil.

Absent from Pepita, I begin to recover my serenity and to think that this first beginning of love was a trial of my virtue.

All these nights I have prayed, I have watched, I have performed many acts of penance.

The persistence of my prayers, the deep contrition of my soul, have found favour with the Lord, who has manifested to me His great mercy.

The Lord, in the words of the prophet, has sent fire to the stronghold of my spirit; He has illumined my understanding, He has kindled my resolution, and He has given me guidance.

The working of the Divine love which animates the Supreme Will has had power, at times, without my deserving it, to lead me to that condition of prayerful contemplation in which the soul enjoys repose. I have cast out from the lower faculties of my soul every image—even her image; and I am persuaded, if pride does not deceive me, that, in perfect peace of mind and heart I have known and enjoyed the Supreme Good that dwells within the depths of the soul.

Compared with this good all else is worthless—compared with this beauty all else is deformity—compared with these heights all else is vile. Who would not forget and scorn every other love for the love of God?

Yes; the profane image of this woman shall depart finally and forever from my soul. I shall make of my prayers and of my penance a sharp scourge, and with it I will expel her therefrom, as Christ expelled the moneylenders from the Temple.

June 18th.

This is the last letter I shall write to you. On the 25th I shall leave this place without fail.

I shall soon have the happiness of embracing you. Near you I shall be stronger. You will infuse courage into me, and lend me the energy in which I am wanting.

A tempest of conflicting emotions is now raging in my soul. The disorder of my ideas may be known by the disorder of what I write.

Twice I returned to the house of Pepita. I was cold and stern. I was as I ought to have been, but how much did it cost me!

My father told me yesterday that Pepita was indisposed, and would not receive.

The thought at once assailed me that the cause of her indisposition might be her ill-requited love.

Why did I return her glances of fire? Why did I basely deceive her? Why did I make her believe I loved her? Why did my vile lips seek hers with ardour, and communicate the ardour of an unholy love to hers?

But no; my sin shall not be followed, as its unavoidable consequence, by another sin!

What has been, has been, and can not be undone; but a repetition of it may be avoided—shall be avoided in future.

On the 25th, I repeat, I shall depart from here without fail.

The impudent Antoñona has just come to see me. I hid this letter from her, as if it were a crime to write to you.

Antoñona remained here only for a moment.

I arose, and remained standing while I spoke to her, that the visit might be a short one.

During this short visit she gave utterance to a thousand mad speeches, which disturbed me greatly. Finally, as she was going away, she exclaimed, in her half-gipsy jargon :

'You deceiver! You villain! My curse upon you! You have made the child sick, and now you are killing her by your desertion. May witches fly away with you, body and bones!'

Having said this, the fiendish woman gave me, in a coarse and vulgar fashion, six or seven ferocious pinches below the shoulders, as if she would like to tear the skin from my back in strips, and then went away, looking daggers at me.

I do not complain. I deserve this brutal jest, granting it to be a jest. I deserve that fiends should tear my flesh with red-hot pincers.

Grant, my God, that Pepita may forget me! Let her, if it be necessary, love another, and be happy with him!

Can I ask more than this of Thee, oh, my God?

My father knows nothing, suspects nothing. It is better thus.

Farewell for a few days, till we see and embrace each other again.

How changed will you find me! How full of bitterness my heart! How soiled my purity! How bruised and wounded my soul!

MARY J. SERRANO

BENITO PÉREZ GALDÓS
[1843–1920]

The great master of the modern Spanish novel is Benito Pérez Galdós, born in the Canary Islands. He delved into painting and law as a young man, but soon dedicated himself entirely to writing, publishing his first novel at the age of twenty-seven. Until his death in 1920 he wrote unceasingly and prodigiously, despite blindness in his later years.

The universal appeal of his works combined with their brilliant execution has given Pérez Galdós a place unique in contemporary Spanish literature. No other modern novelist has been so widely read by all classes of people and at the same time been so admired by critics. His voluminous production includes thirty novels, forty-six episodios nacionales (*semi-historical novels which range in period from the battle of Trafalgar, 1805, to the end of the nineteenth century*), *twenty-two dramas and numerous short stories.*

A crusading reformer, Galdós consistently defends the liberal side of social problems. One of his best novels, Doña Perfecta, *depicts the evils of religious fanaticism, personified by the character of a strong and ruthless woman.*

DOÑA PERFECTA

The Disagreement Continued to Increase and Threatened to Become Discord

... Doña Perfecta and Señor Don Cayetano at this moment made their appearance.

'What a beautiful evening!' said the former. 'Well, nephew, are you getting terribly bored?'

'I am not bored in the least,' responded the young man.

'Don't try to deny it. Cayetano and I were speaking of that as we came along. You are bored, and you are trying to hide it. It is not every young man of the present day who would have the self-denial to spend his youth, like Jacinto, in a town where there are neither theatres, nor opera bouffe, nor dancers, nor philosophers, nor athenaeums, nor magazines, nor congresses, nor any other kind of diversions or entertainments.'

'I am quite contented here,' responded Pepe. 'I was just now saying to Rosario that I find this city and this house so pleasant that I would like to live and die here.'

Rosario turned very red and the others were silent. They all sat down in a summer-house, Jacinto hastening to take the seat on the left of the young girl.

'See here, nephew, I have a piece of advice to give you,' said Doña Perfecta, smiling with that expression of kindness that seemed to emanate from her soul, like the aroma from the flower. 'But don't imagine that I am either reproving you or giving you a lesson —you are not a child, and you will easily understand what I mean.'

'Scold me, dear aunt, for no doubt I deserve it,' replied Pepe, who was beginning to accustom himself to the kindnesses of his father's sister.

'No, it is only a piece of advice. These gentlemen, I am sure, will agree that I am in the right.'

Rosario was listening with her whole soul.

'It is only this,' continued Doña Perfecta, 'that when you visit our beautiful cathedral again, you will endeavour to behave with a little more decorum while you are in it.'

'Why, what have I done?'

'It does not surprise me that you are not yourself aware of your fault,' said his aunt, with apparent good humour. 'It is only natural; accustomed as you are to enter athenaeums and clubs, and academies and congresses without any ceremony, you think that you can enter a temple in which the Divine Majesty is in the same manner.'

'But excuse me, señora,' said Pepe gravely, 'I entered the cathedral with the greatest decorum.'

'But I am not scolding you, man; I am not scolding you. If you take it in that way I shall have to remain silent. Excuse my nephew, gentlemen. A little carelessness, a little heedlessness on his part is not to be wondered at. How many years is it since you set foot in a sacred place before?

'What I assure you is—— There, if you are going to be offended I won't go on. What I assure you is that a great many people noticed it this morning. The Señores de González, Doña Robustiana, Serafinita—in short, when I tell you that you attracted the attention of the bishop—— His lordship complained to me about it this afternoon when I was at my cousin's. He told me that he did not order you to be put out of the church only because you were my nephew.'

Rosario looked anxiously at her cousin, trying to read in his countenance, before he uttered it, the answer he would make to these charges.

'No doubt they mistook me for some one else.'

'No, no! it was you. But there, don't get angry! We are talking here among friends and in confidence. It was you. I saw you myself.'

'You saw me!'

'Just so. Will you deny that you went to look at the pictures, passing among a group of worshippers who were hearing mass? I assure you that my attention was so distracted by your comings and goings that—well, you must not do it again. Then you went into the chapel of San Gregorio. At the elevation of the Host at the high altar you did not even turn around to make a gesture of reverence. Afterward you traversed the whole length of the church, you went up to the tomb of the Adelantado, you touched the altar with your hands, then you passed a second time among the group of worshippers, attracting the notice of every one. All the girls looked at you, and you seemed pleased at disturbing so finely the devotions of those good people.'

'Good Heavens! How many things I have done!' exclaimed Pepe, half angry, half amused. 'I am a monster, it seems, without ever having suspected it.'

'No, I am very well aware that you are a good boy,' said Doña Perfecta, observing the canon's expression of unalterable gravity, which gave his face the appearance of a pasteboard mask. 'But, my dear boy, between thinking things and showing them in that irreverent manner, there is a distance which a man of good sense and good breeding should never cross. I am well aware that your ideas are—— Now, don't get angry! If you get angry, I will be silent. I say that it is one thing to have certain ideas about religion and another thing to express them. I will take good care not to reproach you because you believe that God did not create us in his image and likeness, but that we are descended from the monkeys; nor because you deny the existence of the soul, asserting that it is a drug, like the little papers of rhubarb and magnesia that are sold at the apothecary's——'

'Señora, for Heaven's sake!' exclaimed Pepe, with annoyance. 'I see that I have a very bad reputation in Orbajosa.'

The others still remained silent.

'As I said, I will not reproach you for entertaining those ideas. And, besides, I have not the right to do so. If I should undertake to argue with you, you, with your wonderful talents, would confute me a thousand times over. No, I will not attempt any thing of that kind. What I say is that these poor and humble inhabitants of Orbajosa are pious and good Christians, although they know nothing about German philosophy, and that, therefore, you ought not publicly to manifest your contempt for their beliefs.'

'My dear aunt,' said the engineer gravely, 'I have shown no contempt for any one, nor do I entertain the ideas which you attribute to me. Perhaps I may have been a little wanting in reverence in the church, I am somewhat absent-minded. My thoughts and my attention were engaged with the architecture of the building and, frankly speaking, I did not observe—— But this was no reason for the bishop to think of putting me out of the church, nor for you to suppose me capable of attributing to a paper from the apothecary's the functions of the soul. I may tolerate that as a jest, but only as a jest.'

The agitation of Pepe Rey's mind was so great that, notwithstanding his natural prudence and moderation, he was unable to conceal it.

'There! I see that you are angry,' said Doña Perfecta, casting down her eyes and clasping her hands. 'I am very sorry. If I had known that you would have taken it in that way, I should not have spoken to you. Pepe, I ask your pardon.'

Hearing these words and seeing his kind aunt's deprecating attitude Pepe felt ashamed of the sternness of his last words, and he made an effort to recover his serenity. The venerable Penitentiary extricated him from his embarrassing position, saying with his accustomed benevolent smile :

'Señora Doña Perfecta, we must be tolerant with artists. Oh, I have known a great many of them! Those gentlemen, when they have before them a statue, a piece of rusty armour, a mouldy painting, or an old wall, forget everything else. Señor Don José is an artist, and he has visited our cathedral as the English visit it, who would willingly carry it away with them to their museums, to its last tile, if they could. That the worshippers were praying, that the priest was elevating the Sacred Host, that the moment of supreme piety and devotion had come—what of that? What does all that matter to an artist? It is true that I do not know what art is worth, apart from the sentiments which it expresses, but, in fine, at the present day, it is the custom to adore the form, not the idea. God preserve me from undertaking to discuss this question with Señor Don José, who knows so much, and who, reasoning with the admirable subtlety of the moderns, would instantly confound my mind, in which there is only faith.'

'The determination which you all have to regard me as the most learned man on earth annoys me exceedingly,' said Pepe, speaking in his former hard tone. 'Hold me for a fool; for I would rather be regarded as a fool than as the possessor of that Satanic knowledge which is here attributed to me.'

Rosarito laughed, and Jacinto thought that a highly opportune moment had now arrived to make a display of his own erudition. 'Pantheism or panentheism,' he said, 'is condemned by the Church, as well as by the teachings of Schopenhauer and of the modern Hartmann.'

'Ladies and gentlemen,' said the canon gravely, 'men who pay so fervent a worship to art, though it be only to its form, deserve the greatest respect. It is better to be an artist, and delight in the contemplation of beauty, though this be only represented by nude nymphs, than to be indifferent and incredulous in every thing. The mind that consecrates itself to the contemplation of beauty, evil will not take complete possession of. *Est Deus in nobis. Deus*, be it well understood. Let Señor Don José, then, continue to admire the marvels of our church; I, for one, will willingly forgive him his acts of irreverence, with all due respect for the opinions of the bishop.'

'Thanks, Señor Don Inocencio,' said Pepe, feeling a bitter and rebellious sentiment of hostility springing up within him toward the canon, and unable to conquer his desire to mortify him. 'But let none of you imagine, either, that it was the beauties of art, of which you suppose the temple to be full, that engaged my attention. Those beauties, with the exception of the imposing architecture of a portion of the edifice and of the three tombs that are in the chapel of the apse, I do not see. What occupied my mind was the consideration of the deplorable decadence of the religious arts; and the innumerable monstrosities of which the cathedral is full, caused me not astonishment, but disgust.'

The amazement of all present was profound.

'I cannot endure,' continued Pepe, 'those glazed and painted images that resemble so much—God forgive me for the comparison —the dolls that little girls play with. And what am I to say of the theatrical robes that cover them? I saw a St. Joseph with a mantle whose appearance I will not describe, out of respect for the holy patriarch and for the church of which he is the patron. On the altar are crowded together images in the worst possible taste; and the innumerable crowns, branches, stars, moons, and other orna-ments of metal or gilt paper have an air of an ironmongery that offends the religious sentiment and depresses the soul. Far from lifting itself up to religious contemplation, the soul sinks, and the idea of the ludicrous distracts it. The great works of art which give sensible form to ideas, to dogmas, to religious faith, to mystic exaltation, fulfil a noble mission. The caricatures, the aberrations of taste, the grotesque works with which a mistaken piety fills the churches, also fulfil their object; but this is a sad one enough : They encourage superstition, cool enthusiasm, oblige the eyes of the believer to turn away from the altar, and, with the eyes, the souls that have not a very profound and a very firm faith turn away also.'

'The doctrine of the iconoclasts, too,' said Jacinto, 'has, it seems, spread widely in Germany.'

'I am not an iconoclast, although I would prefer the destruction of all the images to the exhibition of buffooneries of which I speak,' continued the young man. 'Seeing it, one may justly advocate a return of religious worship to the august simplicity of olden times. But no; let us not renounce the admirable aid which all the arts, beginning with poetry and ending with music, lend to the relations between man and God. Let the arts live; let the utmost pomp be displayed in religious ceremonies. I am a partisan of pomp.'

'An artist, an artist, and nothing more than an artist !' exclaimed the canon, shaking his head with a sorrowful air. 'Fine pictures, fine statues, beautiful music; pleasure for the senses, and let the devil take the soul !'

'Apropos of music,' said Pepe Rey, without observing the deplorable effect which his words produced on both mother and daughter, 'imagine how disposed my mind would be to religious contemplation on entering the cathedral, when just at that moment, and precisely at the offertory at high mass, the organist played a passage from "Traviata".'

'Señor de Rey is right in that,' said the little lawyer emphatically. 'The organist played the other day the whole of the drinking song and the waltz from the same opera, and afterward a rondeau from the "Grande Duchesse".'

'But when I felt my heart sink,' continued the engineer implacably, 'was when I saw an image of the Virgin, which seems to be held in great veneration, judging from the crowd before it and the multitude of tapers which lighted it. They have dressed her in a puffed-out garment of velvet, embroidered with gold, of a shape so extraordinary that it surpasses the most extravagant of the fashions of the day. Her face is almost hidden under a voluminous frill, made of innumerable rows of lace, crimped with a crimping-iron, and her crown, half a yard in height, surrounded by golden rays, looks like a hideous catafalque erected over her head. Of the same material, and embroidered in the same manner, are the trousers of the Infant Jesus. I will not go on, for to describe the Mother and the Child might perhaps lead me to commit some irreverence. I will only say that it was impossible for me to keep from smiling, and for a short time I contemplated the profaned image, saying to myself : "Mother and Lady mine, what a sight they have made of you !" '

As he ended Pepe looked at his hearers, and although, owing to the gathering darkness, he could not see their countenances distinctly, he fancied that in some of them he perceived signs of angry consternation.

'Well, Señor Don José !' exclaimed the canon quickly, smiling with a triumphant expression, 'that image, which to your philosophy and pantheism appears so ridiculous, is Our Lady of Help, patroness and advocate of Orbajosa, whose inhabitants regard her with so much veneration that they would be quite capable of dragging any one through the streets who should speak ill of her. The chronicles and history, Señor Don José, are full of the miracles which she has wrought, and even at the present day we receive constantly incontrovertible proofs of her protection. You must know also that your aunt, Doña Perfecta, is chief lady in waiting to the Most Holy Virgin of Help, and that the dress that to you appears so grotesque—well, the dress, I repeat, which, to your impious eyes, appears so grotesque—went out from this house, and that the trousers of the Infant are the work of the skilful needle and the ardent piety combined of your cousin Rosarito, who is now listening to us.'

Pepe Rey was greatly disconcerted. At the same instant Doña Perfecta rose abruptly from her seat, and, without saying a word, walked toward the house, followed by the Penitentiary. The others rose also. Recovering from his stupefaction, the young man was about to get his cousin's pardon for his irreverence, when he observed that Rosarito was weeping. Fixing on her cousin a look of friendly and gentle reproof, she said :

'What ideas you have !'

The voice of Doña Perfecta was heard crying in an altered accent :

'Rosario ! Rosario !'

The latter ran toward the house.

MARY J. SERRANO

EMILIA PARDO BAZÁN
[1851–1921]

The erudite Countess of Pardo Bazán is one of the major figures of modern Spanish literature. An incisive literary critic, she was, in her later years, a professor of literature at the University of Madrid. She is credited with the introduction of French naturalism into Spain. Although she later tended away from this school of writing, her masterpiece is a naturalistic novel, Los Pazos de Ulloa (1886). Set typically in Galicia, pervaded by an atmosphere of gloom and foreboding, the work adheres uncompromisingly to realism in action, detail and dialogue; on this basis are constructed striking descriptions and powerful character portraits.

In addition to some twenty novels, the Countess of Pardo Bazán wrote scores of short stories; she is considered among the best Spanish cuentistas. Indulto ('The Pardon') is an example of her skill in this field.

THE PARDON

Of all the women busily engaged in lathering soiled linen in the public laundry of Marineda, their arms stiff with the biting cold of a March morning, Antonia the charwoman was the most bowed down, the most disheartened, the one who wrung the clothes with the least energy, and rinsed them with the greatest lassitude. From time to time she would interrupt her work in order to pass the back of her hand across her reddened eyelids; and the drops of water and soapy bubbles glistened like so many tears upon her withered cheeks.

Antonia's companions at the tubs eyed her compassionately, and every now and again, in the midst of the confusion of gossip and of quarrels, a brief dialogue would ensue in lowered tones, interrupted by exclamations of astonishment, indignation, and pity. The entire laundry knew, down to the smallest details, the poor washerwoman's misfortunes, which furnished occasion for unending comment. No one was unaware that, after her marriage a few years ago with a young butcher, she had kept house together with her mother and husband in one of the suburbs outside the town wall, and that the family lived in comfortable circumstances, thanks to Antonia's steady industry, and to the frugal savings of the older woman in her former capacity of huckster, second-hand dealer, and money-lender.

Still less had anyone forgotten the tragic evening when the old woman was found assassinated, with nothing but splinters left of the lid of the chest in which she kept her money and a few ear-rings and trinkets of gold; still less, the horror that spread through the neighbourhood at the news that the thief and assassin was none other than Antonia's husband, as she herself declared, adding that for some time past the guilty man had been tormented with a desire for his mother-in-law's money, with which he wished to set up a butcher's shop of his own. The accused, to be sure, attempted to establish an alibi, relying on the testimony of two or three boon companions, and so far confused the facts that, instead of going to the gallows, he got off with twenty years in prison.

Public opinion was less indulgent than the law; in addition to the wife's testimony, there was one overwhelming piece of evidence, namely, the wound itself which had caused the old woman's death, an accurate, clean-cut wound, delivered from above downward, like the stroke used in slaughtering hogs, evidently with a broad, keen blade, like that of a meat knife. Among the people, there was no question but that the culprit should have paid for his deed upon the scaffold. And Antonia's destiny began to evoke a holy horror when the rumour was circulated that her husband had *sworn to get even with her*, on the day of his release, for having testified against him. The poor woman was expecting soon to have a child; yet none the less, he left her with the assurance that, as soon as he should come back, she might count herself among the dead.

When Antonia's son was born, she was unable to nurse him, because of her enfeebled and wasted condition, and the frequent attacks of prostration from which she had suffered since the commission of the crime. And since the state of her purse did not permit her to pay for a nurse, the women of the neighbourhood who had nursing children took turns in caring for the poor little thing, which grew up sickly, suffering the consequences of all its mother's anguish. Before she had fully got back her strength, Antonia was hard at work again, and although her cheeks continually showed that bluish pallor which is characteristic of a weak heart, she recovered her silent activity and her placid manner.

Twenty years of prison! In twenty years, she told herself, either he might die, or she might die, and from now until then was, in any case, a long time. The idea of a natural death did not disturb her; but the mere thought of her husband's return filled her with horror. In vain her sympathetic neighbours tried to console her, suggesting the possibility that the guilty wretch might repent and mend his ways, or, as they expressed themselves, 'think better of it'; but Antonia would only shake her hand, murmuring gloomily: 'What, he? Think better of it? Not unless God Himself came down from Heaven to tear his dog's heart out of him and give him another!'

And at the mere mention of the criminal, a shudder would run throughout Antonia's body.

After all, twenty years contain a good many days, and time alleviates even the cruelest pain. Sometimes it seemed to Antonia as though all that had happened was a dream, or that the wide gates of the prison, having once closed upon the condemned man, would never again reopen; or that the law, which in the end had inflicted punishment for the first crime, would have the power to prevent a second. The law! that moral entity, of which Antonia formed a mysterious and confused conception, was beyond doubt a terrible force, yet one that offered protection; a hand of iron that would sustain her upon the brink of an abyss. Accordingly she added to her illimitable fears a sort of indefinable confidence, founded chiefly upon the time that had already elapsed and that which remained before the expiration of the sentence.

Strange, indeed, is the conception of human events! Certainly it would never have occurred to the king, when, clad in the uniform of general-in-chief and with his breast covered over with decorations, he gave his hand to a princess before the altar, that this solemn act would cost pangs beyond number to a poor washerwoman in the capital of a distant province. When Antonia learned that her husband had been one of the convicts singled out for royal clemency, she spoke not a word; and the neighbours found her seated on the sill of her doorway, with her fingers interlocked and her head drooping forward on her breast; while the boy, raising his sad face, with its stamp of chronic invalidism, kept moaning:

'Mother, mother, warm me some soup, for God's sake, for I am starving!'

The kind-hearted and chattering chorus of neighbours swooped down upon Antonia; some busied themselves in preparing the child's dinner; others tried as best they could to instil courage into the mother. She was very foolish to distress herself like this! Holy Virgin! It wasn't as though the brute had nothing to do but just walk in and kill her! There was a government, God be thanked, and the law courts, and the police; she could appeal to the authorities, to the mayor——

'The mayor's no good!' she answered, with a gloomy look in a hopeless tone.

'Or to the governor, or the regent, or the chief of the city council; you ought to go to a lawyer and find out what the law says.'

One kind-hearted girl, married to a policeman, offered to send for her husband, 'to give the scoundrel a good scare'; another, a swarthy, dauntless sort of woman, insisted on coming every night to sleep at the charwoman's house; in short, so many and so varied were the signs of interest shown by her neighbours that Antonia made up her mind to take a bold step, and without waiting for her counsellors to adjourn, decided to consult a lawyer and find out what he advised.

When Antonia returned from the consultation, paler even than usual, from every basement and ground floor dishevelled women emerged to hear the news, and exclamations of horror arose. Instead of protecting her, the law required the daughter of the murdered woman to live under the same roof with the assassin, as his wife!

'What laws, divine Lord of Heaven! That's how the brigands who make them carry them out!' clamoured the indignant chorus. 'And is there no help for it, my dear, no help at all?'

'He says that I could leave him after I got what they call a divorce.'

'And what is a divorce, my dear?'

'It's a lawsuit that takes a long time.'

All the women let their arms fall hopelessly. Lawsuits never came to an end, or if they did it was all the worse, because they were always decided against the innocent and the poor.

'And to get it,' continued the charwoman, 'I should have to prove that my husband had ill-treated me.'

Lord of mercy! Hadn't the beast killed her own mother? And if that wasn't ill treatment, then what was? And didn't the very cats in the street know that he had threatened to kill her too?

'But since no one heard him—The lawyer says the proof has to be very clear.'

Something akin to a riot ensued. Some of the women insisted that they would certainly send a petition to the king himself, asking to have the pardon revoked; and they took turns at spending the night at the charwoman's house, so that the poor thing could get a chance to sleep. Fortunately, it was only three days later that the news arrived that the pardon was only a partial remission of the sentence, and that the assassin still had some years to drag his chains behind prison bars. The night after

Antonia had learned this was the first that she did not suddenly start up in bed, with her eyes immeasurably wide open, and scream for help.

After this first alarm, more than a year passed, and the charwoman recovered her tranquillity and was able to devote herself to her humble labours. One day the butler in one of the houses where she worked thought that he was doing a kindness to the poor, white-faced thing who had a husband in prison, by telling her that there was soon to be an heir to the throne, and that this would undoubtedly mean some more pardons.

The charwoman was in the midst of scrubbing the floor, but on hearing this announcement she dropped her scrubbing-brush and, shaking down her skirt, which had been gathered up around her waist, she left the house, moving like an automaton, as cold and silent as a statue. To all inquiries from her various employers, she replied that she was ill; although, in reality, she was merely suffering from a sort of general prostration, and inability to raise her arms to any work whatever. On the day of the royal birth, she counted the number of salutes, whose reverberations seemed to jar through to the centre of her brain; and when someone told her that the royal child was a girl, she began to take heart at the thought that a male child would have been the occasion of a larger number of pardons.

Besides, why should one of the pardons be for her husband? They had already remitted part of his sentence once, and his crime had been a shocking one. To kill a defenceless old woman, just for the sake of a few wretched pieces of gold! The terrible scene once more unrolled itself before her eyes. How did they dare to pardon the beast who had inflicted that fearful knife-thrust? Antonia remembered that the lips of the wound were livid, and it seemed as though she could still see the coagulated blood at the foot of the narrow bed.

She locked herself into her house, and passed the hours seated in a low chair before the hearth. Bah! If they were bound to kill her, they might as well come and do it!

Nothing but the plaintive voice of the little boy aroused her from her self-absorption.

'Mother, I am hungry! Mother, who is at the door? Who is coming?'

But at last, on a beautiful, sunny morning, she roused herself and, taking a bundle of soiled clothing, made her way towards the public washing place. To the many affectionate inquiries she answered only in slow monosyllables, and her eyes rested in unseeing absorption on the soapy water that now and again splashed in her face.

Who was it that brought to the laundry the unlooked-for news? It happened just as Antonia was gathering up her washing and preparing to start for home. Did someone invent the story, meaning to be kind, or was it one of those mysterious rumours, of unknown origin, which on the eve of momentous happenings, whether personal or public, palpitate and whisper through the air? The actual facts are that poor Antonia, upon hearing it, raised her hand instinctively to her heart and fell backward upon the wet flooring of the laundry.

'But is he really dead?' demanded the early comers of the more recent arrivals.

'Indeed he is!'

'I heard it in the market-place.'

'I heard it in the shop.'

'Well, and who told you?'

'Me? Oh, I heard it from my husband.'

'And who told your husband?'

'The captain's mate.'

'Who told the mate?'

'His foster-father.'

At this point the matter seemed to be sufficiently authenticated, and no one sought to verify it further, but assumed that the news was valid and beyond question. The culprit dead, on the eve of pardon, and before completing the term of his sentence! Antonia, the charwoman, raised her head, and for the first time her cheeks took on the colour of health, and the fountain of her tears was opened. She wept to her heart's content, and of all who saw her, there was no one that blamed her. It was she who had received her release, and her gladness was justified.

The tears chased each other from the corners of her eyes, and as they flowed her heart expanded; because, from the day of the murder she had been under a weight too heavy for relief in tears. Now once more she could breathe freely, released from her nightmare fear. The hand of Providence had so plainly intervened that it never even occurred to the poor charwoman that the news might be false.

That evening, Antonia returned home later than usual, because she stopped at the primary school for her boy, and bought him some spice cakes and other dainties that he had long been wanting; and the two wandered from street to street, lingering before the shop windows. She forgot the dinner hour, and thought of nothing but of drinking in the air, and feeling herself alive, and little by little taking possession of herself.

So great was Antonia's self-absorption that she did not notice that her outer door was unlatched. Still holding the child by the hand, she entered the narrow quarters that served as parlour, kitchen, and dining-room all in one, then recoiled in amazement at seeing that the candle was lighted. A huge, dark bulk raised itself from the table, and the scream which rose to the charwoman's lips was strangled in her throat.

It was he. Antonia, motionless, riveted to the ground, stared unseeingly at him, although the sinister image was mirrored in her dilated pupils. Her rigid body was for the moment paralysed; her icy hands relaxed their hold upon the boy, who clung in terror to her skirts. The husband spoke :

'You were not counting on me today!' he murmured in a hoarse but tranquil tone; and at the sound of that voice, in which Antonia fancied that she could hear the echo of maledictions and threats of death, the poor woman, waking from her daze, came to life, emitted one shrill wail, and snatching her boy up in her arms, started to run to the door. The man intercepted her.

'Come, come! Where are you off to, my lady?' he asked her, with harsh irony. 'Rousing the neighbourhood at this time of night? Stay home and stop your noise!'

The last words were spoken without any accompanying gesture of intimidation, but in a tone that froze Antonia's blood. Her first stupefaction had by this time given place to fever, the lucid fever of the instinct of self-preservation. A sudden thought flashed through her mind : she would appeal to him through the child. The father had never seen him, but after all he was his father. Catching the boy up, she carried him over to the light.

'Is that the kid?' murmured the convict, and taking up the candle he held it close to the boy's face. The latter, dazzled, blinked his eyes and covered his face with his hands, as if trying to hide from this unknown father whose name he had never heard pronounced excepting with universal fear and condemnation. He shrank back against his mother, and she at the same time nervously held him close, while her face grew whiter than wax.

'What an ugly kid!' muttered the father, setting the candle down again. 'He looks as if the witches had sucked him dry.'

Antonia, still holding the boy, leaned against the wall, half fainting. The room seemed to be circling around her, and the air was full of tiny flecks of blue light.

'Look here, isn't there anything to eat in the house?' demanded her husband. Antonia set the boy on the floor in a corner, where he sat, crying from fear and stifling his sobs, while she proceeded to hurry about the room, setting the table with trembling hands; she brought out some bread and a bottle of wine, and removed the pot of codfish from the fire, making herself a willing slave in the hope of placating the enemy. The convict took his seat and proceeded to eat voraciously, helping himself to repeated draughts of wine. She remained standing, staring in fascination at the hard, parchment-like face, with close-clipped hair, and the unmistakable prison pallor. He filled his glass again and reached it towards her.

'No, I don't want it,' stammered Antonia, for the wine, where the candlelight fell upon it, seemed to her imagination like a pool of blood.

He drank it himself, with a shrug of his shoulders, and replenished his plate with the codfish, which he consumed, greedily, feeding himself with his fingers and devouring huge slices of bread. His wife watched him as he ate, and a faint hope began to dawn in her heart. As soon as he had finished his meal, he might go out without killing her; in that case, she would lock and bar the door, and if he tried to come back to kill her, it would rouse the neighbours and they would hear her screams. Only it was quite likely that she would find it impossible to scream! She hawked repeatedly in order to clear her voice. Her husband, having eaten his fill, drew a cigar from his pocket, pinched off the tip with his finger nail, and tranquilly lighted it with the candle.

'Here, where are you going?' he called, seeing that his wife made a furtive movement towards the door. 'Let's enjoy ourselves in peace.'

'I must put the boy to bed,' she answered, scarcely knowing what she said, and she took refuge in the adjoining room, carrying the child in her arms. She felt sure that the murderer would not dare to enter there. How could he have the dreadful courage to do so? It was the room where the crime was committed, her mother's room; the room that she had shared before her marriage. The poverty that followed the old woman's death had forced Antonia to sell her own bed and use that of the deceased. Believing herself in security, she proceeded to undress the child, who now ventured to sob aloud, and with his face buried on her breast. All at once the door opened and the ex-convict came in.

Antonia saw him cast a side glance around the room; then he proceeded tranquilly to remove his shoes, to undress, and finally stretch himself in the murdered woman's bed. The charwoman felt that she must be dreaming; if her husband had drawn a knife, he would have frightened her less than by this horrible show of tranquillity. He meanwhile stretched and turned between the sheets, sighing with the contentment of a weary man who has obtained the luxury of a soft, clean bed.

'And you?' he exclaimed, turning towards Antonia, 'what are you sitting there for, as dumb as a post? Aren't you coming to bed?'

'No, I—I am not sleepy,' she temporized, with her teeth chattering.

'What if you aren't sleepy? Are you going to sit up all night?'

'No,—no,—there isn't room. You go to sleep. I'll get on here, some way or other.'

He uttered two or three coarse words.

'Are you afraid of me, do you hate me, or what on earth is the trouble? We'll see whether you aren't coming to bed! If you don't——'

He sat up, reached out his hands, and prepared to spring from the bed to the floor. But Antonia, with the fatalistic docility of a slave, had already begun to undress. Her hurrying fingers broke the strings, violently tore off the hooks and eyes, ripped her skirts and petticoats. In one corner of the room could still be heard the smothered sobbing of the boy.

It was the boy who summoned the neighbours the following morning by his desperate cries. They found Antonia still in bed, stretched out as if dead. A doctor, summoned in haste, declared that she was still alive, and bled her, but he could not draw from her one drop of blood. She passed away at noon, by a natural death, for there was no mark of violence upon her. The boy insisted that the man who had passed the night there had called her several times to get up, and seeing that she didn't answer, had gone away, running like a madman.

ANONYMOUS

LEOPOLDO ALAS
[1852–1901]

Leopoldo Alas, who used the pen name Clarín, *is best known for his discerning literary criticism. He also wrote two novels and numerous short stories. His best work, the novel* La Regenta (*1885*), *is a lengthy, detailed, naturalistic study of life in a provincial town. From his short stories, the touching* Adiós, Cordera! *is here presented.*

ADIÓS, CORDERA!

There were three; always the three! Rosa, Pinin and Cordera.

The Somonte meadow was a triangular cutting of velvety green, stretched like a tapestry, down hill across the mountains. The railroad from Oviedo to Gijon cut off one of its corners, the lower one. A telegraph pole, planted there like a standard of conquest, with its little white cups, and it parallel wires to right and left, represented to Rosa and Pinin the wide world, unexplored, mysterious, awful, forever unknown. Pinin, after thinking a good deal about it, and seeing the post day after day, quiet, inoffensive, neighbourly, with resolution, without doubt, accustoming itself to its surroundings and looking exactly like a dry tree, by force of habit got used to it, and his confidence led him to embrace the trunk and to climb up to the wires. But he never reached the porcelain cups aloft, for they reminded him of the little chocolate cups which he had seen in the rectory of Puao. When he realized he was so near the sacred mystery, a panic of veneration overwhelmed him, and he hastened to slip down until he touched the sward with his feet.

Rosa, less bold, but more enchanted with the unknown, was content to press her ear against the telegraph pole, and she passed minutes and even quarters of an hour listening to the tremendous metallic noises which the wind wrested out of the fibres of dry pine in contact with the wires. These vibrations, intense as those of a tuning fork held to the ear, sounded like a conflagration with their rhythmical pulsations, and to Rosa the messages which were passing seemed letters written over the wires in an incomprehensible language which unknown talked with unknown. What did it matter? Her interest was in the noise, for the sake of the noise itself, its tone and its mystery.

La Cordera, much more sedate than her companions, true it is, of an age much more mature, kept away from all communication with the civilized world, and looked from afar at the telegraph pole, as at something which was, in her mind, certainly a dead thing and useless, answering no good purpose unless it were to scratch her back against. She was a cow who had lived much. Reposing hours after hours, experienced in pastures, she knew how to make good use of her time. She meditated more than she ate, she enjoyed the pleasure of living in peace, beneath the grey and tranquil heaven of her native land, and peace nourishes the soul which the brutes have also, as well as we. And if it shall not be thought a profanation, one might say that the thoughts of the matron cow appear very similar to the soothing and bucolic odes of Horace.

She was present at the sports of the little shepherds, whose duty it was to guard her, as a grandmother might. If she could, she would have smiled at the idea that Rosa and Pinin should have as their mission in life to look after her in the meadow, her, Cordera, and to see that she did not go out of bounds, nor put herself in the way of the railroad train, nor jump into the neighbour's farm. What had she to do with jumping? What had she to do with going astray?

To graze each day for a while without losing time in raising her head through idle curiosity, cropping without hesitating the best mouthfuls, and afterwards to recline upon her haunches, either contemplating life or enjoying the delight of not suffering, or allowing herself to exist, that was her task.

Xatu (the bull) with the wide leaps through the pasture ground higher up. That was so long ago! and all the other dangerous adventures. Now, she could not remember when the last fly had bitten her!

The only thing which had disturbed that peace was the opening of the railroad. The first time Cordera saw the trains go by she was crazy. She jumped the hedge on the highest part of Somonte, ran through the neighbouring meadows, and her fright lasted many days, renewing itself more or less violently each time the machine began to appear in the neighbouring cut. Little by little she became accustomed to the harmless din. When she began to convince herself that it was a danger which would pass by, a catastrophe which was threatening without striking, she reduced her precautions to getting upon her feet, and to looking straight forward at the formidable monster, with her head raised. Later she did nothing but look without getting up, with antipathy and lack of confidence; she finished by not paying any attention to the trains at all.

In Pinin and Rosa the novelty of the railroad produced impressions more persistent and agreeable. If in the beginning it was an exhilaration, a mixture of superstitious fear and nervous excitement which caused them to break into screams, and to make gestures and absurd grimaces, afterwards it was a peaceful recreation, sweet, renewed several times a day. It was slow to wear out, that emotion of looking on at the dizzy progress, swift as the wind, of the great iron serpent which carried along within itself so great noise and so many unknown foreign persons.

But telegraph or railroad was of little account—a passing chance which was drowned in the sea of solitude which encircled the Somonte meadow, from whence no human habitation could be seen, and no noises of the world arrived except the passing of the train.

Mornings without end, beneath the passing of the sun, sometimes, amid the humming of the insects, the cow and the children awaited the approach of midday to go to the house. And finally eternal afternoons of sweet, silent sadness, in the same meadow, before the coming of the night, with the evening star as a mute witness on high. The clouds rolled there overhead. The shadows of the trees and of the rocks lengthened on the hill and in the dale; the birds went to bed; some stars began to shine in the darkest part of the blue sky, and Pinin and Rosa, the twins, the children of Anton de Chinta, their souls possessed by the sweet, dreamy serenity of the solemn and serious Nature, were quiet for hours and hours, after their games, never very noisy, seated near Cordera, who accompanied the august silence with the soft sound of her lazy bell.

In this quiet, in this inactive calm, there was love. The brother and sister loved each other like the two halves of a green fruit, united by the same life, with a bare consciousness of that in which they were distinct and of what separated them. Pinin and Rosa loved Cordera, their large, dun-coloured grandmother cow, whose udder appeared to be a foundling hospital. Cordera will remind a poet of the 'Zavala' of Rabayana, the holy cow. She resembled her in the amplitude of her form, in the solemn serenity of her slow and noble movements; the airs and graces of a dethroned idol, fallen but content with her lot, better satisfied to be a true cow than a false god. One might say that Cordera, as well as it is possible to guess those things, also loved the twins, whose duty it was to look after her. She had little gift of expression, but the patience with which she suffered them to use her as a hiding place, and for a mount, and for other things which caught the fancy of the shepherds, tacitly showed the affection of the pacifist and thoughtful animal.

In hard times Pinin and Rosa had given to Cordera the very

limit of solicitude and care. Anton de Chinta had not always had the Somonte meadow. That luxury was comparatively new. Years before Cordera had to go out on the Common, that is, to graze as she could upon mouthfuls of scant herbage along the roads and lanes, which served as both highway and pasturage. Pinin and Rosa in those days of want spied out the best croppings in the neighbourhood, the least disturbed, and guarded her from the thousand ills which cattle that must get their food on public roads are subject to. In the days of hunger in the stable where hay was scarce, and straw to make a warm bed for the cow was not to be had, Cordera owed to the labours of Pinin and Rosa the alleviation of her misery. And in the heroic days of maternity, when her calf arrived, and when the inevitable struggle ensued between the feeding and prosperity of the little one and the nourishing of the Chintas, which consisted of robbing from the mother cow every drop which was not necessary for the life of the new born calf! Rosa and Pinin, in this struggle, were always on the side of Cordera.

Anton de Chinta knew that he had been born to poverty, when he realised the impossibility of accomplishing that gilded dream of keeping a corral of his own with a yoke of oxen, at least. He owned, thanks to a thousand economies, which caused rivulets of sweat and purgatories of privation—yes, he owned one cow, Cordera; and he never got beyond that. Before he was able to buy another, he found himself in arrears to the overseer, who was the landlord of the cottage which he rented, and to pay him he was obliged to take to the market, though it wrung his heart, Cordera, the darling of his children. Chinta's wife had died two years after Anton had brought Cordera to their home. The stable and the marriage bed had a partition wall between, if you can call a web of chestnut branches and cornstalks a wall. Chinta's wife, the muse of economy, in that humble hovel, looking at the cow through a chink in the broken wall of branches, pointed her out as the salvation of her family.

'Take care of her. She is your support,' appeared to say the eyes of the poor, dying woman, who perished, exhausted by hunger and work. The love of the twin children had been centred on Cordera. As the lap of a mother, which the father could not replace, was the warmth of Cordera in the stable and there in Somonte. All this Anton understood in his own way, confusedly. Of the sale that was necessary he need not say a word to the children.

On Saturday, at dawn of day, in bad humour, Anton began

to walk toward Gijon, driving Cordera ahead of him, without more gear than her bell collar. Pinin and Rosa were asleep. On other days he used to wake them at daybreak. When they got up, they found themselves without Cordera. When at dusk Anton and Cordera came up the lane, fretful, tired and covered with dust, the father gave no explanations but the children guessed that there was danger.

He had not sold her because no one was willing to give the price he had put on her head—a price made excessive by a sophistry of affection; he asked much so that no one might dare bid. Those who had come near to try their luck had soon taken their departure, swearing at him while he looked with eyes of hate and distrust on any one who dared to insist on going near the price fixed. Up to the last moment Anton de Chinta stood in the market place of Humedal defying fate.

'They can't say I do not want to sell, only I cannot get for Cordera what she is worth.' Thus he deceived himself, and finally sighing, as though not quite satisfied, he took his way for the high road to Candas, amidst the confusion and noise of pigs and bullocks, oxen and cows which the country people of many parishes were driving with greater or lesser trouble, depending on how old the relationship between master and beast was.

In Natahoyo, at the crossing of two roads, Chinta again ran the risk of losing Cordera; a neighbour of Carrió who had hung around all day offering only a little less than Chinta asked, made a final attack; somewhat drunk he raised his bid higher and higher, struggling between covetousness and desire to get the cow.

They stood motionless, their hands clasped in the middle of the highway, stopping the traffic. At last covetousness won the day; the small amount of fifty centimos kept them apart, like an abyss; they let go their hands, and each went his way, Anton by a little lane which led through honeysuckles which were not in bloom and flowering bramble berries to his home.

From the day on which they suspected danger, Pinin and Rosa were never at ease. In the middle of the week the superintendent came himself to the corral of Anton. He was a countryman of the same parish, ill tempered and cruel to tenants who were in debt. The landlord would not wait any longer. The cow would have to be sold at a low price. He must pay or get out into the street. On the Saturday following, Pinin went to Humedal with his father. The boy looked with horror at the meat contractors, tyrants of the market. Cordera was sold at a fair price to the highest bidder, a man from Castile. They made a brand on her skin, and sent her back to her stable at Puao, mournfully tinkling her bell. Behind her walked Anton de Chinta in silence and Pinin, with eyes like fists. When Rosa heard of the sale, she threw her arms around the neck of Cordera, who submitted to her embraces as she used to do to the yoke.

'We're losing our old friend,' thought the despondent Anton. She was only a dumb animal, but his children had no other mother or grandmother.

Some days afterwards, in the green field of Somonte, the silence was funereal. Cordera, who was ignorant of her fate, was resting and eating *sub specie aeternitatis*, as she would rest and eat until the moment the cruel blow would strike her dead. But Rosa and Pinin remained desolate, stretched on the grass, useless in the future. They looked with anger at the trains which passed and at the telegraph wires. It was that unknown world, on the one side and on the other, which was taking their beloved Cordera away from them.

Friday at dusk was the time of departure. There came an agent of the buyer of Castile for the cattle. He paid; Anton and the agent had a drink and Cordera was led out to the road. Anton had been plying the bottle, and was excited. Also the weight of the money in his purse enlivened him. He wanted to rattle on. He talked much, praised the excellences of the cow. The other smiled, for the praises of Anton were of no concern to him. The cow gave so many quarts of milk? She was obedient under the yoke? Strong under a burden? What did it matter, if in a few days she would be cut up into steaks and other savoury bits? Anton did not like to think of that. He imagined her alive and working, serving some other farmer, forgetful of him and his children, but alive and happy.

Pinin and Rosa, seated on a mound, thinking of nothing but Cordera and her troubles, their hands clasped, looked at the enemy with terror-stricken eyes. At the last moment they threw themselves upon their friend with kisses and hugs, and would not let go of her; while Anton, overcome by the excitement of the wine, looked as if he had suffered a paralytic stroke. He crossed his arms and went into the dark corral. The children followed for quite a distance through the lane of high hedges Cordera and the agent, the former going against her will with a stranger, and at such an unusual hour. At last they had to separate. Anton called from the house.

'Bah, children, come here; I tell you there has been enough of trifles,' he called, with tears in his voice.

Night was falling, and the long lane was growing dark beneath the vault of high hedges. The form of Cordera became black in the distance. Then there remained nothing but the slow tinkle of the bell, vanishing in the distance amidst the melancholy chirrups of countless crickets.

'Adiós, Cordera,' cried Rosa in tears. 'Good-bye, Cordera of my soul !'

'Good-bye, Cordera !' repeated Pinin, as excited as Rosa.

'Good-bye,' answered last of all the bell, in its own way, until its sad lament was lost among the many sounds of a July evening in a country village.

On the following morning at the usual hour, very early, Pinin and Rosa were at the Somonte meadow. That lonely spot never before had seemed desolate to them, but that day, Somonte without Cordera was like the desert.

Suddenly a locomotive whistled, steam appeared, an instant later the train. In an inclosed box car with tall, narrow windows or air vents, were dimly seen the heads of the cows who, bewildered, were looking through the openings.

'Adiós, Cordera,' shouted Rosa, guessing that her friend, the grandmother cow, was there.

'Adiós, Cordera,' shrieked Pinin, in the same belief, shaking his fist at the train which was flying by on its way to Castile. And weeping, the lad cried out, more acquainted than his sister with the ways of the world :

'They are taking her to the slaughter house so that rich gentlemen may eat meat.'

'Adiós, Cordera.'

'Adiós, Cordera.'

Both Rosa and Pinin looked with anger at the railway and the telegraph, the symbols of that enemy, the world, which was carrying off and would devour the companion of so many lonely hours, the sharer of tenderness so great, so silent, in order to convert her into tid-bits for rich gluttons.

'Adiós, Cordera; Adiós, Cordera.'

.   .   .

There passed many years. Pinin grew to be a young man, and was taken as a conscript by the King. The Carlist war was raging. Anton de Chinta was a workman for a boss of the beaten side. He had no influence to get Pinin declared unfit for service. To tell the truth, the young man was like a young oak tree.

And one dreary afternoon in October, Rosa, in the Somonte

meadow, alone, was waiting for the passing of the local train for Gijon, which was taking away from her her only love, her brother. The engine whistled in the distance, the train appeared in the cut, passed like a flash of lightning. Rosa, almost ground by the wheels, could see for an instant in a third-class coach a multitude of heads of poor conscripts who shouted and made gestures, saluting the trees, the soil, the fields, all the familiar country and the humble homes of those who were going to die in fratricidal struggles of the great fatherland in the service of a King, and for ideas of which they knew nothing.

Pinin, with half his body out the window, stretched his arm out to his sister. They almost touched each other, and Rosa could hear amidst the noise of the wheels and the clamour of the recruits, the distant voice of her brother, who cried out as though inspired by a recollection of a far away grief :

'Adiós, Rosa ! . . . Adiós, Cordera !'

'Adiós, Pinin, Pinin of my soul !'

He was going away like the other, like the grandmother cow, The world was taking him away. The cow had been meat for gluttons; her own flesh and blood was to be cannon fodder, on account of the madness of the world, for the ambitions of others.

Amidst the confusion of grief and of ideas, thus thought the poor sister, as she saw the train lose itself in the distance, whistling mournfully, with a whistle which shook the chestnut trees, the open plains and the huge rocks. How all alone she was left; and now the Somonte meadow seemed like a desert.

'Adiós, Pinin ! Adiós, Cordera !'

With what hatred Rosa looked at the road-bed, smirched with dead coals, with what anger at the telegraph wires. Oh, Cordera was right not to go near them. Such was the world, the unknown, which was taking everything away from her. And without thinking, Rosa leaned her head against the telegraph pole, rising like a standard on the promontory of Somonte, and listened to its inward chant. And now she understood it. It was the tune of tears, of leave-taking, of loneliness, of death.

In the swift vibrations, almost lamentations, she seemed to hear a far away voice which was sobbing along the track :

'Adiós, Rosa ! Adiós, Cordera !'

CHARLES B. MᶜMICHAEL

(Revised by the Editors)

ARMANDO PALACIO VALDÉS
[1853–1938]

One of Spain's most popular novelists, both in that country and abroad, Armando Palacio Valdés is noted for the readability of his works. His style is easy and uncluttered; his tone, good-humoured; his characterizations, interesting. In particular he is adept at the art of description, drawing word-pictures of such compelling charm that the reader feels almost literally transported into the scene.

Among his best-known novels are La hermana San Sulpicio (*1889*), José (*1885*) *and* Marta y María (*1883*). La hermana San Sulpicio *concerns the courtship of an Andalusian novice by a Galician poet.* José *tells a tale of life among Asturian fishermen.* Marta y María *deals with two sisters, one of whom becomes fanatically steeped in mysticism.*

MARTA AND MARIA

HOW THE MARQUIS OF PEÑALTA BECAME THE DUKE OF THURINGEN

'*Mi Queridisimo Ricardo,*—

'For some time I have been anxious to tell you a thought that has filled my mind, but I have not had the courage. I know your nature well : you are extremely impetuous, and thus many times, instead of reflecting on my words and trying to understand their meaning, you would flare up like gunpowder, spoil everything, and frighten me terribly, as on the evening when we celebrated mamma's fête-day. Accordingly, after much vacillation, I have decided to tell you by letter and not by word of mouth.

'The thought that disturbs me of late is to ask you to postpone our wedding still a little longer. Don't get angry, Ricardo *mio*, and read on calmly. I am sure that the first thought that will occur to your mind is that I don't love you. How mistaken you would be to think such a thing ! If you could read in my soul, you would see that your love holds my conscience in its sway, and this I deplore bitterly. But that is not the question now.

'Are you sure, Ricardo, that you and I are properly trained to enter upon a state which entails so many and such serious responsibilities? Have you thought well of what the sacrament of marriage means? Is there not in our hearts rather an unreflecting inclination, mixed, perhaps, with carnal impulses, than a serious desire to undertake an austere, religious life, becoming in a Christian family, educating our children in the fear of God and in the practice of virtue? If you reflect a little on how frivolous hitherto our love has been, and on the sins which we are constantly committing, you cannot but agree with me that two young people, so wanting in gravity and genuine virtue, are not authorized by God to bring up and direct a family. I should feel a great smiting of the conscience if I were married now (and you ought to feel the same), and I believe that God could not bless or make our union happy. If it is to be blessed, we must make ourselves worthy of celebrating it, by leaving forever behind us our frivolous, worldly manner of loving, for another, more lofty and spiritual, by refraining absolutely from certain earthly manifestations to which we are impelled by our great love, and by making preparations for it, during a few months at least, by a virtuous and devout life, by performing a few sacrifices and works of charity, and by constantly imploring God to illumine our minds, and give us power to fulfil the duties imposed upon us by the new state.

'There is an example in history which ought to encourage us greatly in doing what I propose. The beloved Saint Isabel of Hungary had been betrothed from early youth to the Duke Luis of Thuringen, but the nuptials were not celebrated until both reached the proper age. After the betrothal was celebrated, Isabel and Luis did not separate, but lived in the same palace, as though they had been brother and sister, until, by the will of God, they became husband and wife. The pious sentiments of the lovers, together with the austere education which was given them, made their affection always pure and upright, founding the unchangeable union of their hearts, not on the ephemeral sentiments of a purely human attraction, but on a common faith and the stern observance of all the virtues inculcated by this faith. Until they were united by the indissoluble bond of matrimony, they always called each other brother and sister; and even after they were married, they frequently used to apply this sweet name to each other.

'I confess, Ricardo, that the spectacle of those noble and holy young people has an unspeakable attraction for me. Love sanctified in such a way is a thousand times more beautiful, and bestows upon the heart purer and loftier pleasures. Why should we not follow, as far as possible, the steps of that illustrious husband and wife, the pattern of abnegation and tenderness, as well as of purity and fidelity? Why should you not imitate, my beloved Ricardo, the stern virtue of the young Duke of Thuringen, the nobleness and dignity of all his actions, the innocence and modesty of his soul, never found guilty of falsehood,—virtues which in no respect were opposed to the valour and boldness of which he always gave eminent proofs? For my part, I promise you to imitate, according to the measure of my feeble strength, the tenderness, the obedience, and the faithfulness of his saintly spouse Isabel, living subject to the law of God, within the affection which I profess for you.

'This is what I propose to you, and desire to do. Don't get angry, for God's sake, dear Ricardo. Reflect over what I have just said, and you will see how right I am. Doubt not that I love you much, much,—I, who am, for the time being,

'Your sister,
'Maria.'

THE ROAD TO PERFECTION

The letter which we have just read led to a very important crisis in the lives of our lovers. Ricardo at first was furious, and wrote a long answer to his betrothed, announcing the end of their acquaintance, but he did not send it. Then he held a consultation with her in which he overwhelmed her with recriminations and insults, saying that all she had written in her letter was nothing but a tissue of follies and absurdities, manufactured on purpose to hide her treachery; that she might have dismissed him in some way not so grotesque; that although he had no claim upon her love, at least he might and ought to demand the frankness and loyalty which he had always shown; that for a long time back he had noticed her coldness and indifference, but he could never have believed that she would make use of a pretext so ridiculous and so absurd for breaking the tie that united them, etc., etc. Maria received this storm of contumely with great humility, assuring him with gentle words of persuasion, when he left her a moment's chance to speak, that she still loved him with all her soul; that he might put her love to the test as often as he pleased, since she was ready to make whatever sacrifice he demanded, except what went against her conscience; that his suspicions of her untruth and treachery cut her to the heart, but she forgave him because she was aware of his excited state of mind; that she likewise felt it keenly that he should call the motives of her resolution grotesque and ridiculous when she found them so worthy; and, in fine, that she begged him to calm himself.

After the young marquis had thoroughly vented his ill-feeling without result, he began to get off his high horse and try the effect of skilful reasoning, and then he changed to entreaties, but without any better results. He employed all the devices of genius and all the tender and expressive words dictated by his honourable heart, in order to convince her that neither of them was fortunately under the necessity of mourning for their sins like two criminals; since if they were not better than the average of humanity, they were at least as good; and as for their skill and judgment in governing themselves and their children in matrimony, he believed that they were no less fitted than the rest, and that in the end they would come out as well as other people. All was useless. The young woman met argument with argument, and her lover's prayers, sprinkled with endearments, with a firm and obstinate silence. Ricardo, in a state of tribulation . . . went straight to Don Mariano, whom he loved like a father, to tell him the state of things, and ask his aid and advice. The latter was highly surprised and disturbed when he read his daughter's letter. He read it over many times as though he could not get the key of it, and at each new reading he found it more obscure and inexplicable. Finally he handed it back with a gesture of dismay, signifying that his daughter must have lost her wits, for he could not understand any such nonsense. . . .

. . . It is easy to imagine the effect made upon him by his daughter's letter. He looked upon it as one of those many extravagant hobbies which she had passed through in her life, and he solemnly promised Ricardo to make her desist from such folly. But after he had called her to his room and spent about two hours closeted with her, he began to suspect that the thing was not so easy as it appeared at first sight. Neither by turning her austere plan into ridicule by his jests, nor by showing that he was annoyed, nor by descending to entreaties, was our worthy *caballero* able to accomplish anything. Maria met these attacks like her lover's, with a humble but resolute attitude impossible to overcome. No other way was left them but to resign themselves, and this they both did perforce with the secret hope that the girl would very soon change of her own accord when once her caprice was satisfied. Accordingly the wedding was indefinitely postponed, and poor Ricardo began to play his part as Duke of Thuringen almost as ill as a Spanish actor.

From that time forth his interviews with Maria became less frequent and familiar. The girl seemed to shun him and to avoid opportunities of talking confidentially with him as she used. Ricardo eagerly sought them, sometimes employing them in bitter expostulations, at others in softly whispering a thousand passionate phrases. She always appeared sweet and affectionate, but endeavoured to turn the conversation to serious subjects. Ricardo still caressed her whenever he had an opportunity, but he no longer obtained from her the usual reciprocation in spite of the incredible efforts which he made to obtain it. And not only he did not obtain this grace, but little by little the girl came to avoid his familiarities by always talking with him in the presence of others. One day when he found her alone in the dining-room, he said to himself with inward delight, 'She is mine.' And creeping up behind her carefully, he gave her a ringing kiss on her neck. Maria sprang suddenly from her chair and said, with a certain sweetness not free from severity,

'Ricardo, don't do that again !'

'Why not?'

'Because I don't like it.'

'How long since?'

'I never did; don't be foolish.' She said these words with asperity, and another unpleasant stage in Ricardo's love was signalized. Almost absolutely ceased those happy moments of fond raptures, sweet and delicious as the pleasures of the angels in which the poesy of spirit and matter is indistinguishable, the prospect of which kindles and stirs the deepest roots of our being, and their remembrance throws over all our lives, even for the most prosaic of men, a vague and poetic melancholy helping us to endure the rebuffs of existence and to contemplate without envy the felicity of others. The most that the young marquis obtained grudgingly from his sweetheart was the permission to give her a brotherly kiss on the forehead from time to time. And there is no need of telling my experienced readers, for they must be able to imagine it, that with this enforced fast the young man's love far from growing less, increased and became violent beyond all power of words.

Maria was able fully to devote herself to the life of perfection toward which she had felt such vehement aspiration. The hours of the day seemed to her too few for her prayers, both at church and at home, and for the repentance of her sins. She attended the sacraments more and more, and she was present and assisted with her sympathy and money in all the religious solemnities which were celebrated in the town. The time left free from her prayers she spent in reading books of devotion, which, in a short time, formed a library almost as numerous as her novels. The lives of the saints pleased her above all, and she soon devoured a multitude of them, paying most attention, as was logical, to the lives of those who reached the greatest glory and brough the greatest splendour to the Church,—the life of Saint Teresa, that of Saint Catalina of Siena, of Saint Gertrudis, of Saint Isabel, Saint Eulalia, Saint Monica, and many others who, without having been canonized, were celebrated for their piety and for the spiritual grace which God bestowed upon them, like the holy Margarita of Alacoque, Mademoiselle de Melun, and others. These works made a very profound impression on our young lady's ardent and enthusiastic mind, driving her farther and farther along the road to perfection. The incredible and marvellous powers of those heroic souls, who, through love and charity, succeeded in lifting themselves to heaven, and in enjoying through anticipation, while still on earth, the delights reserved for the blessed, filled her with deep, fervent admiration. She felt an ecstasy over the most insignificant incidents in the lives of the saints, where God often showed them that He held them as His chosen ones, and would not let the world entice them away, as, for example, the scene of the miraculous toad which Saint Teresa saw talking in the garden with a *caballero* toward whom she felt a drawing; the sudden death of Buenaventura, Saint Catalina's sister, who was leading that holy woman along the worldly path of bodily adornments and pleasures; and many others which filled the books aforesaid. Maria regarded these notable heroines of religion with the same emotion and astonishment as one regards the phenomena and marvels of Nature. A long time passed before she dared to lift her eyes toward them in the way of imitation; she contented herself with beseeching them, through interminable prayers, to intercede with God to pardon her sins. She bought the finest effigies that she found and, when she had caused them to be richly framed, she hung them up on the walls of her room. To do this she had to take down Malec-Kadel and many other warriors of the Middle Ages which had invaded them. She was especially carried away by the scenes of their infancy, and by the first steps which these blessed women had taken along the road to perfection; but when she reached that part of their lives which marked the apogee of their glory on earth, when God, overcome by their steadfast love, their fidelity, and the wonderful penances imposed upon themselves, began to grant them favours and spiritual gifts by means of ecstasies and visions, she remained somewhat disturbed and even cast down. She did not as yet comprehend the mystic delight of direct communication through the senses between the soul and God, and she confessed with great compunction that if one of these miraculous visions were to be vouchsafed her, she should feel much greater fear than pleasure.

Nevertheless, before long, the desire to imitate them sprang up in her heart. It is always a short step from admiration to imitation. She began where it was proper, that is, by imitating their humility. Hitherto she had been modest, but not to such a degree as not to enjoy being flattered and applauded; but from this time forth she not only carefully avoided all praise, but she repelled those who offered it, and even tried to hide her talents so as to give her friends no chance to praise her. She began to talk as little as possible with friends or members of the family, and to do on the instant whatever they asked her to, lamenting in her heart that they did not give her harsh commands. She managed to have the servants help her at table after all the rest, and always give her stale bread instead of fresh. To conquer the natural impulses of selfishness she showed those who had offended her more affability than others, and anyone had only to offend her pride more or less for her immediately to overwhelm them with attentions, as though she owed them gratitude. On the other hand, to those who, as she knew, loved and admired her, she took delight in seeming peevish, so that they might not think her better than she really was.

Having started out on this pious path, which had been travelled by all the saints for the glory of God and of the human race, since the virtue of humility raises man above his own nature, conquering the passion deepest rooted in the human heart, and, of all virtues is the one that best proves the power of the spirit, and inspires respect even in the most unbelieving of men; having started out, I say on this pious path, and being aided by vivid imagination, she performed a number of strange deeds, well-nigh incomprehensible to those whose attention is turned to the world and not to religious things, deeds which the illustrious biographers of Saint Isabel call *secret and holy fancies*, serving as the mystic steps whereby the soul mounts to perfection and communicates with God. One day, for example, it came into her mind to eat humbly with the servants as though she were one of them. In order to do this, when dinner-time came, she pretended to have a headache, and kept in her chamber; but when the family were gathered in the dining-room, she softly ran downstairs to the kitchen, and there she stayed all through the dinner-hour, helping herself to the remains of the food, to the surprise and admiration of the servants. Another day, when it seemed to her that she had not answered her father with sufficient respect, she suddenly presented herself in his office, fell on her knees, and begged his pardon. Don Mariano lifted her from the floor, with startled eyes :

'But, my daughter, suppose you have not offended me or committed any fault? And even if you had, there is no need of going to these extremes. What nonsense ! Come, give me a kiss, and go and sew with your sister, and don't frighten me again with such absurdities !'

Maria did not meet with the contrarieties in the bosom of her family that she would have liked, in the way of test. Her father and sister, though they did not encourage her in her devotions, said nothing to oppose her; and each day they showed her more and more affection, which was the natural consequence of the growing sweetness and gentleness of her character. Her mother adored her with foolish frenzy, blindly applauded all her acts of piety, and never wearied of praising to the skies the virtue and talent of her first-born. The servants likewise joined their voices in a chorus of flatteries, spreading all over town the fame of her virtues, and crowning her with a halo of respect and sanctity. As far as such things influenced her salvation, our maiden would have preferred a cruel, tyrannical father, who laid harsh commands upon her, or a disagreeable mother or an envious sister, who would not let her live in peace, since, according to the biographies which she read, no saint had been free from suffering persecutions in her own family. She grieved inwardly at the ease and comfort which she enjoyed at home, and she thought that she suffered nothing for the God who had redeemed us with His blood. She would have liked it had a calumny been breathed about her, such as Palmerina caused Saint Catalina of Siena to suffer, so that she might be scorned and maltreated; but no one in the house or out of it dreamed of doing such a thing.

To compensate for this absence of persecutions, she mortified her flesh with fasting and penances, always performing those which were more unpleasant to her. Some dish on the table was distasteful to her; then she imposed upon herself the penance of eating it, leaving others, of which she was extremely fond, untouched. She went so far as to put aloes in some, in imitation of what was done by Saint Nicolas of Tolentino. On Fridays she fasted rigorously on bread and water, performing miracles of shrewdness to prevent her father from discovering it; for she felt certain that if he knew it, he would not give his consent.

She always wore a locket around her neck, containing the picture of her betrothed. One day, when he had succeeded in having a moment's conversation alone with her, she said to him,

'Listen, Ricardo; if you would not be vexed, I would tell you something.'

'What is it?' hastily asked the young man, with the sudden alarm of one who is always afraid of some misfortune.

'I see that I am going to offend you—but I will tell you. I have taken your picture out of the locket.'

Ricardo's face expressed amazement.

'And the worst is, that I have put another in its place.'

The expression of amazement changed into one of such pain, that Maria, on looking in his contracted and grief-stricken face, could not refrain from breaking out into a fresh, ringing peal of merry laughter, such as in former times used to ripple from her lips all the time, and which little by little had decreased, as though the fire of light and joy from which they came had died down.

'Good heavens! what a long face! Wait! Now I'll show your substitute, so as to make you suffer more.'

And taking the locket from her neck she showed it to him. It held the effigy of Jesus crowned with thorns. Ricardo, half satisfied and half vexed, answered with a smile.

'Now kiss it!'

The young man obeyed instantly, placing his lips on the picture of the Lord, and at the same time touching the rosy fingers that held it out to him. Maria withdrew them and ran away.

NATHAN HASKELL DOLE

JOSÉ ECHEGARAY
[1832–1916]

A remarkable man who had been a brilliant mathematician, engineer and politician before turning to the theatre, José Echegaray wrote his first drama after the age of forty. During the next thirty years he poured out more than sixty plays.

They are for the most part exaggerated, moralizing melodramas. But Echegaray was Spain's most popular dramatist during the last quarter of the nineteenth century, and in 1904 he was awarded the Nobel Prize for literature, thus becoming the first Spaniard to be so honoured.

His masterpiece, El gran Galeoto (1881), is a powerful drama whose theme is the destruction of a happy home by the consuming force of slander. It is written in verse, with a prose prologue.

THE GREAT GALEOTO

PROLOGUE

Ernesto's *study. To the left, a french window; to the right, a door.—Nearly in the centre, a table on which are books, papers, and a lighted lamp.—To the right is a sofa. It is evening.* Ernesto *is seated at the table, as though about to write.*

ERN. There's no use. I can't do it. It is impossible. I am simply contending with the impossible. The idea is here; it is stirring in my brain; I can feel it. Sometimes a light from within illumines it and I see it with its shifting form and vague contours, and suddenly there sound in the hidden depths voices that give it life; cries of grief, sighs of love, sardonic, mocking laughter—a whole world of living, struggling passions. They break from me, and spread out, and fill the air all about me! Then, then, I say to myself, the moment has come, and I take up my pen, and with eyes gazing into space, with straining ears, with fast-beating heart, I bend over my paper.—But oh, the irony of impotence! The contours become blurred, the vision disappears, the shouts and sighs die away, and nothingness, nothingness surrounds me! The desolation of empty space, of meaningless thought,' of deadly weariness! More than all that, the desolation of an idle pen and a barren page—a page bereft of all life-giving thought. Ah, how many forms has nothingness, and how it mocks, dark and silent, at creatures of my sort! Many, many forms :—the colourless canvas, the shapeless piece of marble, the discordant sound, but none more irritating, more mocking, more blighting, than this worthless pen and this blank paper. Ah, I cannot cover you, but I can destroy you, vile accomplice in my wrecked ambitions and my everlasting humiliation!—So, so,—smaller, still smaller. (*Tearing the paper— then, a pause.*) Well, it's fortunate that no one saw me, for at best such ranting is foolish, and it's all wrong. No—I will not give in; I will think harder, harder, until I conquer or blow up in a thousand pieces. No, I will never admit I am beaten. Come, let's see whether now——

(*Enter Don Julian, right, wearing a frock coat and carrying his overcoat on his arm. He looks in at the door but doesn't come in.*)

JUL. Hello, Ernesto!

ERN. Don Julian!

JUL. Still working? Am I disturbing you?

ERN. Disturbing me? Indeed, no. Come in, come in, Don Julian. Where's Teodora?

JUL. We've just come from the opera. She went up to the third floor with my brother and his wife to see some purchases of Mercedes, and I was on my way to my own room, when I saw a light in yours and looked in to say good night.

ERN. Were there many people there?

JUL. A good many—as usual. All my friends were asking for you. They were surprised at your not going.

ERN. How kind of them!

JUL. Not so very, considering all that you deserve. But how about you? Have you made good use of these three hours of solitude and inspiration?

ERN. Solitude, yes; inspiration, no. That would not come to me, though I called upon it desperately and with passion.

JUL. It wouldn't obey the summons?

ERN. No, and this was not the first time. But I did make a profitable discovery, though I accomplished nothing.

JUL. What?

ERN. Simply this—that I am a poor good-for-nothing.

JUL. Good-for-nothing! Well, that's a profitable discovery, indeed.

ERN. Precisely.

JUL. And why so disgusted with yourself? Isn't the play you told about the other day going well?

ERN. I'm the one who is going—out of my mind!

JUL. And what is all this trouble that inspiration and the play together are making for my Ernesto?

ERN. The trouble is this : when I conceived it I thought the idea a good one; but when I give it form and dress it out in the proper stage trappings the result is extraordinary; contrary to all laws of the drama; utterly impossible.

JUL. But why impossible? Come, tell me about it. I am curious.

ERN. Imagine, then, that the principal character, the one who creates the drama, who develops, who animates it, who brings about the catastrophe, and who thrives upon that catastrophe and revels in it—that person cannot appear on the stage.

JUL. Is he so ugly? Or so repulsive? Or so wicked?

ERN. It's not that. He is no uglier than any one else—than you or I. Nor is he bad. Neither bad nor good. Repulsive? No indeed. I am not such a sceptic, nor such a misanthrope, nor so at odds with the world that I would say such a thing or commit such an injustice.

JUL. Well, then, what is the reason?

ERN. Don Julian, the reason is that there probably wouldn't be room on the stage for the character in question.

JUL. Good heavens, listen to the man! Is this a mythological play, then, and do Titans appear on the stage?

ERN. They are Titans; but a modern variety.

JUL. In short?

ERN. In short this character is—*Everybody*.

JUL. *Everybody!* Well, you are right! There's not room in the theatre for everybody. That is an indisputable fact that has often been demonstrated.

ERN. Now you see how right I was.

JUL. Not altogether. *Everybody* can be condensed into a certain number of types, or characters. I don't understand these things myself, but I have heard that authors have done it more than once.

ERN. Yes, but in my case, that is, in my play, it can't be done.

JUL. Why not?

ERN. For many reasons that it would take too long to explain; especially at this time of night.

JUL. Never mind, let's have some of them.

ERN. Well then, each part of this vast whole, each head of this thousand-headed monster, of this Titan of today whom I call *Everybody*, takes part in my play only for the briefest instant, speaks one word and no more, gives one glance; perhaps his entire action consists in the suggestion of one smile; he appears for a moment and goes away again; he works without passion, without guile, without malice, indifferently, and absently—often *by* his very abstraction.

JUL. And what then?

ERN. From those words, from those fleeting glances, from those indifferent smiles, from all those little whispers, from all those peccadilloes; from all these things that we might call insignificant rays of dramatic light, when brought to a focus in one family, result the spark and the explosion, the struggle and the victims. If I represent the whole of mankind by a given number of types or symbolic characters, I have to ascribe to each one that which is really distributed among many, with the result that a certain number of characters must appear who are made repulsive by vices that lack verisimilitude, whose crimes have no object. And, as an additional result, there is the danger that people will believe I am trying to paint society as evil, corrupt, and cruel, when I only want to show that not even the most insignificant acts are really insignificant or impotent for good or evil; for, gathered together by the mysterious agencies of modern life, they may succeed in producing tremendous results.

JUL. Come, stop, stop! That is all dreadfully metaphysical. I get a glimmering, but the clouds are pretty thick. In fact, you understand more than I do about these things. Now, if it were a question of drafts, of notes, of letters of credit, of discount, it would be another matter.

ERN. Oh, no, you have common sense, which is the main thing.

JUL. Thanks, Ernesto, you are very kind.

ERN. But are you convinced?

JUL. No, I'm not. There must be some way of getting round the difficulty.

ERN. If only there were!

JUL. Is there something more?

ERN. I should say so! Tell me, what is the moving force of the drama?

JUL. I don't know exactly what you mean by the moving force of the drama, but I will say that I don't find any pleasure in plays in which there are no love-affairs; preferably unhappy love-affairs, for I have plenty of happy love-making in my own house with my Teodora.

ERN. Good. Splendid! Well, in my play there is hardly any love-making at all.

JUL. Bad, very bad indeed, I say. Listen, I don't know what your play is about, but I am afraid that it won't interest anybody.

ERN. That's just what I told you. Still, love-making might be put in, and even a little jealousy.

JUL. Well, with that, with an interesting and well-developed intrigue, with some really striking situation . . .

ERN. No, señor, certainly not that. Everything must be quite commonplace, almost vulgar. This drama can have no outward manifestation. It goes on in the hearts and minds of the characters; it progresses slowly; today it is a question of a thought; tomorrow of a heartbeat; gradually the will is undermined . . .

JUL. But how is all this shown? How are these inner struggles expressed? Who tells the audience about them? Where are they seen? Are we to spend the whole evening in pursuit of a glance, a sigh, a gesture, a word? My dear boy, that is no sort of amusement. When a man wants to meddle with such abstractions he studies philosophy.

ERN. That's it, exactly. You repeat my thoughts like an echo.

JUL. I don't want to discourage you, however. You probably know what you are doing. And, even though the play may be a little colourless, even though it may seem a bit heavy and uninteresting, so long as it has a fine climax and the catastrophe . . . eh?

ERN. Catastrophe—climax! They have hardly come when the curtain falls.

JUL. You mean that the play begins when the play ends?

ERN. I'm afraid so—though, of course, I shall try to put a little warmth into it.

JUL. Come now, what you ought to do is write the second play, the one that begins when the first ends; for the first, judging by what you say, isn't worth the trouble—and plenty of trouble it's bound to give you.

ERN. I was convinced of that.

JUL. And now we both are—thanks to your cleverness and the force of your logic. What is the title?

ERN. Title! Why, that's another thing. It has no title.

JUL. What! What did you say? No title, either?

ERN. No, señor.

JUL. Well, Ernesto, you must have been asleep when I came in— you were having a nightmare and now you are telling me your dreams.

ERN. Dreaming? Yes. A nightmare? Perhaps. And I am telling you my dreams, good and bad. You have common sense, and you always guess right in everything.

JUL. It didn't take much penetration to guess right in this case. A play in which the principal character doesn't appear, in which there is almost no love-making, in which nothing happens that doesn't happen every day, which begins as the curtain falls on the last act, and which has no title.—Well, I don't see how it can be written, how it can be acted, or how any one can be found to listen to it,—or, indeed, how it is a play at all.

ERN. Ah, but it is a play. The only trouble is that I must give it form, and that I don't know how to do.

JUL. Do you want my advice?

ERN. Your advice? The advice of my friend, my benefactor, my second father! Oh, Don Julian!

JUL. Come, come, Ernesto, let us not have a little sentimental play of our own here in place of yours which we have pronounced impossible. I only asked you whether you wanted to know my advice.

ERN. And I said, Yes.

JUL. Well, forget all about plays—go to bed—go to sleep—go shooting with me tomorrow, kill any number of partridges instead of killing two characters, and perhaps having the audience kill you —and when all is said and done, you'll be thankful to me.

ERN. That can't be : I must write the play.

JUL. But, my dear fellow, you must have thought of it by way of penance for your sins.

ERN. I don't know why it happened, but think of it I did. I feel it stirring in my mind, it begs for life in the outer world, and I am bound to give it that.

JUL. Can't you find some other plot?

ERN. But what about this idea?

JUL. Let the devil take care of it.

ERN. Ah, Don Julian, do you think that when an idea has been hammered out in our minds, we can destroy it and bring it to naught whenever we choose? I should like to think of another play, but this accursed one won't let me until it has been born into the world.

JUL. There's no use talking, then. I only hope you get some light on the subject.

ERN. That is the question, as Hamlet says.

JUL. (*In a low voice, with mock mystery.*) Couldn't you put it in the literary orphanage for anonymous works?

ERN. Don Julian, I am a man of conscience. My children, good or bad, are legitimate, and shall bear my name.

JUL. I'll say no more. It must be—it is written.

ERN. I only wish it were. Unfortunately it is not written, but no matter, if I don't write it, someone else will.

JUL. Well, to work! Good luck, and don't let any one get ahead of you.

TEO. (*Without.*) Julian! Julian!

JUL. There's Teodora!

TEO. Are you here, Julian?

JUL. Yes, here I am. Come in !

(Enter Teodora.)

TEO. Good evening, Ernesto.

ERN. Good evening, Teodora. Did they sing well?

TEO. As usual. Have you done a lot of work?

ERN. As usual; nothing.

TEO. Why, you might better have gone with us. All my friends were asking for you.

ERN. It seems that everybody is taking an interest in me.

JUL. I should say so; since you are going to make *Everybody* the principal character in your play, naturally it is to his interest to have you for his friend.

TEO. A play?

JUL. Hush, it's a great mystery; you mustn't ask anything about it. It has no title, no actors, no action, no catastrophe! Oh, how sublime! Good night, Ernesto.—Come, Teodora.

ERN. Good-bye, Julian.

TEO. Until tomorrow.

ERN. Good night.

TEO. (*To* Julian.) How preoccupied Mercedes seemed !

JUL. And Severo was in a rage.

TEO. I wonder why.

JUL. I'm sure I don't know. Pepito, on the other hand, was lively enough for both.

TEO. He always is—and speaking ill of every one.

JUL. A character for Ernesto's play.

(*Teodora and* Julian *go out, right.*)

ERN. Let Julian say what he likes, I am not going to give up my undertaking. It would be rank cowardice. No, I will not retreat. Forward! (*He rises and walks up and down in agitation. Then he goes over to the french window.*) Night, lend me your protection, for against your blackness the luminous outlines of my inspiration are defined more clearly than against the blue cloak of day. Lift up your roofs, ye thousands of houses in this mighty city; for surely you should do as much for a poet in distress as for that crooked devil who mischievously lifted your tops off. Let me see the men and women coming back to your rooms to rest after the busy hours of pleasure-seeking. As my ears become more sensitive, let them distinguish the many words of those who were asking Julian and Teodora about me; and as a great light is made from scattered rays when they are gathered into a crystal lens, as the mountains are formed from grains of sand and the sea from drops of water, so from your chance words, your stray smiles, your idle glances, from a thousand trivial thoughts which you have left scattered in cafés, in theatres, in ball-rooms, and which are now floating in the air, I shall shape my drama, and the crystal of my mind shall be the lens that brings to a focus the lights and shadows, so that from them shall result the dramatic spark and the tragic explosion. My drama is taking shape. Now it has a title, for there in the lamp-light I see the work of the immortal Florentine poet, and in Italian it has given me the name which it would be madness or folly to write or speak in plain Spanish. Paolo and Francesca, may your love help me! (*Sitting down at the table and beginning to write.*) The play! the play begins! The first page is no longer blank. (*Writing.*) Now it has a title. (*Writes madly.*) *The Great Galeoto*!

(*Curtain.*)

ELEANOR BONTECOU

TWENTIETH CENTURY

VICENTE BLASCO IBÁÑEZ
[1867–1928]

Vicente Blasco Ibáñez began his prolific writing career as a regionalist, vividly portraying scenes from his native Valencia. To this early period belong his best novels: La barraca *(1898) and* Cañas y barro *('Reeds and Mud') (1902). There followed a number of novels on social themes in which Blasco Ibáñez projects his own attitudes. The best known are the anti-clerical* La catedral *(1903), set in Toledo, and* Sangre y arena *('Blood and Sand'), depicting the brutality of bullfighting, set in Seville. Blasco Ibáñez finally undertook novels of international scope, and one of them,* Los cuatro jinetes del Apocalipsis *('The Four Horsemen of the Apocalypse') (1916), a war novel favouring the Allies, brought him great fame and fortune. His style is vigorous and he is a master of realistic description. Blasco Ibáñez was extremely popular in his own country, and he is no doubt one of the most translated of all Spanish authors.*

THE CABIN

BATISTE'S TRIAL

It was Thursday, and according to a custom which dated back for five centuries, the Tribunal of the Waters was going to meet at the doorway of the Cathedral named after the Apostles.

The clock of the Miguelete pointed to a little after ten, and the inhabitants of the *huerta* were gathering in idle groups or seating themselves about the large basin of the dry fountain which adorned the *plaza*, forming about its base an animated wreath of blue and white cloaks, red and yellow handkerchiefs, and skirts of calico prints of bright colours.

Others were arriving, drawing up their horses, with their rush-baskets loaded with manure, satisfied with the collection they had made in the streets; still others, in empty carts, were trying to persuade the police to allow their vehicles to remain there; and while the old folks chatted with the women, the young went into the neighbouring café, to kill time over a glass of brandy, while chewing at a three-centime cigar.

All those of the *huerta* who had grievances to avenge were here, gesticulating and scowling, speaking of their rights, impatient to let loose the interminable chain of their complaints before the syndics or judges of the seven canals.

547

The bailiff of the tribunal, who had been carrying on this contest with the insolent and aggressive crowd for more than fifty years, placed a long sofa of old damask which was on its last legs within the shadow of the Gothic portal, and then set up a low railing, thereby closing in the square of sidewalk which had to serve the purpose of an audience-chamber. . . .

The bailiff finished arranging the Tribunal, and placed himself at the entrance of the enclosure to await the judges. The latter arrived solemnly, dressed in black, with white sandals, and silken handkerchiefs under their broad hats, they had the appearance of rich farmers. Each was followed by a cortège of canal-guards, and by persistent supplicants who, before the hour of justice, were seeking to predispose the judges' minds in their favour.

The farmers gazed with respect at these judges, come forth from their own class, whose deliberations did not admit of any appeal. They were the masters of the water : in their hands remaimed the living of the families, the nourishment of the fields, the timely watering, the lack of which kills a harvest. And the people of these wide plains, separated by the river, which is like an impassable frontier, designated the judges by the number of the canals.

A little, thin, bent, old man, whose red and horny hands trembled as they rested on the thick staff, was Cuart de Faitanar; the other, stout and imposing, with small eyes scarcely visible under bushy white brows, was Mislata. Soon Roscaña arrived; a youth who wore a blouse that had been freshly ironed, and whose head was round. After these appeared in sequence the rest of the seven : Favara, Robella, Tornos and Mestalla.

Now all the representatives of the four plains were there; the one on the left bank of the river; the one with the four canals; the one which the *huerta* of Rufaza encircles with its roads of luxuriant foliage ending at the confines of the marshy Albufera; and the plain on the right bank of the Turia, the poetic one, with its strawberries of Benimaclet, its *cyperus* of Alboraya and its gardens always overrun with flowers.

The seven judges saluted, like people who had not seen each other for a week; they spoke of their business beside the door of the Cathedral : from time to time, upon opening the wooden screens covered with religious advertisements, a puff of incense-laden air, somewhat like the damp exhalation from a subterranean cavern, diffused itself into the burning atmosphere of the *plaza*.

At half-past eleven, when the divine offices were ended and only some belated devotee was still coming from the temple, the Tribunal began to operate.

The seven judges seated themselves on the old sofa; then the people of the *huerta* came running up from all sides of the *plaza*, to gather around the railing, pressing their perspiring bodies, which smelled of straw and coarse sheep's wool, close together, and the bailiff, rigid and majestic, took his place near the pole topped with a bronze crook, symbolic of aquatic majesty.

The seven syndics removed their hats and remained with their hands between the knees and their hats upon the ground, while the eldest pronounced the customary sentence :

'Let the Tribunal begin.'

Absolute stillness. The crowd, observing religious silence, seemed here, in the midst of the *plaza*, to be worshipping in a temple. The sound of carriages, the clatter of tramways, all the din of modern life passed by, without touching or stirring this most ancient institution, which remained tranquil, like one who finds himself in his own house, insensible to time, paying no attention to the radical change surrounding it, incapable of any reform.

The inhabitants of the *huerta* were proud of their tribunal. It dispensed justice; the penalty without delay, and nothing done with papers, which confuse and puzzle honest men.

The absence of stamped paper and of the clerk of court who terrifies, was the part best liked by these people who were accustomed to looking upon the art of writing of which they were ignorant with a certain superstitious terror. Here were no secretary, no pens, no days of anxiety while awaiting sentence, no terrifying guards, nor anything more than words.

The judges kept the declarations in their memory, and passed sentence immediately with the tranquillity of those who know that their decisions must be fulfilled. On him who would be insolent with the tribunal, a fine was imposed; from him who had refused to comply with the verdict, the water was taken away forever, and he must die of hunger.

Nobody played with this tribunal. It was the simple patriarchal justice of the good legendary king, coming forth mornings to the door of his palace in order to settle the disputes of his subjects; the judicial system of the Kabila chief, passing sentences at his tent-entrance. Thus are rascals punished, and the honourable triumph, and there is peace.

And the public, men, women, and children, fearful of missing a word, pressed close together against the railing, moving, sometimes, with violent contortions of their shoulders, in order to escape from suffocation.

The complainants would appear at the other side of the railing, before the sofa as old as the tribunal itself.

The bailiff would take away their staffs and shepherds' crooks, which he regarded as offensive arms incompatible with the respect due the tribunal. He pushed them forward until with their mantle folded over their hands they were planted some paces distant from the judges, and if they were slow in baring their head, the handkerchief was wrested from it with two tugs. It was hard, but with this crafty people it was necessary to act thus.

The line filing by brought a continuous outburst of intricate questions, which the judges settled with marvellous facility.

The keepers of the canals and the irrigation-guards, charged with the establishment of each one's turn in the irrigation, formulated their charges, and the defendants appeared to defend themselves with arguments. The old men allowed their sons, who knew how to express themselves with more energy, to speak; the widow appeared, accompanied by some friend of the deceased, a devoted protector, who acted as her spokesman.

The passion of the south cropped out in every case.

In the midst of the accusation, the defendant would not be able to contain himself. 'You lie! What you say is evil and false! You are trying to ruin me!'

But the seven judges received these interruptions with furious glances. Here nobody was permitted to speak before his own turn came. At the second interruption, he would have to pay a fine of so many *sous*. And he who was obstinate, driven by his vehement madness, which would not permit him to be silent before the accuser, paid more and more *sous*.

The judges, without giving up their seats, would put their heads together like playful goats, and whisper together for some seconds; then the eldest, in a composed and solemn voice, pronounced the sentence, designating the fine in *sous* and pounds, as if money had suffered no change, and majestic Justice with its red robe and its escort of plumed crossbow-men were still passing through the centre of the *plaza*.

It was after twelve, and the seven judges were beginning to show signs of being weary of such prodigious outpouring of the stream of justice, when the bailiff called out loudly to Bautista Borrull, denouncing him for infraction and disobedience of irrigation-rights.

Pimentó and Batiste passed the railing, and the people pressed up even closer against the bar.

Here were many of those who lived near the ancient land of Barret.

This trial was interesting. The hated newcomer had been denounced by Pimentó, who was the *'atandador'** of that district. The bully, by mixing up in elections, and strutting about like a fighting cock all over the neighbourhood, had won this office which gave him a certain air of authority and strengthened his prestige among the neighbours, who made much of him and treated him on irrigation days.

Batiste was amazed at this unjust denunciation. His pallor was that of indignation. He gazed with eyes full of fury at all the familiar mocking faces, which were pressing against the rail, and at his enemy Pimentó, who was strutting about proudly, like a man accustomed to appearing before the tribunal, and to whom a small part of its unquestionable authority belonged.

'Speak,' said the eldest of the judges, putting one foot forward, for according to a century-old custom, the tribunal, instead of using the hands, signalled with the white sandal to him who should speak.

Pimentó poured forth his accusation. This man who was beside him, perhaps because he was new in the *huerta,* seemed to think that the apportionment of the water was a trifling matter, and that he could suit his own blessed will.

He, Pimentó, the *atandador,* who represented the authority of the canals in his district, had set for Batiste the hour for watering his wheat. It was two o'clock in the morning. But doubtless the señor, not wishing to arise at that hour, had let his turn go, and at five, when the water was intended for others, he had raised the flood-gate without permission from anybody (the *first* offence), and attempted to water his fields, resolving to oppose, by main force, the orders of the *atandador,* which constituted the *third* and last offence.

The thrice-guilty delinquent, turning all the colours of the rainbow, and indignant at the words of Pimentó, was not able to restrain himself.

'You lie, and lie doubly!'

The tribunal became indignant at the heat and the lack of respect with which this man was protesting.

If he did not keep silent he would be fined.

But what was a fine for the concentrated wrath of a peaceful man! He kept on protesting against the injustice of men, against the tribunal which had, as its servants, such rogues and liars as Pimentó.

The tribunal was stirred up; the seven judges became excited.

* One in charge of the *tanda,* or turn in irrigating.

Four *sous* for a fine !

Batiste, realizing his situation, suddenly grew silent, terrified at having incurred a fine, while laughter came from the crowd and howls of joy from his enemies.

He remained motionless, with bowed head, and his eyes dimmed with tears of rage, while his brutal enemy finished formulating his denunciation.

'Speak,' the tribunal said to him. But little sympathy was noted in the looks of the judges for this disturber, who had to trouble the solemnity of their deliberations with his protests.

Batiste, trembling with rage, stammered, not knowing how to begin his defence because of the very fact that it seemed to him perfectly just.

The court had been misled; Pimentó was a liar and furthermore his declared enemy. He had told him that his time for irrigation came at five, he remembered it very well, and was now affirming that it was two; just to make him incur a fine, to destroy the wheat upon which the life of his family depended. . . . Did the tribunal value the word of an honest man? Then this was the truth, although he was not able to present witnesses. It seemed impossible that the honourable syndics, all good people, should trust a rascal like Pimentó !

The white sandal of the president struck the square tile of the sidewalk, as if to avert the storm of protests and the lack of respect which he saw from afar.

'Be silent.'

And Batiste was silent, while the seven-headed monster, folding itself up again on the sofa of damask, was whispering, preparing the sentence.

'The tribunal decrees . . .' said the eldest judge, and there was absolute silence.

All the people around the roped space showed a certain anxiety in their eyes, as if they were the sentenced. They were hanging on the lips of the eldest judge.

'Batiste Borrull shall pay two pounds for penalty, and four *sous* for a fine.'

A murmur of satisfaction arose and spread, and one old woman even began to clap her hands, shouting 'Hurrah ! hurrah !' amid the loud laughter of the people.

Batiste went out blindly from the tribunal, with his head lowered as though he were about to fight, and Pimentó prudently stayed behind.

If the people had not parted, opening the way for him, it is certain that he would have struck out with his powerful fists, and given the hostile rabble a beating on the spot. . . .

FRANCIS HAFFKINE SNOW
and BEATRICE M. MEKOTA

RAMÓN DEL VALLE-INCLÁN
[1869–1936]

The most polished stylist of the modernist novelists is probably Ramón María del Valle-Inclán. Endowed with a fantastic imagination and exquisite sensitivity, he creates a moody, exotic atmosphere for the many novels set in his native Galicia. His style is musical and poetic (he was a poet and dramatist, as well as a novelist) and is flavoured by numerous literary, archaic and popular expressions.

Valle-Inclán's most famous novels are the four Sonatas *(1902–1905), one for each season of the year, symbolizing the four phases of man's amatory life as seen in the memoirs of a sentimental Don Juan, the Marquis de Bradomín. Some of Valle-Inclán's novels deal with the Carlist wars, and in his later writings he developed a satirical, grotesque style—the* esperpento—*reminiscent of Quevedo.*

SONATA OF SPRING

CHAPTER XVI

That night the daughters of the Princess gathered in the moonlight on the terrace; they were like sprites in the fairytales as they surrounded a beautiful young friend who from time to time gazed on me in curiosity. In the salon the older ladies were carrying on a discreet conversation, smiling at the sound of the young voices that came in eddies with the perfume of lilies from the openings on the terrace. The garden stretched out motionless in the moonlight which wove magic over the pallid tops of the cypresses and the balconies, where a peacock was spreading his fantastic fan of feathers.

I tried at various times to approach Maria Rosario. It was useless; she divined my intentions and cautiously and noiselessly defeated them with her eyes lowered and her hands crossed on the conventual scapular she was already wearing. The sight of her timidity so aroused, flattered my pride as a Don Juan, and sometimes merely to torment her I would pass from one side to another. The poor child prepared for flight on the instant. I would pass apparently without seeing her. I had all the impetuosity of my twenty years. Again I would enter the salon and approach the old ladies who received my intentions with the timidity of damsels. I remember I was once talking with the devout old Marquise de Téscara when intuitively I turned my head toward the white form of Maria Rosario, and suddenly found my saint had gone.

A cloud of gloom came over me; I left the elderly lady and hurried to the terrace. I remained a long time leaning on the marble baluster, gazing on the garden. A nightingale was singing amid the silent perfume and its voice seemed to harmonize with the fountains. The moon shone down the path of roses I had followed the night before; the breeze was light and soft as though it carried sighs and would murmur them far among the myrtle groves and over the stirring waters of the pool. With Maria Rosario's face in my memory I incessantly asked myself : 'What does she think? What does she think of me?'

Light clouds gathered about the moon and followed her on her fantastic journey; suddenly in a heap they blinded her and left the garden in darkness. The pool lost its gleam among the still myrtles; only the tops of the cypresses held the light. As if to harmonize with the darkness a breeze arose and swept in a great gust across the scene, bringing the scent of scattered roses. I returned to the Palace; one of the windows was lighted up and a strange presentiment caused my heart to palpitate. The window was raised only a little above the terrace and the wind was waving its curtains. It seemed to me that a pale shadow crossed the room. I wished to draw closer but the sound of steps on the avenue of the cypresses held me back; it was the old major-domo walking in his dreams of art. I stood still in the depths of the garden. Gazing on her lighted window, my heart repeated : 'What does she think? What does she think of me?'

Poor Maria Rosario! I believe she was in love and yet her heart forewarned her of some strange confused adventure. I wished to lose myself in my amorous dreams but the croak of a frog, monotonously sounding under the arching cypresses, distracted and disturbed my thoughts. I remember that as a child I had read many times in my grandmother's prayerbook that the devil used to take the form of a frog to interrupt the devotions of a holy monk. It seemed natural that the same thing should occur to me. I, the calumniated and misunderstood, was just such another mystical gallant as Saint John of the Cross! In the flower of my youth I would gladly have given up all other early glories to be able to inscribe on my cards : 'The Marquis de Bradomín, Confessor of Princesses.'

CHAPTER XXIV

What a sad memory that day has become to me! Maria Rosario was filling the flower-jars of the chapel at the end of the salon; when I entered she stood undecided for a moment. With a timid, ardent light her eyes looked in fear on the door and back again at me. As she was filling the last jar, a rose broke over her hand. I smiled and said to her : 'Even the roses die in kissing your hands.'

She also smiled, seeing the petals between her fingers, and gave a slight sigh as they drifted away. We remained silent. It was nightfall, and the sun shone in its last golden glow upon the window. The cypresses lifted their pensive points in the twilight azure below. Within, one could hardly make out the arrangement of things; throughout the salon the roses scattered a perfume as light as the light words that died away with the sun. My eyes sought the eyes of Maria Rosario with the hope of imprisoning them in the shadows. She sighed heavily as though for want of air, and drawing back her locks with both hands from her forehead she took refuge by a window. I was afraid to assist her, and without following her merely said after a long silence : 'Are you not going to give me a rose?'

She turned and answered softly : 'Would you like one?'

I hesitated a moment and then drew nearer. I managed to appear calm, but I could see her hands trembling over the jars as she selected the flower. With a sorrowful smile she said : 'I shall give you the most beautiful one.'

She continued to search among the roses. I sighed romantically : 'The loveliest would be your lips.'

She drew back and looked at me in pain : 'You are not kind. Why do you say such things to me?'

'To see your anger.'

'And that delights you? Sometimes I think you are the devil.'

'The devil does not know what love is.'

Silence fell again. I could hardly make out her face in the dying light, and I only knew from her soft sobs that she wept. I came closer to console her : 'Oh! forgive my faults.'

My voice was tender and passionate. I myself as I heard it felt its strange seductive power. The supreme moment had arrived; my heart was seized with anxiety over the great adventure that faced me. Maria Rosario closed her eyes in dread, as though she were on the brink of an abyss. Her colourless lips expressed a painful voluptuousness. I seized her hands, which were lying inert. She abandoned them to me, sobbing in her grief : 'Why do you take pleasure in making me suffer? You know that everything is impossible!'

'Impossible! I know I shall never obtain your love! I know I do not deserve it! Only I want you to pardon me and to know that you will pray for me when I am far away.'

'Silence! Silence!'

'I regard you as so high, so far above me, so ideal, that I want your prayers as I should want those of a saint.'

'Silence! Silence!'

'My heart suffers, without a single hope. Perhaps I may learn to forget you, but your love will always be a purifying fire.'

'Silence! Silence!'

There were tears in my eyes and I knew that with tears the hands may show some boldness. Poor Maria Rosario seemed pale as death and I thought she was about to faint in my arms. This maiden was really a saint; seeing the extremity of my grief she did not wish to show me any more cruelty. She closed her eyes and murmured in agony : 'Leave me! Leave me!'

I whispered to her : 'Why do you abhor me so?'

'Because you are the devil!'

She gazed at me in terror, and as if the sound of my voice were awakening her she broke from my arms and fled toward the window, which was golden with the sunset. She leaned her forehead against the glass and sobbed. From the garden came the song of the nightingale, stirring in the twilight some innocent memory of holiness.

MAY HEYWOOD BROUN
and THOMAS WALSH

PÍO BAROJA
[1872–1956]

The Basque Pío Baroja was a doctor and baker before he turned to writing as his exclusive occupation. He is one of the most original and unorthodox of modern authors. His numerous novels cover a wide variety of themes, but he has a penchant, in particular, for writing about the lower classes of society, and reflects in his novels a sceptical and pessimistic view of our civilization. His style is careless and abrupt, perhaps deliberately so, and his plots are, by design, often incomplete.

A number of Baroja's novels deal with the Carlist wars. The swift-moving Zalacaín el aventurero *(1909) belongs in this category, as well as some of the twenty-two novels of the series* Memorias de un hombre de acción. *Among the works in which Baroja best reveals his iconoclastic ideas are* Camino de perfección *(1902),* Paradox Rey *(1906) and* El árbol de la ciencia *(1911). Baroja has termed the latter 'probably my most finished and complete book'.*

THE TREE OF KNOWLEDGE

UNIVERSAL CRUELTY

Andrés felt a great desire to comment philosophically on the lives of these lodgers in Lulu's house; but his friends were not interested in these comments or philosophies, and one morning, a holiday, he resolved to pay a visit to his Uncle Iturrioz.

When he first knew him—he had not met him till he was about fifteen—Iturrioz seemed to him a dry and selfish man who looked on everything with indifference; later, without exactly knowing how far his dryness and egoism went, he found he was one of the few persons with whom one could discuss transcendental subjects.

Iturrioz lived on the fifth floor of a house in the Argüelles quarter, a house with a fine flat roof.

He was attended by a servant who had been a soldier when Iturrioz was an army doctor.

Between them they had set the house-top in order, painted the tiles with pitch to make them waterproof, and set up steps for the wooden boxes and tubs full of earth in which they kept their plants.

The morning on which Andrés paid him a visit, Iturrioz was having his bath, and the servant took Andrés up to the roof.

Between two tall houses one had a view of the Guadarrama

Mountains; to the west the roof of the Montaña barracks concealed the hills of the Casa del Campo; and on one side of the barracks appeared the Torre de Móstoles and the highroad to Extremadura with some windmills near it. Farther to the south shone in the April sun the green patches of the cemeteries of San Justo and San Isidro, the two towers of Getafe, and the hermitage of the Cerrillo de los Angeles.

After a little Iturrioz came out on to the house-top.

'Well, is anything the matter?' he asked, when he saw his nephew.

'Nothing; I came to have a talk with you.'

'Very good. Sit down; I am going to water my flower-pots.'

Iturrioz opened a tap at a corner of the terrace and filled a tub with water, and then with a piece of pot began to throw water on to the plants.

Andrés spoke of Lulu's neighbours and of the scenes at the hospital as strange things requiring a commentary, of Manolo the Buffoon, Old Skinflint, Don Cleto, and Doña Virginia.

'What inference can one draw from all these lives?' he asked.

'For me the inference is easy,' answered Iturrioz, waterpot in hand : 'that life is a constant struggle, a cruel carnage in which we devour one another. Plants, microbes, animals.'

'Yes,' answered Andrés, 'the same idea occurred to me, but I do not think it will hold water. In the first place the conception of life as a struggle among animals, plants and even minerals is an anthropomorphic idea; and then what kind of a struggle for life is that of Don Cleto, who refuses to fight, or of Brother Juan, who gives his money to the poor?'

'I will answer the two questions separately,' said Iturrioz, setting down his watering-pot, for such questions were his delight. 'You say the idea of a struggle is an anthropomorphic idea. Well, of course, we give to all the various conflicts the name of a struggle because it is the human idea best fitted to express the relations which with us produce a victor and a vanquished. If that were not, essentially, what we meant we would not speak of a struggle. The hyena picking clean the bones of a carcass, the spider sucking the life out of a fly, is acting precisely in the same way as the kindly tree which takes from the earth the moisture and salts necessary to its life. An indifferent spectator like myself watches the hyena, the spider, and the tree and understands them; a man with a sense of justice shoots the hyena, crushes the spider under his foot, and sits down under the shade of the tree, imagining that he has done a good deed.'

'Then you consider there is no struggle and no justice?'

'In an absolute sense there is none; in a relative sense there is. Every living thing has first to gain possession of space, of a place to exist, and then of the means to grow and multiply; this process carried on by the energy of the living against the obstacles which surround it is what we call a struggle. As to justice I think that, essentially, it is what happens to suit us. Suppose, for instance, that the hyena, instead of being killed, kills the man, or that the tree falls upon him and kills him, or that the spider gives him a poisonous bite; nothing in all that seems to us just, because it does not suit us. Yet, although essentially it is no more than a question of utilitarian interest, who can doubt that the idea of justice and equity is a tendency which exists in us? But how are we to put it into practice?'

'That's what I ask myself, how put it into practice?'

'Are we to grow indignant because a spider kills a fly?' went on Iturrioz. 'What are we to do—kill the spider? If we kill it, that will not prevent spiders from devouring flies. Are we to cure mankind of these ferocious instincts to which you object? Are we to erase the Latin writer's verdict that man is a wolf to man : *homo homini lupus*? Very well; in four or five thousand years we shall be able to do so. Man has converted a carnivorous animal like the jackal into an omnivorous animal like the dog; but it requires centuries to effect this. You may have read that Spallanzini taught a dove to eat meat, and an eagle to eat and digest bread. That is the case of these great religious and lay apostles : they are eagles eating bread instead of raw meat; they are wolves turned vegetarians. Brother Juan for instance.'

'I don't think he's an eagle, nor a wolf.'

'He may be an owl or a martin, a perverted one.'

'Possibly,' answered Andrés, 'but I think we have wandered from the point; I don't see what inference is to be drawn.'

'The inference that I wished to draw is this : that a man of clear mind confronted with life has but two practical courses open, either to abstain from action and contemplate everything with indifference, or to limit his action to a small area; in other words one may be quixotic in an anomalous case but to be so as a general rule is absurd.'

'Then you think that a man of action must limit his love of justice within narrow bounds?'

'Of course he must; you may include in your view your house, your town, your region, society, the world, every dead and living thing; but if you attempt to act, and to act in a spirit of justice,

you must restrict yourself more and more, even perhaps within
your own conscience.'

'That is the beauty of philosophy,' said Andrés bitterly. 'It
convinces one that it is best to do nothing.'

Iturrioz walked up and down the house-top and then said:
'That is the only objection you can bring against me, and it's not
my fault.'

'I know it.'

'To entertain an idea of universal justice is fatal,' continued
Iturrioz. 'Adapting Fritz Müller's principle that the embryology
of an animal reproduces its genealogy, or, as Haeckel says, that
ontogenesis is but a recapitulation of phylogenesis, one may say
that human psychology is but a synthesis of animal psychology.
Thus we find in man all the forms of struggle and development:
that of the microbe, the insect, the wild beast. How many incar-
nations cannot zoology show of that usurer you have described
to me, Old Skinflint! We see the acinetids sucking the protoplasm
from other infusoria; and the various animals that fatten on
decaying matter. And the mutual antipathy of those people: is
it not seen perfectly in the obstinate antagonism of a certain
bacillus for certain bacteria?'

'Possibly,' murmured Andrés.

'And among the insects how many Old Skinflints and Victorios!
How many Manolos! There is the ichneumon which lays its
eggs in a worm and gives it an injection of a substance which acts
like chloroform; there is the sphex which takes small spiders, holds
them down, winds thread round them and places them alive in
the cells of its larvae for their food; there are the wasps which do
the same thing with other insects which they paralyse with their
sting; there is the estafilino which treacherously hurls itself upon
another individual of its own species, holds it down, wounds it
and sucks out its life; there is the insect which penetrates surrepti-
tiously into the honeycomb of the bees, enters the queen's cell,
eats its fill of honey, and then devours the queen's larva; there
is——'

'Yes, yes, you need say no more: life is a horrible carnage.'

'It is characteristic of Nature that when it intends to ruin you, it
does so thoroughly. Justice is a human illusion: essentially everything is destruction and creation. Hunting, war, digestion,
breathing are instances of simultaneous creation and destruction.'

'But what must one do?' murmured Andrés. 'Become indifferent?
Digest, fight, and hunt with the serenity of a savage?'

'You believe in the serenity of the savage? What an illusion!

That is another of our inventions. The savage has never been serene.'

'Is there no possible plan to live with a certain decency?' asked Andrés.

'Only if one invents one for one's own use. And, today, I believe that whatever is spontaneous and natural is bad, that only the artificial, man's creation, is good. If I could I would live in a London club; I would never go into the country except to a park; the water I drank would be filtered, the air sterilized——'

But Andrés was no longer listening to Iturrioz, who had begun to follow the bent of his fancy. He got up and leant upon the balustrade running around the roof.

Some doves were flying above the neighbouring roofs; on a large gutter cats were running and playing.

In front, separated by a high wall, were two gardens; one belonged to a girls' college, the other to a monastery.

The convent garden was surrounded by shady trees; that of the college had nothing but plots of grass and flowers; and it was a strange thing, not without a certain impression of allegory, to see at one and the same time the girls running and shouting and the friars walking silently round their court, in rows of five or six.

'Both the one and the other are life,' said Iturrioz philosophically, and began to water his plants.

Andrés went out into the street.

What should he do? How order his life? he asked himself searchingly. And with this problem in his mind the people he met, the things he saw, the sun itself seemed to lack reality.

AUBREY F. G. BELL

MIGUEL DE UNAMUNO
[1864–1936]

In the opinion of many scholars Miguel de Unamuno was the outstanding Spaniard of the twentieth century. Professor, philosopher, essayist, poet and novelist, he exerted an important influence upon Spanish intellectuals.

His most famous work, Del sentimiento trágico de la vida (*1913*), *develops one of the author's main themes, the struggle between faith and reason. Since his novels do not conform to conventional novelistic requirements, Unamuno invented the term 'nivolas'. One of his most popular 'nivolas' is* Niebla (*1914*), *from which our excerpt comes. It is of unusual interest for it presents a lively argument between the author and one of his characters.*

MIST

AUGUSTO HAS AN INTERVIEW WITH THE AUTHOR

The storm in the soul of Augusto ended in a terrible calm : he had resolved to kill himself. He wanted to put an end to that self which had been the cause of all his misery. But before carrying out his plan it occurred to him, like a drowning sailor who grasps at a straw, to come and talk it over with me, the author of this whole story. Augusto had read an essay of mine in which I made a passing reference to suicide and this, together with some other things of mine that he had read, had evidently made such an impression upon him that he did not wish to leave this world without having met me and talked with me for a while. Accordingly, he came here to Salamanca, where I have been living for twenty years past, to pay me a visit.

When his call was announced I smiled enigmatically, and I had him come into my study. He entered like a ghost. He looked at a portrait of me in oil which presides over the books of my library, and then at a sign from me he took a seat opposite me.

He began by speaking of my literary works, in particular of those that were more or less philosophical, showing that he knew them very well; which, of course, did not fail to please me. Then he began to tell me of his life and of his misfortunes. I interrupted him by telling him to spare himself the trouble; I was as familiar with the vicissitudes of his life as he himself; and this I demonstrated to him by citing some of the most intimate details, and in particular some things that he thought to be utterly hidden. He looked at me with genuine terror in his eyes, as one looks at some incredible being. I seemed to see a change in the colour and in the lines of his face, and I saw that he even trembled. I had him fascinated.

'It hardly seems true,' he kept repeating, 'it hardly seems true. I shouldn't believe it if I had not seen it. I don't know whether I am awake or dreaming——'

'Neither awake nor dreaming,' I replied.

'I can't explain it—I can't explain it,' he went on. 'But since you seem to know as much about me as I know myself, perhaps you guess my purpose in coming.'

'Yes,' I said. 'You'—and I gave to this 'you' the emphasis of authority—'you, oppressed by the weight of your misfortunes, have conceived the diabolical idea of killing yourself; and before doing it, impelled by something you have read in one of my last essays, you have come to consult me about it.'

The poor man shook like a drop of mercury and looked at me with the stare of one possessed. He tried to rise, perhaps with the idea of flight, but he could not. He could not summon the strength.

'No, don't move,' I commanded him.

'Do you mean—do you mean——' he stammered.

'I mean that you cannot commit suicide even if you wish to do so.'

'What!' he cried, finding himself so flatly opposed and contradicted.

'Yes, if a man is going to kill himself what is the first thing that is necessary?' I asked him.

'That he should have the courage to do it,' he replied.

'No,' I said, 'that he should be alive.'

'Of course!'

'And you are not alive.'

'Not alive! What do you mean? Do you mean that I have died?' And without clearly knowing what he was doing he began to pass his hands over his body.

'No, my man, no!' I replied. 'I told you before that you were neither waking nor sleeping; now I tell you that you are neither alive nor dead.'

'Tell me all of it at once; God, tell me all,' he begged me in terror. 'With what I am seeing and hearing this afternoon I am afraid of going mad.'

'Very well, then. The truth is, my dear Augusto,' I spoke to him the softest of tones, 'you can't kill yourself because you are not alive; and you are not alive—or dead either—because you do not exist.'

'I don't exist! What do you mean by that?'

'No, you do not exist except as a fictitious entity, a character of fiction. My poor Augusto, you are only a product of my imagination and of the imagination of those of my readers who read this story which I have written of your fictitious adventures and misfortunes. You are nothing more than a personage in a novel, or a *nivola*, or whatever you choose to call it. Now, then, you know your secret.'

Upon hearing this the poor man continued to look at me for a while with one of those perforating looks that seem to pierce your own gaze and go beyond; presently he glanced for a moment at the portrait in oil which presides over my books, then his colour returned and his breathing became easier, and gradually recovering, he was again master of himself. He rested his elbows on the arm of the sofa opposite me, against which he was leaning; and then with his face in the palms of his hands he looked at me with a smile and he said slowly :

'Listen to me, Don Miguel—it can't be that you are mistaken, and that what is happening is precisely the contrary of what you think and of what you have told me?'

'And what do you mean by the contrary?' I asked, rather alarmed to see him regaining his self-possession.

'May it not be, my dear Don Miguel,' he continued, 'that it is you and not I who are the fictitious entity, the one that does not really exist, who is neither living nor dead? May it not be that you are nothing more than a pretext for bringing my history into the world?'

'Really this is too much!' I cried, now becoming irritated.

'Please don't get so excited, Señor de Unamuno,' he replied. 'Keep calm. You have expressed doubts about my existence——'

'Doubts? No!' I interrupted. 'Absolute certainty that you do not exist outside of the novel that I have created.'

'Very well; then please don't be disturbed if I in turn doubt your existence rather than my own. Let us come to the point. Are you not the person who has said, not once but several times, that Don Quixote and Sancho are not only real persons but more real than Cervantes himself?'

'I can't deny it, but the sense in which I said it was——'

'Very well, never mind in what sense. Let us come to another point. When a man who is lying asleep in his bed dreams of something, which is it that more truly exists, he as the consciousness that dreams or the dreams themselves?'

'And what if the dreamer dreams that he himself exists?'—I turned the question on him.

'In that case, friend Don Miguel, my own question would be, in what fashion does he exist? As the dreamer who dreams of himself or as something dreamed by himself? And note this, moreover: in entering this discussion with me you are already recognizing me as an existence independent of yourself.'

'Not at all. Not at all,' I said quickly. 'In entering this discussion I am merely satisfying a private need of my own. Apart from discussion and contradiction I am never alive; and when there is no one outside of me to question and contradict me I invent some one to do it within me. My monologues are dialogues.'

'And perhaps the dialogues that you fabricate are nothing more than monologues.'

'It may be. But in any case I tell you, and I wish to repeat it, that you do not exist outside of me——'

'And I will again suggest this to you, namely, that you do not exist outside of me and of the other characters that you think you have invented. I am certain that Don Avito Carrascal would be of my opinion and the great Don Fulgencio——'

'You needn't mention them——'

'Very well, then, I won't; but you shouldn't make fun of them. And now let us see; what do you really think about my suicide?'

'I think, then, that since you do not exist except in my imagination—as I tell you again—and since you neither ought nor are you able to do anything but just what I please, and since it does not really suit me that you should kill yourself—well, you are not going to kill yourself. And that settles it.'

'Your saying that "it does not really suit me" is very Spanish, Señor de Unamuno, but it is far from edifying. Moreover, even granting your strange theory that I do not really exist and that you do, that I am nothing but a character of fiction, the product of your imagination as a novelist—or as a "nivolist"—even so there is no reason why I should submit to "what really suits you", that is, to your caprice. For even those whom we call characters of fiction have their own inwrought logic——'

'Yes, I know that song.'

'But, really, it is a fact that neither a novelist nor a playwright is at all able to do anything that happens to occur to him, to a character that he creates. That a fictitious character in a novel should do that which no reader would ever expect him to do, is forbidden by all of the established principles of art——'

'Doubtless a character in a novel——'

'Well, then?'

'But a character in a *nivola*—a "nivolistic" character——'

'Let us drop these buffooneries. They are offensive, and they wound me where I am most sensitive. Whether of myself, as I think, or because you have given it to me, as you suppose, I have my own character, my own manner of being, my own inwrought logic, and this logic demands that I kill myself——'

'You may think so, but you are wrong.'

'Let us see. Why am I wrong? And where am I wrong? Show me where my mistake lies. Since the most difficult knowledge that there is, is knowing yourself, I may easily be mistaken and it may be that suicide is not the logical solution of my problem. But prove it to me. For though this self-knowledge be difficult, Don Miguel, there is another kind of knowledge that seems no less difficult——'

'And that is?——' I asked.

He looked at me with a smile that was shrewd and enigmatic and then he said slowly :

'Well, that which is more difficult than self-knowledge is this : that a novelist or a playwright should know the characters that he creates or thinks he creates.'

These sallies of Augusto were beginning to make me uneasy and I was losing my patience.

'And I insist,' he added, 'that even granting you have given me my being—a fictitious being, if you please—even so, and because it is so, you cannot prevent me from killing myself just because, as you say, it does not really suit you.'

'Very well, that will do—enough !' I cried, bringing my fist down on the sofa. 'Hold your tongue ! I don't wish to hear any more impertinence ! And from a creature of mine, too ! And since I have had enough of you and I don't know, moreover, what more to do with you, I have now decided, not that you may not now kill yourself, but that I shall kill you. You are to die, then, but soon ! Very soon !'

Augusto was horror-struck. 'What !' he cried. 'Do you mean that you are going to let me die, make me die—you are going to kill me?'

'Yes, I am going to cause you to die.'

'Oh, never ! never ! never !' he shrieked.

'Ah !' I said, looking at him with mingled pity and rage. 'And so you were ready to kill yourself, but you don't want me to kill you? And you were about to take your own life, but you object to my taking it?'

'Yes, it is not the same thing——'

'To be sure, it is not. I have heard of cases of that kind. I heard of a man who went out one night armed with a revolver, intending to take his own life, when some thieves undertook to rob him. They attacked him, he defended himself, killed one of them and the others fled. And then, seeing that he had bought his life at the cost of another's, he renounced his intention.'

'One can understand that,' observed Augusto. 'It was a matter of taking the life of somebody, of killing a man; and after he had killed another, what was the use of killing himself? Most suicides are frustrated homicides; men kill themselves because they have not the courage to kill others——'

'Ah! now I understand you, Augusto, I understand. You mean that if you had had the courage to kill Eugenia* or Mauricio, or both, you would not be thinking of killing yourself, isn't that so?'

'Let me tell you, it is not precisely of them that I am thinking—no!'

'Of whom, then?'

'Of you'—and he looked me straight in the eye.

'What!' I cried, rising to my feet. 'What! Have you conceived the idea of killing me? You? And of killing me?'

'Sit down and keep cool. Do you think, Don Miguel, that it would the first case in which a fictitious entity, as you call me, had killed him whom he believed to have given him his being—his fictitious being, of course?'

'This is really too much,' I said, walking up and down my study. 'This passes all limits. This couldn't happen except——'

'Except in *nivolas*,' Augusto completed with a drawl.

'Very well, enough! enough! enough! This is more than I can stand. You came here to consult me—me, you understand—and you? You begin by disputing my own existence, forgetting that I have the right to do with you anything that suits me—yes, just what I say, anything that may happen to occur to——'

'Don't be so Spanish, Don Miguel——'

'And now this too, you idiot! Well, yes, I am indeed a Spaniard, Spanish by birth, by education, by profession and occupation; Spanish above everything and before everything. Spanishism is my religion, the heaven in which I wish to believe is a celestial and eternal Spain, and my God is a Spanish God, the God of our Lord Don Quixote, a God who thinks in Spanish and who said in Spanish, Let there be light! *Sea luz!*—His word was a Spanish word——'

* Augusto's fiancée, who ran off with Mauricio just before the wedding day.

'Well, and what of it?' he interrupted, recalling me to reality.

'And now you have conceived the idea of killing me. Of killing me—*me*? And you? Am I to die at the hands of one of my creatures? I'll stand no more of it. And so to punish you for your insolence, and to put an end to these disintegrating, extravagant, and anarchistic ideas with which you have come to me, I hereby render judgment and pass the sentence that you are to die. As soon as you reach home you shall die. You shall die, I tell you, you shall die.'

'But—for God's sake!' cried Augusto, now in a tone of supplication, pale and trembling with fear.

'There is no God that can help you. You shall die.'

'Yes, but I want to live, Don Miguel, I want to live—I want to live——'

'Weren't you just now thinking of killing yourself?'

'Oh! if that is why, Don Miguel, then I swear to you that I will not kill myself, I will not take away this life which God, or yourself, has given me; I swear it to you—now that you wish to kill me I myself want to live—to live—to live——'

'What a life!' I exclaimed.

'Yes, whatever it may be. I want to live even though I am again to be mocked at, even though another Eugenia and another Mauricio tear my heart out. I wish to live—live—live——'

'Now it cannot be—it cannot be——'

'I want to live—live—I want to be myself, myself, myself.'

'But what if that self is only what I wish to be——?'

'I wish to be myself—to be myself! I wish to live!' and his voice was choked with sobs.

'It cannot be—cannot be——'

'Listen, Don Miguel, for the sake of your children, of your wife, of whatever is dearest to you! Remember that you will then cease to be yourself—that *you* will die——'

He fell on his knees at my feet, begging and imploring me : 'Don Miguel, for God's sake! I want to live. I want to be myself.'

'It cannot be, my poor Augusto,' I said, taking him by the hand and lifting him up. 'It cannot be. I have now decreed it—it is written—and irrevocably; you can live no longer. I no longer know what to do with you. God, when he does not know what to do with us, kills us. And I do not forget that there passed through your mind the idea of killing me——'

'But, Don Miguel, if I——'

'It makes no difference. I know where I stand. And really I

am afraid that if I do not kill you soon, you will end by killing me.'

'But are we not agreed that——?'

'It cannot be, Augusto, it cannot be. Your hour has come. It is now written, and I cannot now recall it. And for all that your life can now be worth to you——'

'But——good God!'

'There is neither "but" nor "God" that can avail you. Go!'

'And so you won't?' he said. 'You refuse? You are unwilling to let me be myself, come out of the mist and live, live, live; to see myself, hear myself, touch myself, feel myself, feel my own pain, be myself—you are unwilling, then? And so I am to die as a fictitious character? Very well, then, my lord creator Don Miguel, you too are to die, you too! And you will return to that nothing from which you came! God will cease to dream you! You are to die, yes, you are to die, even though you do not wish to; and die shall all of those who read my story, all of them, all, all, without a single exception. Fictitious entities like myself—just like myself! All of them are to die; all, all. And it is I who tell you this—I, Augusto Pérez, a fictitious entity, a "nivolistic" entity, and your readers are "nivolistic" entities, just like me, just the same as Augusto Pérez, your victim——'

'Victim!' I cried.

'Victim, yes! To create me only to let me die! Well, you too are to die! He who creates creates himself, and he who creates himself dies. You will die, Don Miguel, you will die, and all those who think me, they are to die too! To death, then!'

This supreme effort of the passion for life—of the thirst for immortality—left poor Augusto utterly weak.

I pushed him towards the door. He walked out with his eyes fixed upon the ground, passing his hands wonderingly over himself as if he were uncertain of his own existence. I wiped away a furtive tear.

WARNER FITE

AZORÍN
[b. 1874]

José Martínez Ruiz, who wrote under the pseudonym Azorín, is one of the foremost essayists and prose stylists of the twentieth century. Although Azorín has tried his hand at the novel and drama, it is as a sensitive essayist and impressionistic critic that he is most important. As a leader of the Generation of '98 he blames some of Spain's shortcomings on the past. Yet no one better than Azorín can evoke wistful and whimsical reminiscences of Spain's history, geography and literature. His style is highly personal, but clear and precise. Nubes ('Clouds') comes from the collection Castilla (*1912*).

CLOUDS

Calisto and Melibea were married, as the reader will know (if he has read *La Celestina*) a few days after the discovery of their stolen interviews in the garden. Calisto had become enamoured of the maiden, who was destined to be his wife, on a certain day when he entered her garden in pursuit of a falcon. Eighteen years ago it was. Twenty-three had been Calisto then. The two are living now as man and wife in Melibea's ancestral mansion; a daughter has been born to them, named like her grandmother, Alisa. From the broad verandah in the rear of the dwelling is to be seen the whole of the garden, wherein Melibea and Calisto had held their sweet colloquies of love. The house is large and stately; a carved staircase of stone ascends from the far end of the vestibule. Above are spacious retiring-rooms, silent and secluded bed-chambers, dimly-lighted galleries, and in the rear a small doorway with squares of glass in its upper part, giving a glimpse, as in *Las Meninas* of Velasquez, of an inner court bathed in light. A carpet of green branches and yellow fir-cones, worked on a crimson ground, is stretched over the floor of the chief drawing-room, where, on silken cushions, noble dames may sit at ease. Here and there are small divans covered with red leather, or folding-chairs with Moorish inlaid-work. A sculptured cabinet with painted and soft-lined drawers contains papers and jewels. In the centre of the apartment, on a walnut table with carved legs and framework, and with bars of wrought-iron, lies a delicately-fashioned box of chessmen with reliefs of ivory, mother-of-pearl, and silver; while in the crystal border of a broad mirror are reflected from a background of gold the elongated faces of a painting on wood, hanging on the wall that fronts the door of entrance.

All is peace and silence in the house. Melibea moves gently from room to room, sees to all things, thinks of all things. The presses are full of smooth and sweet-smelling linen, redolent of juicy quinces. In the pantry a sunbeam lights up a row of capacious and glazed Talaveran bowls. In the kitchen the brazen pots and pans hanging upon the dresser are as mirrors, and canakins and pitchers wrought by the hands of a craftsman of the potteries near by, display their round, smooth, and shining bellies. Over all things watches Melibea with untiring diligence; nothing escapes those soft green eyes of hers.

Ever and again, breaking upon the silence of the house is heard the sweet and languorous sound of a harpsichord; it is Alisa, who is making music. Ere long upon the garden-paths is seen in gentle movement a maiden's tall and slender figure; it is Alisa walking amid the trees.

The garden is sweet to look upon and full of verdure. Oleanders and jasmine-plants grow side by side. At the foot of the never-changing cypresses rose-bushes lay their offering, fleeting as life itself, of their yellow, white, and crimson flowers. Three colours meet the eye where'er it turns : the intense blue of the sky, the white coating of the walls, and the green of the trees and shrubs. In the silence is heard, like diamond upon crystal, the shrill note of the swallows in their rapid flight through the deep indigo of the firmament. From the marble basin of a fountain trickles the water peacefully into the trough below. In the air rises the penetrating fragrance of the jasmines, roses and magnolias. 'Climb over my garden wall,' said Melibea in soft tones to Calisto, eighteen years ago.

Calisto is basking in the sun near one of the balconies, his elbow is on the arm of his chair, and his chin is in his hand. In his house are beautiful pictures; if he has a mind for music, his daughter, Alisa, delights his ear with sweet melodies, or if it is poetry that his soul desires, from his book-shelves he can cull the choicest poets of Spain and Italy. His fellow citizens love him well; the careful hands of Melibea tend him; he sees his race continued, though not by a son, yet for the present by a lovely girl of bright intelligence and gentle heart. Nevertheless, Calisto sits lost in thought, with his head resting in his hand. Juan Ruiz, Archpriest of Hita, wrote in his book :

> . . . 'Et crei la fabrilla
> Que dis : Por lo pasado no estés mano en mejilla.'

'And I believed the saying which says : Do not for that which is past sit with your cheek in hand.'

Calisto has indeed small need to mourn the past; past and present are for him alike rich in blessings. Nothing exists to trouble or to sadden him; and yet Calisto, chin in hand, gazes thoughtfully at the distant clouds, drifting over the blue sky.

Clouds inspire us with a feeling of instability, and of eternity. Clouds are, like the sea, ever changing yet ever the same. While watching their flight we feel that our life and all things earthly are hastening into nothingness, while they, fugitive though they be, are yet eternal. The clouds, which we now see above us, were seen five hundred, one thousand, three thousand years ago by other men with the passions and the carking cares that we find in ourselves. When in a moment of happiness we would fain make time our captive, we find weeks, months, and years already slipping away from us. But the clouds, the same yet not the same, each moment and each day are chasing one another over the heavens. Clouds there are, round, and full and dazzling white of colour, that in spring mornings float over the translucent sky. Others, like delicate gauze, spread themselves horizontally over a milky background; others are grey and veil grey distances; others, again, are crimson and gold in those sunsets of the great plains, sunsets interminable, full of deep melancholy. Others there are, like little fleeces, countless in number, and alike in form, revealing through some break in their midst a fragment of blue sky. Some go their way slowly and solemnly, some course along swiftly. Some again, ashy in colour, darken the whole face of the sky, casting upon the earth beneath a certain grey, opaque, and subdued light that lends a charm of its own to the autumnal landscape.

Hundreds of years after the day when Calisto is sitting chin in hand, a great poet, Campoamor, will dedicate to the clouds a canto in one of his poems named *Columbus*. 'Clouds', says the poet, 'mirror our own existence. What is existence but the sporting of clouds? . . . Life consists in seeing that which passes.' Yes, to live is to see things passing, passing as above the clouds up yonder. Rather might we say; 'To live is to see things returning, for ever returning, griefs, joys, and hopes, even as these clouds, distinct yet ever one, fugitive yet unchangeable.' Clouds are the image of Time. Can there be sensation more tragic than that of the fleetingness of Time, as when one sees in the present the past, and in the past the future?

In the garden, full of silence, is heard the shrill note of the swallows in their rapid flight. The water of the fountain peacefully trickles from the marble basin; at the foot of the cypresses short-lived roses, white, yellow, and crimson, open their petals to the light. The heavy fragrance of jasmine and magnolia perfumes the air. The green of the foliage contrasts with the white walls, and above both green and white is seen the indigo blue of the sky. Alisa is seated in the garden book in hand; her little feet peep from beneath her skirt of finest cloth. They are shod in black velvet slippers, trimmed with lace-edging and with buckles of burnished silver. Alisa's eyes are green, like those of her mother, her face is long rather than round. Who could find words for the softness and delicacy of her hands? Who could praise as it deserves the sweetness of her speech?

In the garden all is peace and silence. Above, in the sunshine, leaning against a balustrade, Calisto watches his daughter with a fond delight. Suddenly he sees a falcon, circling in rapid and frenzied movement amidst the trees. In hot pursuit of him appears an excited youth. Brought face to face with Alisa, he halts, lost in contemplation of her, smiles and begins to speak.

Calisto sees him from the verandah, and guesses his words. Far above him a few round, white clouds pass slowly over the blue sky.

IDA FARNELL

JOSÉ ORTEGA Y GASSET
[1883–1955]

Professor of metaphysics for many years at the University of Madrid, José Ortega y Gasset was Spain's leading contemporary philosopher. With brilliant, forceful style, he attacked and analysed Spain's many problems—usually from a pessimistic point of view. His most famous essays are included in España invertebrada (*1922*) *and* La rebelión de las masas (*1930*).

INVERTEBRATE SPAIN

THE INCREASING MENACE OF SOCIETY

Ever since the middle of the last century, life in Europe has become more and more public, and in these last few years that tendency has increased at a rate that is positively dizzy. A life which is private, hidden, solitary, closed to public view, becomes more difficult every day.

The situation has certain characteristics which are obvious to the senses. Noise in the street, for instance—the street has become stentorian. One of the privileges which man used to take for granted was silence. Now his right to a certain amount of silence is recognized no more. The street penetrates into our own private corners and fills them with public clamour. He who wishes to meditate must get used to doing it submerged in the midst of a public racket, a diver in an ocean of collective noise. Man is never left alone by himself. Whether he likes it or not, he must be with others. The public square and the avenue force their anonymous clamour in through the very walls of his home.

Confronted with unlimited public invasion, everything that used to signify reverence has become less and less important. Especially the theory that a man's house is his castle. Family life, that society in miniature erected outside of and opposed to society in the large, is reduced to a minimum. The more advanced a country is, the less important the family.

The immediate cause of its disappearance is curious. It has always been recognized that the heart of the family was the hearth. But then, as usual, man began surrounding it with an aura of romance. The hearth was altar as well as cooking place; the haven of the family, of fatherhood, of the lares. But the fact is that just as soon as it began to be difficult to get domestic servants, the lares, fatherhood, and the family altar commenced to disappear. One began to realize that in the last analysis the cornerstone of the family was not the household gods, nor the paterfamilias, but the hired girl. It became possible to reduce the fact to a formula almost as exact as a functional law—in every country, family life today is important in direct ratio to the available amount of domestic service. In the United States, where it is harder to keep a good maid than to keep a giraffe, family life has contracted to a minimum. And so has the size of the house. Why have a large house if you cannot stay in it? Without servants, some simplification of domestic existence is essential, and when you simplify it you make it uncomfortable. The complicated, semi-religious rite of seasoning food—the rite of the kitchen-altar—was reduced to a minimum. Man was thrust out of domestic seclusion into public life. The real god Lar was the soup kettle.

The modern family tends to fly apart. There is a vast difference between the hours that used to be passed at home and those that are passed there now. In those long, slow hours of another day, man used to assist in the crystallization of a part of himself which was private, non-public and which easily became anti-public.

The physical change in the thickness of walls since the Middle Ages could be shown by a diagram. In the 14th century each house was a fortress. Today, each many-storied house is a beehive. It is a city in itself, and its walls are thin partitions which barely shut us off from the street. Even as late as the 18th century, houses were still spacious and deep. Man spent the major portion of his day in them, in secret and well-defended solitude. That solitude, working on the soul hour after hour, forged it, like a transcendent blacksmith, into a compact and forceful character. Under its treatment, man consolidated his individual destiny and sallied forth with impunity, never yielding to contamination from the public. It is only in isolation that we gain, almost automatically, a certain discrimination in ideas, desires, longings, that we learn which are ours, and which are anonymous, floating in the air, falling on us like dust in the street.

No one knows what the end of this process will be. Until very recently the whole of European development was focused on the education and encouragement of the individual. With increasing intensity it insisted that life should take individual form. That is to say, that by the very act of living each one should feel himself unique. Unique in joy, as in duty and in sorrow. And is this not the truth, the pure transcendental truth about human life? Whether humble or magnificent, to live is to be alone—to have this consciousness of the singleness, the exclusiveness of man's own individual destiny, a destiny which he alone possesses. Life is not lived in company. Each must live his own life by himself, taste it with his own lips, whether the cup be full of bitter or of sweet. Some of us find ourselves with partners, but this does not mean that we allow another to participate in the secret life which is ours and only ours.

Yet, today, there is no doubt that the direction of social evolution has changed. For the last two generations, life in Europe has tended to be less and less individual. Everything forces man to lose that sense of being unique and to make himself less compact. Just as the house has been opened up, made more porous and better ventilated, so people and ideas, tastes, opinions blow back and forth across us until each one of us begins to think that perhaps he is someone else.

Is this just a phase, a passing change, a step backwards in order to make a still higher leap toward greater intensifying of the individual? No one knows; but it is a fact that right now a great number of Europeans are feeling a sense of luxurious fruition in ceasing to be individuals and dissolving themselves into the mass.

There is a delicious epidemic of feeling oneself part of the mass, of ceasing to have any individual destiny. Man is becoming part of society.

Throughout the long course of human history there is no novelty in this. It has been the thing that has happened with the greatest frequency. The unusual was the opposite—the desire to be individual, non-transferable, unique. What is happening now, clarifies the situation of man in the good old days of Greece and Rome. Liberty to live by and for oneself was not conceded then. The State had a right to the whole of one's existence. When Cicero wanted to retire to his Tuscan villa and devote himself to the reading of Greek books, he had to justify himself publicly, and to obtain pardon for momentarily seceding from the collective body. The great crime which cost Socrates his life was the pretension that he possessed a particular and private daemon; that is, an inspiration which was individual.

The process of making man a social animal is terrifying. It is not content with demanding of me that what is mine be given to others—an excellent idea which causes me no annoyance whatever—but it also insists that what is theirs be mine. For example, that I adopt their tastes and their ideas. Everything private and apart is forbidden, including the right of having convictions for one's own exclusive use.

The abstract divinity of 'the collective' is coming back to exercise its tyranny; indeed it is already creating havoc in Europe. The press believes it has the right to publicize our private lives, to judge them, to condemn them. Day by day the government forces us to give a larger part of our existence to society. Man is left no corner to retire to, no solitude for himself. The masses protest angrily against any reserve which we hold back for ourselves.

Probably the origin of this anti-individual fury lies in the fact that in their inmost hearts the masses feel themselves weak and defenceless in the face of their destiny. On a bitter and terrible page Nietzsche notes how, in primitive societies which were weak when confronted with the difficulties of existence, every individual and original act was a crime, and the man who tried to lead a solitary life was a malefactor. He must in everything comport himself according to the fashion of the tribe.

Now, apparently, many men are again feeling homesick for the herd. They devote themselves passionately to whatever there is left in them of the sheep. They want to march through life together, along the collective path, shoulder to shoulder, wool rubbing wool, and the head down. This is the reason why so many European peoples are looking for a shepherd and a sheep dog. Hatred of liberalism comes from this and nothing else. For liberalism, before it becomes a question of this or that in politics, is a fundamental idea about life. It is believing that every human being ought to be free to fulfil his individual and non-transferable destiny.

MILDRED ADAMS

JACINTO BENAVENTE
[1866–1954]

When Jacinto Benavente began to write, towards the end of the nineteenth century, the exaggerated melodramas of José Echegaray dominated the Spanish stage. Benavente's art was a radical and refreshing change. Most of his plays fall into the category of social satire and deal mainly with the upper classes of his native Madrid. The dialogue, in prose, is calm and sophisticated, with frequent ironic and sceptical overtones.

Benavente's masterpiece, Los intereses creados (*1907*), *takes its stock characters from the old Italian* commedia dell'arte. *Two of Benavente's powerful dramas have a rural setting:* Señora ama (*1908*) *and* La malquerida (*1913*). *The latter, translated for the American stage as* The Passion Flower, *is the gripping story of a stepfather's illicit love for his beautiful stepdaughter.*

One of the most prolific of modern dramatists, Benavente received the Nobel Prize in 1922. Many of his plays have been translated into English by John Garrett Underhill.

THE BONDS OF INTEREST

ACT I

SCENE I

A plaza in a city. The façade of an Inn is at the right, having a practicable door, with a knocker upon it. Above the door is a sign which reads Inn.

(Leander *and* Crispin *enter from the left.*)

LEANDER. This must be a very great city, Crispin. Its riches and its power appear in everything.

CRISPIN. Yes, there are two cities. Pray God that we have chanced upon the better one!

LEANDER. Two cities do you say, Crispin? Ah! Now I understand —an old city and a new city, one on either side of the river.

CRISPIN. What has the river to do with it, or newness or age? I say two cities just as there are in every city in the world; one for people who arrive with money and the other for persons who arrive like us.

LEANDER. We are lucky to have arrived at all without falling into the hands of Justice. I should be heartily glad to stop here awhile and rest myself, for I am tired of this running about the world so continually.

CRISPIN. Not I! No, it is the natural condition of the freeborn subjects of the Kingdom of Roguery, of whom am I, not to remain seated long in any one place, unless it be through compulsion, as to say in the galleys, where, believe me, they are very hard seats. But now since we have happened upon this city, and to all appearances it is a well-fortified and provisioned one, let us like prudent captains map out our plan of battle beforehand, if we are to conquer it with any advantage to ourselves.

LEANDER. A pretty army we shall make to besiege it.

CRISPIN. We are men and we have to do with men.

LEANDER. All our wealth is on our backs. You were not willing to take off these clothes and sell them, when by doing so we could easily have obtained money.

CRISPIN. I would sooner take off my skin than my good clothes. As the world goes nothing is so important as appearances, and the clothes, as you must admit, are the first things to appear.

LEANDER. What are we going to do, Crispin? Hunger and fatigue have been too much for me. I am overcome; I cannot talk.

CRISPIN. There is nothing for us to do but to take advantage of our talents and our effrontery, for without effrontery talents are of no use. The best thing, as it seems to me will be for you to talk as little as possible, but be very impressive when you do, and put on the airs of a gentleman of quality. From time to time then I will permit you to strike me across the back. When anybody asks you a question, reply mysteriously, and if you open your mouth upon your own account, be sure that it is with dignity, as if you were pronouncing sentence. You are young; you have a fine presence. Until now you have known only how to dissipate your resources; this is the time for you to begin to profit by them. Put yourself in my hands. There is nothing so useful to a man as to have some one always at his heels to point out his merits, for modesty in one's self is imbecility, while self-praise is madness, and so between the two we come into disfavour with the world. Men are like merchandise; they are worth more or less according to the skill of the salesman who markets them. I tell you, though you were but muddy glass, I will so contrive that in my hands you shall pass for pure diamond. And now let us knock at the door of this inn, for surely it is the proper thing to have lodgings on the main square.

LEANDER. You say at this inn? But how are we going to pay?

CRISPIN. If we are to be stopped by a little thing like that, then we had better search out an asylum or an almshouse or else beg on the streets, if so be that you incline to virtue. Or if to force, then back to the highway and cut the throat of the first passer-by. If we are to live upon our means, strictly speaking, we have no other means to live.

LEANDER. I have letters of introduction to persons of importance in this city, who will be able to lend us aid.

CRISPIN. Then tear those letters up; never think of such baseness again. Introduce yourself to no man when you are in need. Those would be pretty letters of credit indeed! Today you will be received with the greatest courtesy; they will tell you that their houses and their persons are to be considered as yours. The next time you call, the servant will tell you that his master is not at home. No, he is not expected soon . . . and at the next visit nobody will trouble so much as to open the door. This is a world of giving and taking, a shop, a mart, a place of exchange, and before you ask you have to offer.

LEANDER. But what can I offer when I have nothing?

CRISPIN. How low an opinion you must have of yourself! Is a man in himself, then, worth nothing? A man may be a soldier, and by his valour win great victories. He may be a husband or a lover, and with love's sweet, oblivious medicine, restore some noble dame to health, or some damsel of high degree, who has been pining away through melancholy. He may be the servant of some mighty and powerful lord, who becomes attached to him and raises him up through his favour, and he may be so many other things besides that I have not the breath even to begin to run them over. When one wants to climb, why, any stair will do.

LEANDER. But if I have not even that stair?

CRISPIN. Then accept my shoulders, and I will lift you up. I offer you the top.

LEANDER. And if we both fall down upon the ground?

CRISPIN. God grant that it may be soft! . . .

ACT III

SCENE IX

(Leander *and* Crispin *enter*.)

CRISPIN. What is this sadness, this dejection? I expected to find you in better spirits.

LEANDER. I was never unfortunate till now; at least it never mattered to me whether or not I was unfortunate. Let us fly, Crispin, let us fly from this city before any one can discover us and find out who we are.

CRISPIN. If we fly it will be after every one has discovered us and they are running after us to detain us and bring us back in spite of ourselves. It would be most discourteous to depart with such scant ceremony without bidding our attentive friends good-bye.

LEANDER. Do not jest, Crispin; I am in despair.

CRISPIN. So you are. And just when our hopes are under fullest sail.

LEANDER. What could you expect? You wanted me to pretend to be in love, but I have not been able to pretend it.

CRISPIN. Why not?

LEANDER. Because I love—I love in spirit and in truth!

CRISPIN. Silvia? Is that what you are complaining about?

LEANDER. I never believed it possible a man could love like this. I never believed that I could ever love. Through all my wandering life along the dusty roads, I was not only the one who passed, I was the one who fled, the enemy of the harvest and the field, the enemy of man, enemy of sunshine and the day. Sometimes the fruit of the wayside tree, stolen, not given, left some savour of joy on my parched lips, and sometimes, after many a bitter day, resting at night beneath the stars, the calm repose of heaven would invite and soothe me to a dream of something that might be in my life like that calm night sky, brooding infinite over my soul— serene! And so tonight, in the enchantment of this fête, it seemed to me as if there had come a calm, a peace into my life—and I was dreaming! Ah! How I did dream! But tomorrow it will be again the bitter flight with justice at our heels, and I cannot bear that they should take me here where she is, and where she may ever have cause to be ashamed at having known me.

CRISPIN. Why, I thought that you had been received with favour! And I was not the only one who noticed it. Doña Sirena and our good friends, the Captain and the poet, have been most eloquent in your praises. To that rare excellent mother, the Wife of

Polichinelle, who thinks of nothing but how she can relate herself by marriage to some nobleman, you have seemed the son-in-law of her dreams. As for Signor Polichinelle . . .

LEANDER. He knows . . . he suspects. . . .

CRISPIN. Naturally. It is not so easy to deceive Signor Polichinelle as it is an ordinary man. An old fox like him has to be cheated truthfully. I decided that the best thing for us to do was to tell him everything.

LEANDER. How so?

CRISPIN. Obviously. He knows me of old. When I told him that you were my master, he rightly supposed that the master must be worthy of the man. And upon my part, in appreciation of his confidence, I warned him not to permit you under any circumstances to come near to or speak with his daughter.

LEANDER. You did? Then what have I to hope?

CRISPIN. You are a fool! Why, that Signor Polichinelle will exert all his authority to prevent you from meeting her.

LEANDER. I do not understand.

CRISPIN. In that way he will become our most powerful ally, for if he opposes it, that will be enough to make his wife take the opposite side, and the daughter will fall in love with you madly. You have no idea what a young and beautiful daughter of a rich father, who has been brought up to the gratification of her every whim, can do when she finds out for the first time in her life that somebody is opposing her wishes. I am certain that this very night, before the fête is over, she will find some way of eluding the vigilance of her father at whatever cost, and return to speak with you.

LEANDER. But can't you see that Signor Polichinelle is nothing to me, no, nor the wide world either? It is she, only she! It is to her that I am unwilling to appear unworthy or mean, it is to her—to her that I cannot lie.

CRISPIN. Bah! Enough of this nonsense! Don't tell me that. It is too late to draw back. Think what will happen if we vacillate now and hesitate in going on. You say that you have fallen in love? Well, this real love will serve us better than if it were put on. Otherwise you would have wanted to get through with it too quickly. If insolence and effrontery are the only qualities which are of use elsewhere, in love a faint suggestion of timidity is of advantage to a man. Timidity in a man always makes the woman bolder. If you don't believe it, here is the innocent Silvia now, skulking in the shadows and only waiting for a chance to come near until I retire or am concealed.

LEANDER. Silvia, do you say?

CRISPIN. Hush! You may frighten her. When she is with you,
remember, discretion—only a few words, very few. Adore her,
admire her, contemplate her, and let the enchantment of this night
of pallid blue speak for you, propitious as it is to love, and whisper
to her in the music whose soft notes die away amid the foliage and
fall upon our ears like sad overtones of this festival of joy.
LEANDER. Do not trifle, Crispin! Do not trifle with my love! It
will be my death.
CRISPIN. Why should I trifle with it? I know, too, it is not always
well to grovel on the ground. Sometimes we must soar and mount
up into the sky better to dominate the earth. Mount now and soar
—and I will grovel still. The world lies in our hands!

(He goes out to the right.)

JOHN GARRETT UNDERHILL

ANTONIO MACHADO
[1875-1939]

*Antonio Machado, though born in Seville, is intimately associated with
Castile, where he spent most of his life. His verse, small in quantity, is serious,
intense and restrained. His most characteristic work is contained in* Campos
de Castilla *(1912), in which he exalts the austere beauty of the plains of
Castile. Some critics believe him to be Spain's greatest poet of the twentieth
century.*

FIELDS OF SORIA

III

An undulating country, where the roads
Do now conceal the travellers, astride
Their dusky-coated asses,
Now, in the crimson light of dying day,
Uplift in full relief their rustic forms,
Darkening the golden canvas of the West.
Climb now yon mount, and from those jagged peaks
Where dwells the eagle, gaze upon the scene;
And see the leaden plains and silvery slopes
All bathed in carmine, shot with steely grey,
Circled by mountains of deep violet,
With snowy summits blushing like the rose.

IV

Lo, these are they that move 'twixt land and sky;
Two oxen, slowly ploughing
Upon a hillside, touched by Autumn's breath,
The while between their sturdy heads, low bent
Beneath the heavy yoke,
A basket hangs woven of reeds and broom—
An infant's rustic cradle;
And, following the team,
A man, who bows him down towards the earth,
Likewise a woman, who in the gaping furrows
Scatters the precious seed.
Beneath a cloud of crimson and of flame
See in the West, all liquid gold and green,
Their shadows slowly lengthen as they pass.

IDA FARNELL

TO DON FRANCISCO GINER DE LOS RIOS

Now, when the Master left us,
There came that morning's light,
Whispering : 'Three days have fled,
And lo, my brother Francis worketh not!
Died he?' We only know
That he went hence upon a shining path,
And spake : 'Mourn me with works,
Mourn me with hopes, I would no dole of tears;
Only be good. Be, as I strove to be
While in this life—a soul.
Live on, life hath no end;
The dead alone shall die, and shadows pass;
Who sowed is reaping now, who lived yet liveth;
Let the good anvils sound, let bells be dumb!'
Then to a purer light
The brother of the light of dawn went forth,
Forth from the scene of toils
That bright and glad old man of saintly life.

. . . Yea, comrades, let us bring
His body to the mountains,
Up to those azure heights
Where Guadarrama towers.

Yonder are shadowy gorges
With pine-trees, where the winds make melody.
Let his great heart repose
Beneath this sacred oak,
Where beds of thyme scatter their fragrance sweet,
And golden butterflies play.
'Tis there of old our Master
Dreamt his sweet dream of Spain's new blossoming.

IDA FARNELL

COUNSELS

Learn how to hope, to wait the proper tide—
   As on the coast a bark—then part without a care;
He who knows how to wait wins victory for bride;
   For life is long and art a plaything there.
But should your life prove short
   And never come a tide,
   Wait still, unsailing, hope is on your side,
Art may be long or, else, of no import.

THOMAS WALSH

SONGS OF SEVERAL LANDS

I

By the sierra gardens
The wide seas break in foam,
And grains of salt I find
Within the honeycomb.

II

By waters in darkness flowing—
Night over Málaga—
Sea foam and jasmine blowing.

III

Suddenly—spring is here!
No one saw her appear.

IV

Now comes the spring.
Blossoms of briers upon the air
White hosannas fling!

V

Full moon, full moon,
Glory-crowned, so very round,
In this peaceful, springtime night,
White bees are building you,
A honeycomb of light!

VI

Castilian evening . . .
The music will begin,
Or better, cease to sing.
To the window will I come
When all are slumbering.

VII

Singing and keeping time,
River willow and green
Almond bough sing a rhyme.

They sing of grey oak tree
With branch for axe to fell,
And flowers none may see.

White flowers of the pear,
Pink flowers of the peach,
In gardens everywhere.

And of this perfume
By winged, wet winds carried
From bean fields in bloom.

VIII

Above the little square
The sun no longer burns.
With the four acacias
To dusk the fountain turns.
O happy afternoon!
Sing, nightingale, thy rue!
In my heart this hour
It is twilight too.

IX

On whitewashed walls
Of traveller's cell,
My shadow falls!

XIII

In meadows green they dance
To sound of fifes and drums.
With sandals gold and crook
In bud, a shepherd comes.

From hills in haste came I,
Only to dance with her;
Back to the hills I'll hie.

Among the garden trees
There is a nightingale.
By night and day, to sun
And moon he tells his tale.
The bird in garden close
Is hoarse with song. The maid
Will come to pluck a rose.

Among the oak trees black
There is a fountain stilled,
A little jar of clay
That never has been filled.

With the white moon
Through groves of oak,
She will come soon.

XV

While you dance in a ring,
Maidens, sing.
Now green the meadows are,
Now comes the wooing spring.

Among the oak trees black,
By river murmuring,
Where tread his sandalled feet,
The silver traces cling.
Now green the meadows are,
Now comes the wooing spring.

FLORENCE LEWIS MAY

MANUEL MACHADO
[1874–1947]

Manuel Machado, born in Seville but brought up in Madrid, retains in his poetry the lyricism of his native Andalusia. Though neither as deep nor as original as his brother Antonio, Manuel Machado is one of the outstanding modernist poets of Spain, following the path of Rubén Darío. Alma (1902), Apolo (1911) and Cante hondo (1912) are among his best works.

ADELPHOS

I am kindred to those people who made this land their own;
I spring from the Moorish race, born lovers of the sun.
A scion of that nation who won and lost a throne,
My soul like the Spanish Arab's is a pale sweet-scented one.

My failing will died in me beneath the moonlight's spell—
Sweet the release from reason and from love's tyrant claim;
My joy to lie at ease where no illusions dwell—
From time to time embraces or the music of a name.

In my soul as in the twilight, all shapes inconstant change,
And the rose which is a symbol of my one abiding passion
Shall be a flower opened in distant lands and strange
And have no certain perfume, no colour, nor rightful fashion.

Kisses—but not to give them. Glory—what the world owes,
Let all this like an aura descend around my head.
May the tide still bear me with it as it softly ebbs and flows,
And never need I choose the road which I must tread.

Ambition I have none, and love I have not known;
I never burned with faith nor glowed with gratitude.
I had towards art vague yearnings, now forever flown;
I am not swayed by vice, with virtue not imbued.

In loftiness of lineage to no man need I yield;
Innate and not acquired are breeding and blazon proud.
But the emblem of my house, the device upon my shield
Is a futile sun half-hidden in a faint uncertain cloud.

I ask nought, love nor hate, only by going now
Can you grant to me the boon that I to you would give.
And let life take the trouble to kill, I care not how,
Since I'll not bestir myself to take the pains to live.

My failing will died in me beneath the moonlight's spell—
Sweet the release from reason and rest from love to earn;
From time to time a kiss, where no illusions dwell,
The kind and generous kiss that asks for no return.

BEATRICE GILMAN PROSKE

FIGURINES

With loveliness the little princess
Fairly seems to glow,
Completely charming,
Small, disarming,
The princess of Watteau!

When the princess is before me,
I admire, I adore!
If she is sighing,
I am crying,
If she smiles, I laugh once more.

At times, as now, she smiles on me,
And oh, her smile is gay!
Her eyes are dancing,
Roguish, glancing,
Then lost in thought she looks away.

The little princess of Watteau,
She really seems to live!
All who view her
Find allure there,
Those who know her their love give.

Her sweet face echoes each emotion,
There I can divine
Sorrow blending
With love, ending
In death, her fate like mine.

ALICE JANE M^CVAN

PHILIP THE FOURTH

None could more gracious nor more courtly be
Than our King Philip, may God keep him well!
With raven night his sombre clothes agree.
Pallid his face as is the twilight's spell;

Heavy his hair with golden ringlets drest;
In furtive eyes faint sapphire shadows dwell.
Above his generous and noble breast
No flash of gems nor clink of littering chains
Disturbs the hush where folds of velvet rest.
The sceptre laid aside, he now sustains,
With languid grace, a single glove within
His ivory hand enlaced with frail blue veins.

BEATRICE GILMAN PROSKE

JUAN RAMÓN JIMÉNEZ
[1881–1958]

At first a follower of the modernist innovations of Rubén Darío, the Andalusian Juan Ramón Jiménez soon developed a highly personal and original style. His numerous poems, contained in more than twenty volumes, are notable for their imagery, delicate romanticism and musicality. His earlier poems were inspired by Nature and beauty; more recently Jiménez sought to achieve 'pure poetry'. He is also the author of a number of prose works, among them the delightful tale about a child and his pet donkey, Platero y yo (*1914*). *Juan Ramón Jiménez has exerted a tremendous influence on the younger poets of Spain and Spanish America. He was awarded the Nobel Prize for Literature in 1956.*

GREEN

Green was the maiden, green, green!
Green her eyes were, green her hair.

The wild rose in her green wood
was neither red nor white, but green.

Through the green air she came.
(The whole earth turned green for her.)

The shining gauze of her garment
was neither blue nor white, but green.

Over the green sea she came.
(And even the sky turned green then.)

My life will always leave unlatched
a small green gate to let her in.

J. B. TREND

AUTUMNAL ARIA

XVIII

Idly sings the shepherd,
Trusty crook in hand,
And eyes the veiled horizon
Where dim the pine trees stand.

The sheep in drowsy flock
Raise dusty clouds and soon
Their little bells are crying
Beneath the golden moon.

Over the town in the valley
Trembles a cloud of white;
All that was gay in the sun
Dreams of lost love by night.

If lovers sad should pass
There where the river lies,
There would be warm salt tears
And secrets in their eyes.

The countryside would tell them,
Sweet are the pangs of love,
Within the shadow, gilded
By the autumn moon above.

The smoke cloud lifts; alone
And sad the vale is lying;
Beneath the golden moon
The little bells are crying.

ALICE JANE MᶜVAN

ONE NIGHT

The ancient spiders with a flutter spread
  Their misty marvels through the withered flowers,
The windows, by the moonlight pierced, would shed
  Their trembling garlands pale across the bowers.

The balconies looked over to the South;
  The night was one immortal and serene;
From fields afar the newborn springtime's mouth
  Wafted a breath of sweetness o'er the scene.

How silent! Grief had hushed its spectral moan
  Among the shadowy roses of the sward;
Love was a fable—shadows overthrown
  Trooped back in myriads from oblivion's ward.

The garden's voice was all—empires had died—
  The azure stars in languor having known
The sorrows all the centuries provide,
  With silver crowned me there, remote and lone.

THOMAS WALSH

DREAM NOCTURNE

The earth leads by the earth.
But, sea,
You lead by the heavens.
With what security of gold and silver light
Do the stars mark the road for us!
One would think
That the earth was the road
Of the body,
That the sea was the road
Of the soul.
Yes. It seems
That the soul is the only traveller
Of the sea; that the body, alone,
Remains behind, on the beach,
Without her, saying goodbye,
Heavy, cold, as though dead.
How like
Is a journey by sea
To death,
To eternal life!

THOMAS M^CGREEVY

I WOULD THAT ALL MY VERSES

I would that all my verses
could be such as the sky is in the night-time :
truth of the moment—now—without history.

That, like the sky, they would yield at every instant
all things, with all their streaming stars, and
neither childhood, nor youth, nor age could rob them,
nor cast a spell on the immensity of their beauty.

A thrill, a bright flash, music,
before my eyes and upon me!
The thrill, the bright flash, the music, right between my eyes,
—the whole sky in my heart—the naked book!

J. B. TREND

PEDRO SALINAS
[1892–1951]

One of the finest of the newer poets was the cultured professor and critic, Pedro Salinas. His poetry is intimate and intellectual; his style, simple and lyric. From 1940 until his untimely death, Salinas was Professor of Spanish at Johns Hopkins University. Many of his poems have been translated into English by Eleanor L. Turnbull.

IT MIGHT BE ÁVILA

Walls unbroken rise
In undisputed reign
And gaze in still surprise
Upon the lonely plain.
And the foe?

The towered height commands
The quiet roads below
Where sheep in dusty bands
Pass humbly to and fro.
And the foe?

Beneath the valiant arch
Now comes the farmer's spoil;
In dreary legions march
Wine casks, wheat bags, and oil.
And the foe?

Where stands the battlement
The winds a refuge take,
And storks on nesting bent
A peaceful murmur make.
And the foe?

Towers that from the height
A faithful vigil keep
While centuries take flight
And farms in stillness sleep,
        And thy foe?

                    ANNE SAWYER DURAND

SOIL

Soil. Nothing more.
Soil. Nothing less.
And let that suffice you.
Because on the soil the feet are planted,
on the feet body erect,
on the body the head firm,
and there, in the lee of the forehead,
pure idea and in the pure idea
the tomorrow, the key
—tomorrow—of the eternal.
Soil. No more no less.
And let that suffice you.

                    ELEANOR L. TURNBULL

HOW GENTLY YOU ROCK MY CHILD
TO SLEEP

How gently you rock my child to sleep,
enormous cradle of the world,
cradle of the August night!
The wind caresses his cheeks for me
and that which sings in the tree-tops
has the soothing sound of a lullaby
which quiets and puts him to sleep.
Tranquil stars watch over him,
from too much light and darkness
they guard and protect his eyes.
The earth seems to turn very slowly,
I feel it revolve on its axis
with no more motion than needful
to lull the child to sleep,
son of mine and son of yours.

                    ELEANOR L. TURNBULL

SWIMMER OF NIGHT

Swimmer of night, swimmer between
waves and shadows.
White arms submerging and rising
with a rhythm
governed by unknown designs,
you advance 'gainst
the double, silent resistance
of darkness and sea, world of gloom.
At the shipwreck of day,
you, voyager
crossing through April and May,
wished to save, are saving yourself,
not from death, from resignation.
The waves break over you, their fierceness gone,
their war repented of,
their wonder turned to foam,
when you offer them as a pact,
your strong, virgin breast.
The broad, dense billows of the night
break against
that desire for light that you seek,
by uplifting arms, that raises
in the heavens a great foaming;
a foam of lights, yes, of stars,
which sprinkle your face
with a riot of constellations,
of worlds. By your bare
innocence, seas of centuries defied,
centuries of shadows.
Your rhythmic bodily motion
supports, impels and saves
much more than your flesh. Thus your triumph
will be your end, and at last, sea,
night and conventions passed over,
on the far side of the black world,
on the shore of the day which breaks,
you will die in the dawn you have won.

ELEANOR L. TURNBULL

JORGE GUILLÉN
[b. 1893]

Jorge Guillén is regarded by many critics as the initiator of 'pure poetry' in the intellectual manner. His verse is of classic perfection and great lyric beauty—his one volume of poetry, Cántico (1928, and expanded several times), sings the joy and wonder of life. Guillén is at present Professor of Spanish at Wellesley College.

NAMES

It is dawn. The horizon
Peeps between its eyelashes,
And begins to see. What?
Names written on the surface,

The patina of things.
The rose is still called rose
Today, and the memory
Of its passing is haste.

Haste to be living more.
To abundant love we are
Raised by that unripe power
Of the Moment, so nimble

That on reaching its goal
It hastes to impose the Aftermath.
Be alert, on your guard!
I shall be, I shall be!

And the roses? Eyelashes
Fast closed : final horizon.
If perchance there is nothing?
But the names still remain.

ELEANOR L. TURNBULL

PERFECTION

The firmament, a dense blue,
Is overarching the day.
'Tis the rounding out of splendour,
Midday. All is curving dome.

At the centre lies, unwilling,
The rose, subject to a sun
At its zenith. And the present
So yields itself up that the
Foot that is moving now feels
The completeness of the planet.

ELEANOR L. TURNBULL

SLENDER SPRING

When the formless infinite enshrouds
        With the clouds
Its vast uncertainty and drifting soars . . .
        To what shores,

While the river curving as it goes
        Ever flows
Pursuing then with etched, oblique caprice
        Its release,

While the water hides in folds of green
        Fish unseen
Below the deep reflections trembling there
        Of the air . . .

When morning lingers on her misty way
        All the day
Along a silver wake which glimmering weaves
        Among the leaves,

Then sinuous spring unites in her design
        The smooth line
Of clouds wind-borne that swaying in the sky
        Circle by

With bubbles which a pointed pattern make
        And crystal break . . .
For a moment seen in the oars that flashing swing—
        Slender spring.

ANNE SAWYER DURAND

FEDERICO GARCÍA LORCA
[1899–1936]

Undoubtedly the most popular Spanish writer of this century was the brilliant and versatile Andalusian, Federico García Lorca. A spontaneous and gifted poet and dramatist, whose works have been widely translated, Lorca was in addition an excellent painter and musician. His tragic death at the outbreak of the Civil War cut short a truly remarkable career.

In the traditions and folk songs of Andalusia Lorca found his main inspiration. (Libro de poemas, *1921;* Canciones, *1927;* Romancero Gitano, *1928;* Poema del cante jondo, *1931.) His favourite metre is the traditional ballad, but he also wrote extensively in the modernistic style, notably the surrealistic* Poeta en Nueva York *(1929). His dramatic production includes light, lyric pieces as well as gripping tragedies.*

RIDER'S SONG

Cordoba.
Distant and lonely.

Black my pony, full the moon
and olives stowed in my saddle-bags.
Though well I may know the way
I'll never arrive at Cordoba.

Across the plain, through the wind,
black my pony, red the moon,
stark death is staring at me
from the tall towers of Cordoba.

Alas, how long is the way!
Alas, for my brave black pony!
Alas, stark death awaits me
before I arrive at Cordoba!

Cordoba.
Distant and lonely.

ELEANOR L. TURNBULL

SIX STRINGS

The guitar
makes the dreams weep.

The sobbing of souls
that are lost
escapes from its round
open mouth.
And like the tarantula
it weaves a great star
to catch the sighs
that float on its dark
pool of wood.

ELEANOR L. TURNBULL

THE GUITAR

Now begins the cry
Of the guitar,
Breaking the vaults
Of dawn.
Now begins the cry
Of the guitar.
Useless
To still it.
Impossible
To still it.
It weeps monotonously
As weeps the water,
As weeps the wind
Over snow.
Impossible
To still it.
It weeps
For distant things,
Warm southern sands
Desiring white camelias.
It mourns the arrow without a target,
The evening without morning.
And the first bird dead
Upon a branch.
O guitar !
A wounded heart,
Wounded by five swords.

ELIZABETH DU GUÉ TRAPIER

SOMNAMBULE BALLAD

Green, how I want you green.
Green wind. Green branches.
The ship upon the sea
and the horse in the mountain.
With the shadow on her waist
she dreams on her verandah,
green flesh, hair of green,
and eyes of cold silver.
Green, how I want you green.
Beneath the gipsy moon,
all things look at her
but she cannot see them

Green, how I want you green.
Great stars of white frost
come with the fish of darkness
that opens the road of dawn.
The fig-tree rubs the wind
with the sand-paper of its branches,
and the mountain, a filching cat,
bristles its bitter aloes.
But who will come? And from where?
She lingers on her verandah,
green flesh, hair of green,
dreaming of the bitter sea.
—Friend, I want to change
my horse for your house,
my saddle for your mirror,
my knife for your blanket.
Friend, I come bleeding,
from the harbours of Cabra.
—If I could, young man,
this pact would be sealed.
But I am no more I,
nor is my house now my house.
—Friend, I want to die
decently in my bed.
Of iron, if it be possible,
with sheets of fine holland.
Do you not see the wound I have
from my breast to my throat?

—Your white shirt bears
three hundred dark roses.
Your pungent blood oozes
around your sash.
But I am no more I,
nor is my house now my house.
—Let me climb at least
up to the high balustrades :
let me come ! let me come !
up to the green balustrades.
Balustrades of the moon
where the water resounds.

Now the two friends go up
towards the high balustrades.
Leaving a trail of blood,
Leaving a trail of tears.
Small lanterns of tin
were trembling on the roofs.
A thousand crystal tambourines
were piercing the dawn.
Green, how I want you green,
green wind, green branches.
The two friends went up.
The long wind was leaving
in the mouth a strange taste
of gall, mint and sweet-basil.
Friend ! Where is she, tell me,
where is your bitter girl?
How often she waited for you !
How often did she wait for you,
cool face, black hair,
on this green verandah !

Over the face of the cistern
the gipsy girl swayed.
Green flesh, hair of green,
with eyes of cold silver.
An icicle of the moon
suspends her above the water.
The night became as intimate
as a little square.
Drunken civil guards
were knocking at the door.

Green, how I want you green.
Green wind. Green branches.
The ship upon the sea.
And the horse in the mountain.

J. L. GILI and STEPHEN SPENDER

RAFAEL ALBERTI
[*b.* 1902]

Like Lorca, Rafael Alberti is a talented Andalusian who has cultivated both popular and modern themes. His first book of verse, Marinero en tierra, *was awarded the National Prize for Literature in 1925. In 1929 he published the Gongoristic* Cal y canto *and the surrealistic* Sobre los ángeles. *He has written some dozen volumes of poetry; his work is characterized by perfection of form.*

THE SEA

The sea, the sea,
the sea, only the sea!

Father, oh why to the city
did you drag me?

Why, oh why, did you pull me
out of the sea?

In dreams, the swell of the sea
tugs at the strings of my heart,
and away with it would flee.

here from the sea?
Father, why did you drag me

ELEANOR L. TURNBULL

STREET CRY UNDER SEA

How happy now would I be
with you, my fair young gardener,
in a garden under sea!

In a cart of cockle-shell,
drawn by a trout, oh what glee
for me, love, your wares to sell
under the salty blue sea!

—Fresh seaweed here from the sea,
seaweed, seaweed!

ELEANOR L. TURNBULL

STREET CRY

I sell clouds of many colours:
dark clouds to cool heat of summers!

I sell fleecy clouds of violet,
clouds that rosy flush at dawning,
gilded clouds of evening sunset!

Buy the yellow star of morning,
plucked from green boughs still dew-wet,
the heavenly peach tree adorning!

I sell snow and flames of fire,
and the call of the street crier!

ELEANOR L. TURNBULL

THE ANGEL OF NUMERALS

Virgins with T-squares
and compasses, guarding
celestial blackboards.

And the angel of numerals
pensively flying
from 1 to 2, from 2
to 3, from 3 to 4.

Dull chalk and wet sponges
erased and crossed out
the light of spaces.

Neither sun, moon, nor stars,
nor the sudden green
of flash of lightning,
nor air. Only mist.

Virgins without squares
and compasses, weeping.

And on the blurred blackboards
the angel of numerals,
lifeless, shrouded, lying
on 1 and on 2,
on 3 and on 4.

ELEANOR L. TURNBULL

BIBLIOGRAPHY

I. HISTORIES OF SPANISH LITERATURE IN ENGLISH

Aubrey F. G. Bell, *Castilian Literature*, Oxford, 1938.
——, *Contemporary Spanish Literature*, New York, 1933.
Gerald Brenan, *The Literature of the Spanish People*, Cambridge, 1952.
James Fitzmaurice-Kelly, *Chapters on Spanish Literature*, London, 1908.
——, *A History of Spanish Literature*, New York, 1898.
J. D. M. Ford, *Main Currents of Spanish Literature*, New York, 1919.
Ernest Mérimée and S. Griswold Morley, *A History of Spanish Literature*, New York, 1930.
Maxim Newmark, *Dictionary of Spanish Literature*, New York, 1956.
George Tyler Northup, *An Introduction to Spanish Literature*, Chicago, 1936.
George Ticknor, *History of Spanish Literature*, 3 vols., New York, 1849.

II. SPANISH LITERATURE IN ENGLISH TRANSLATION

John Bowring, *Ancient Poetry and Romances of Spain*, London, 1824.
Barrett H. Clark, *Masterpieces of Modern Spanish Drama*, New York, 1917.
Harriet de Onís, *Spanish Stories and Tales*, New York, 1954.
Ida Farnell, *Spanish Prose and Poetry*, Oxford, 1920.
Angel Flores, *Great Spanish Stories*, New York, 1956.
——, *Spanish Literature in English Translation: a bibliographical syllabus*, New York, 1926.
Mildred E. Johnson, *Spanish Poems of Love*, New York, 1955.
Willis Knapp Jones, *Spanish One Act Plays in English*, Dallas, 1934.
James Kennedy, *Modern Poets and Poetry of Spain*, London, 1852.
John Gibson Lockhart, *Ancient Spanish Ballads*, London, 1841.
Henry Wadsworth Longfellow, *The Poets and Poetry of Europe*, Philadelphia, 1845.
Charles B. McMichael, *Short Stories from the Spanish*, New York, 1920.
Paul T. Manchester, *Joyas Poéticas: Spanish and Spanish-American Poetry*, New York, 1951.
Remigio U. Pane, *English Translations from the Spanish, 1484–1943: a bibliography*, New Brunswick, 1944.
Samuel Putnam, *The European Caravan*, New York, 1931.
Thomas Roscoe, *The Spanish Novelists*, London, 1832.

Tales from the Italian and Spanish, New York, 1920.
Susette M. Taylor, *The Humour of Spain*, London, 1894.
Translations from Hispanic Poets, New York, 1938.
J. B. Trend, *Spanish Short Stories of the 16th Century in Contemporary Translation*, London, 1928.
Eleanor L. Turnbull, *Contemporary Spanish Poetry*, Baltimore, 1945.
——, *Ten Centuries of Spanish Poetry*, Baltimore, 1955.
J. F. Vingut, *Selections from the Best Spanish Poets*, New York, 1856.
Thomas Walsh, *Hispanic Anthology: Poems Translated from the Spanish by English and North American Poets*, New York, 1920.
Warre B. Wells, *Great Spanish Short Stories*, New York, 1932. (Published in England as *The Spanish Omnibus*, London, 1932.)

III. A BRIEF ENGLISH BIBLIOGRAPHY OF SPANISH-AMERICAN LITERATURE

Germán Arciniegas, *The Green Continent*, New York, 1944.
Alice Stone Blackwell, *Some Spanish-American Poets*, Philadelphia, 1937.
Alfred Coester, *The Literary History of Spanish America*, New York, 1928.
G. Dundas Craig, *The Modernist Trend in Spanish-American Poetry*, Berkeley, 1934.
Harriet de Onís, *The Golden Land*, New York, 1948.
Dudley Fitts, *Anthology of Contemporary Latin-American Poetry*, Norfolk (Conn.), 1942.
Isaac Goldberg, *Studies in Spanish-American Literature*, New York, 1920.
Pedro Henríquez-Ureña, *Literary Currents in Hispanic America*, Cambridge (Mass.), 1945.
E. Herman Hespelt and others, *An Outline History of Spanish-American Literature*, New York, 1942.
Jefferson Rea Spell, *Contemporary Spanish-American Fiction*, Chapel Hill, 1944.
Arturo Torres-Ríoseco, *New World Literature*, Berkeley and Los Angeles, 1949.

INDEX

[AUTHORS AND MAJOR ANONYMOUS WORKS]

AN ANTHOLOGY
OF
SPANISH LITERATURE
in English Translation

Edited by Seymour Resnick
and Jeanne Pasmantier

Except for Cervantes' immortal *Don Quixote*, the rich and varied literature of Spain is almost unknown to the average English-speaking reader. This new anthology is the first to encompass the entire range of Spanish literature—prose, verse, drama—in English translation. For the reader who dips into it at his leisure, for the student who traces the themes and character types so influential in the work of writers of many nations, a whole new world of pleasure and knowledge is in store.

This anthology offers a discerning selection from almost all of the major works Spain has produced in eight centuries, from the magnificent twelfth-century epic *The Cid* to the novelists, poets, dramatists, and essayists of our own time. Many of the quoted works were put into English by noted writers who, like Lord Byron, were attracted by the poetic beauty of Spanish writing. Among well-known translators are John Masefield, Robert Southey, Edward